Disability, Equality, and Human Rights

Oxfam GB

Oxfam GB, founded in 1942, is a development, humanitarian, and campaigning agency dedicated to finding lasting solutions to poverty and suffering around the world. Oxfam believes that every human being is entitled to a life of dignity and opportunity, and it works with others worldwide to make this become a reality.

From its base in Oxford, UK, Oxfam GB publishes and distributes a wide range of books and other resource materials for development and relief workers, researchers, campaigners, schools and colleges, and the general public, as part of its programme of advocacy, education, and communications.

Oxfam GB is a member of Oxfam International, a confederation of 12 agencies of diverse cultures and languages which share a commitment to working for an end to injustice and poverty – both in long-term development work and at times of crisis.

For further information about Oxfam's publishing, and online ordering, visit www.oxfam.org.uk/publications

For further information about Oxfam's development, advocacy, and humanitarian relief work around the world, visit www.oxfam.org.uk

ADD

Action on Disability and Development (ADD) has a vision of a world where all disabled people are able to participate as fully as they choose, at every level of society. To achieve this, it works in partnership with networks of disabled people in some of the poorest communities in the world, to help them to campaign for the rightful inclusion of disabled adults and children in society.

ADD is the only British-based agency supporting self-help development work, exclusively, with groups of disabled people in Africa and Asia. Since 1985 it has supported more than 75,000 disabled people in their self-help activities and their fight for basic rights and equal opportunities.

ADD's aim is to see democratic, representative, and active networks of disabled people who are campaigning for the rights of all their members, whatever their disability. Through facilitating the growth of these organisations, locally and nationally, ADD aims to help to promote a vibrant people's movement.

For more information about the work of ADD, visit www.add.org.uk

Disability, Equality, and Human Rights

A Training Manual for Development and Humanitarian Organisations

Alison Harris with Sue Enfield

Oxfam

Action on Disability
and Development

First published by Oxfam GB in 2003

© Oxfam GB 2003

ISBN 0 85598 485 6

A catalogue record for this publication is available from the British Library.

Available from:
Bournemouth English Book Centre, PO Box 1496, Parkstone, Dorset, BH12 3YD, UK
tel: +44 (0)1202 712933; fax: +44 (0)1202 712930; email: oxfam@bebc.co.uk

USA: Stylus Publishing LLC, PO Box 605, Herndon, VA 20172-0605, USA
tel: +1 (0)703 661 1581; fax: +1 (0)703 661 1547; email: styluspub@aol.com

For details of local agents and representatives in other countries, consult our website:
http://www.oxfam.org.uk/publications
or contact Oxfam Publishing, 274 Banbury Road, Oxford OX2 7DZ, UK
tel: +44 (0)1865 311 311; fax: +44 (0)1865 312 600; email: publish@oxfam.org.uk

Our website contains a fully searchable database of all our titles, and facilities for secure on-line ordering.

Published by Oxfam GB, 274 Banbury Road, Oxford OX2 7DZ, UK in association with
Action on Disability and Development, Vallis House, 57 Vallis Road, Frome, Somerset, BA11 3EG, UK.

Printed by Hobbs the Printers Ltd., Totton.

Oxfam GB is a registered charity, no. 202 918, and is a member of Oxfam International.

Contents

Foreword vi
Barbara Frost

Preface viii
Barbara Stocking

Acknowledgements x
Abbreviations and acronyms xi

Introduction 1

Part One: The principles of Disability Equality training 9
Alison Harris with Sue Enfield

Chapter 1   Disability and development: an overview of the issues 11
Chapter 2   What is 'Disability Equality'? 27
Chapter 3   Working with disabled people's organisations 33
Chapter 4   Guidelines for good practice 49

Part Two: The practice of Disability Equality training 59
Alison Harris

Chapter 5   The Disability Equality Training of Trainers (DETOT) course 61
Chapter 6   Outline of the training materials 69
Chapter 7   Preparing for the workshop and forming the group 76
Chapter 8   Facilitation skills 112
Chapter 9   Disability Equality in practice 167
Chapter 10   Action planning 277
Chapter 11   Evaluation 284
Chapter 12   Case studies 300
Chapter 13   Some useful quotations 319
Chapter 14   Sample workshop agendas 321
Chapter 15   Conclusion 326

Resources 329
Appendix   Oxfam's policy on disability 331
General index 333
Index of training methods 341

Foreword

For too long disabled people – most particularly disabled women and children – have been marginalised and excluded from mainstream society. There is no country in the world which can confidently claim that its disabled citizens have realised equal rights and equal opportunities. Rarely are disabled people equally able to exercise the vote, attend school or college, gain employment, use public transport, and live independently – the basic rights that most non-disabled people take for granted.

The United Nations Standard Rules on Equalisation of Opportunities for Persons with Disabilities, adopted by the UN General Assembly in 1993, imply a strong political commitment by member states to take measures to ensure that disabled people can realise equal rights. However, implementation of these measures is patchy – despite the fact that many international agencies acknowledge the links between disability and poverty.

International development organisations and policy makers have yet to adopt and implement policies which are fully inclusive and which affirm the value of social diversity. While it is acknowledged that disabled people are among the poorest members of their communities, many agencies consider their needs to be related solely to their impairments (in line with 'the medical model of disability'), rather than considering their needs in the context of their rights as equal members of society ('the social model').

In the United Kingdom, legislation now requires public services, facilities, and buildings to be accessible to disabled people. Disability-rights activists campaigned for years for changes in legislation to outlaw discrimination and to gain recognition. But the fundamental principle that society needs to change if disabled people are to realise their full potential has yet to be internalised fully by development and humanitarian agencies, although policies to this effect do exist.

There are a few examples of countries in receipt of development assistance which do themselves have excellent policies in place to promote the rights of disabled people. (South Africa is one such.) Much could be learned from these examples. In recent years the shift to rights-based development and the struggle of the disability-rights movement around the world to ensure that its voice is heard (*'nothing about us without us'* – Disabled Peoples' International) have led to an acknowledgement that practice does need to change.

In the UK, the Department for International Development published an issues paper in February 2000, entitled 'Disability, Poverty and Development'. It stated: 'Disability is both a cause and consequence of poverty. Eliminating world poverty is unlikely to be achieved unless the rights and needs of disabled people are taken into account.' There is a clear need to ensure that the most marginalised people are included in development work. This requires planners and all development workers to think multi-dimensionally, rather than to categorise people on the basis of single identities, such as gender, disability, urban/rural provenance, or HIV status. We need to be truly committed to diversity and to consider the whole person, remembering in our analyses that a disproportionate number of those experiencing social exclusion and poverty will be women, and especially disabled women and women living with HIV/AIDS. We need to look at the world through more than one lens.

However, until we are familiar with the institutional, environmental, and attitudinal barriers that exclude marginalised groups from full participation in society, we will be unable to ensure appropriate responses. That is why this manual is so important. It helps practitioners in development and humanitarian organisations to understand the issues confronting disabled children and adults, and ways in which we can go about breaking down the barriers and including people with disabilities in our work. It presents disability as a matter of human rights and moves away from the charitable and medical models of disability to argue that it is society that needs to change.

Disabled people themselves are powerful advocates for social change. Development practitioners need to hear the voices of disabled women, children, and men, in order to plan inclusive development.

Barbara Frost
Chief Executive, Action on Disability and Development

Preface

Oxfam's mandate is to overcome poverty and suffering. As this manual makes very clear, all around the world disabled people are among the poorest and most marginalised members of their communities. We need to understand why this is, and to devise ways of supporting them to take action to overcome their poverty and achieve their civil, political, social, and economic rights.

Disabled people, and particularly disabled women, are among those least likely to escape from the trap of poverty. Prejudice denies them the opportunity to develop the necessary skills, knowledge, and confidence, and to make effective use of the resources that they may already have. Many people working in development agencies are, often unwittingly, guilty of discriminating against people with physical or mental impairments, and disabled people are therefore less likely than others to benefit from development interventions – for the very same reasons that explain why they are poor in the first place.

This means that people with impairments are likely to remain among the chronically poor, and when progress towards the Millennium Development Goals is measured in 2015, it will be interesting to see how many disabled people are among those who have been enabled to edge above the poverty line.

Disabled people are often made invisible by society, and invisibility can be lethal in situations of armed conflict or natural calamity. Organisations such as Oxfam must enlist the support of people with disabilities in designing and delivering their humanitarian responses, if they are to ensure that all people are able to benefit equally from them. We have some excellent examples of good practice in this regard, but we cannot afford to be complacent. This manual identifies some of that good practice and helps us to understand how to replicate it.

It is only relatively recently that disability has been considered as an issue to be taken seriously by development or humanitarian agencies. Now, when major institutions such as the World Bank, the European Commission, and the British government's Department for International Development are making explicit their analysis of the relationship between disability, poverty, and the abuse of human rights, Oxfam GB and Action on Disability and Development (ADD) offer this practical toolkit for disseminating that analysis more widely.

In this era of globalisation, one of Oxfam's priorities is to ensure that the relationship between local and global causes of poverty is understood, and that the capacity of our partners to address these causes at every level is increased. Among those partners, we are fortunate to count disability-rights organisations which have had some notable successes in this regard: campaigning and advocacy have resulted in legislative change in Albania, Kosovo, Lebanon, and Uganda, for example. The struggle continues, however, to ensure that laws are implemented and that disabled people actually benefit from them.

The Disability Movement, like any movement of people marginalised because of their identity, needs allies and deserves the support of development and humanitarian organisations. There is a growing realisation that rights-based approaches to overcoming poverty and suffering are essential, but awareness of the abuses endured by specific groups in this regard is often low. People working in the fields of development and relief often assume that they need specialist skills in order to work with disabled people, but a good start can easily be made by ensuring that we apply our existing skills and principles to the task.

I am pleased to introduce this, Oxfam's fourth book about the rights and needs of disabled people, and its second publication in collaboration with ADD, in the hope that it will help to raise awareness of these vital issues among workers in development and in the fields of humanitarian protection and response.

Barbara Stocking
Director, Oxfam GB

Acknowledgements

This manual was inspired and improved by many people. Heartfelt thanks are due to Rachel Wareham-Bell and Liz Hughes, my fellow trainers on the Disability Equality Training Of Trainers course in Kosovo, who provided ideas and designed activities for many of the sessions which are described in Part Two. Halit Ferizi, President of the Kosovo Association of People with Paraplegia (now called Handikos), and Gordana Rajkov, Oxfam's Disability Adviser in Yugoslavia, also contributed ideas and helped to develop activities: my thanks are due to them, and to the participants on the Kosovo course, whose experiences and feedback kept the principles firmly connected to reality.

My thanks are due also to the reviewers of the first draft, whose insightful comments and suggestions made this a more comprehensive and logical book than it would otherwise have been. Their enthusiasm and encouragement were much appreciated. I hope they will find their ideas adequately and accurately conveyed through the manual. The reviewers were Jacqui Christy James, formerly Regional Disability Adviser for Oxfam in the Caucasus; Peter Coleridge, UNDP/UNOPS Comprehensive Disabled Afghans' Programme; Anita Eisenbeis, Mennonite Social Assistance Association, Brazil; Fiona Gell, formerly of Oxfam GB's Emergencies Department, now a Programme Policy Adviser on Gender Equity; Jon Horsley, Programme Development Manager for Oxfam GB in the Middle East and Eastern Europe; Liz Hughes, former Programme Manager for Oxfam GB in Kosovo; Agnes Kalibbala, of Action on Disability and Development (Uganda); and Chris Mason, formerly of Oxfam GB's Eastern Europe Desk.

Helpful comments on the second draft were contributed by Rachel Hastie, formerly Oxfam's Deputy Representative for Bosnia; Helen Lee, a freelance consultant on disability issues; and Caroline Roseveare, formerly Senior Policy Adviser in Oxfam GB's Programme Policy Team. Hannah Chandler of ADD helped to keep the project on track. Jon Horsley's support and advice have been invaluable.

Sue Enfield, a freelance consultant, redrafted Part One to bring it into line with current international thinking about Disability Equality. Chapter 3 incorporates findings from an evaluation written by Adrienne Hopkins, with contributions from Dukagjin Kelmendi, formerly Oxfam's Disability Programme Manager in Pristina.

Finally, I am eternally grateful to the Oxfam editor, Catherine Robinson, who stuck by this project, gave it time to mature, and was a constructive yet honest critic.

Alison Harris

Abbreviations and acronyms

ADD	Action on Disability and Development
CBR	community-based rehabilitation
DETOT	Disability Equality Training of Trainers
DFID	Department for International Development
DPI	Disabled Peoples' International
DPO	disabled people's organisation
HI	Handicap International
INGO	international non-government organisation
KAPP	Kosovo Association of People with Paraplegia (now known as Handikos)
LAG	Local Active Group
NGO	non-government organisation
UDHR	Universal Declaration of Human Rights
UNDP	United Nations Development Programme
UN	United Nations

Introduction

This manual is derived from the experience of working with a disabled people's organisation originally known as KAPP (Kosovo Association of People with Paraplegia) and later renamed Handikos, which was supported by Oxfam GB in Kosovo between 1994 and 2001. Although the programme operated within the particular political and social context of Kosovo – a UN Protectorate located in south-east Europe – the challenges that it confronted are typical of those encountered by development and humanitarian organisations in many countries when they seek to respond to the special needs of sub-groups within a diverse population.

Over time, agencies have become more attuned to the concerns of vulnerable groups who will not necessarily benefit from generic, across-the-board approaches to meeting basic needs. The needs of women, children, orphans, older people, and ethnic minorities are now frequently considered when any intervention is being planned: it is an accepted fact that these groups may have specific problems of access which must be addressed if they are to benefit from the project. Less regularly, although the issue is equally pertinent, the particular needs of disabled people in a community are considered, and measures are taken to allow for their inclusion.

The work done by KAPP/Handikos, in partnership with Oxfam, before, during, and after the recent crisis in Kosovo, enabled both partners to learn from the reality of disability-focused work based on the principles of equality and empowerment. Theoretical models were compared with the actual situation of disabled people, and responses were developed to include disabled people in the definition and delivery of programmes to meet their needs. The cornerstone to this inclusive approach was the social model of disability and the application of Disability Equality principles. Useful lessons were learned about the process of changing attitudes towards disability, both within a humanitarian and development agency (Oxfam) and in the beneficiary community. This manual seeks to distil the theory and practice used in the programme. It also provides extensive details of methods and materials that were used as part of a training programme to raise awareness of disability.

Why this manual?

Worldwide, the current *status quo* for disabled people can only be described as 'disability inequality'. Humanitarian and development organisations have failed to ensure that disabled people are equal participants in their programmes. For agencies whose mandate requires them to reach those most in need, the (often inadvertent) exclusion of disabled people means that many organisations are currently failing to honour their obligations. Disabled people are among the poorest of the poor, and the most powerless in virtually every community in the world. Programmes which do not include them on an equal basis with their non-disabled counterparts are inherently ineffective.

This book's basic premise is that the time is right to improve the *status quo*: Disability Equality must become part of the everyday reality of humanitarian and development work. If communities and organisations are to benefit from becoming disability-aware, and if disabled people are to be empowered to participate on an equal basis, existing ways of thinking and working must change. This manual provides information and training materials which will support this change.

It is important to emphasise, however, that the book is a starting point, rather than a definitive prescription. One of the reasons for publishing it is that the authors believe that Oxfam GB, like most other aid organisations, is seriously inadequate in its knowledge of and response to disability issues. The manual reflects Oxfam GB's commitment to improving its performance on disability, but Oxfam GB does not claim expertise on the subject. The text has benefited from contributions by ADD (Action on Disability and Development), which is the only British-based agency supporting self-help development work exclusively with groups of disabled people in Africa and Asia.

There is an urgent need for a manual such as this. In 1995, when Oxfam staff began to support the introduction of concepts of Disability Equality in Kosovo and Banja Luka, they could find no single publication which brought together, in one easily obtainable and simple-to-use resource, the materials that were needed. Existing materials on disability either lacked a rights-based approach, or they did not focus on group work or workshop activities, or they failed to take gender into account. Most literature on disability either views it from a Northern perspective or perceives it in exclusively development-related terms, rather than seeing it as an issue that is integral to both humanitarian and development work. Existing materials on human rights and gender (both theoretical and practice-based) pay scant attention to the existence and rights of disabled people. Disability issues are not covered at all, or they are inappropriately covered. Most training and group-work activities make the assumption that all participants are non-disabled.

Gathering and creating the materials while working in a geographically and technologically isolated area was a fascinating process, but it took a lot of time and effort. In order not to reinvent too many wheels, staff borrowed heavily from other sources and adapted existing materials to suit the circumstances. The training materials that form Part Two of this manual present the results of this labour and the lessons that were learned by using the materials.

The geo-political context

Can lessons learned from programmes in Europe be applied to other countries, especially developing countries of the South? For aid workers with experience of, say, Africa or Latin America, but not of Bosnia or Kosovo, this is a very legitimate concern.

In response, one could argue first that, while details differ from society to society, the root causes and effects of the poverty and marginalisation of disabled people are similar worldwide. And there are many commonalities in the range of responses which can lead to positive change. This is borne out by reviewers' comments on the first draft of this book, and contributions included in the manual from diverse countries, including Uganda, Bangladesh, and Mali.

Second, it is a mistake to see 'Europe' as a homogeneous entity. On the one hand, abject poverty can and does exist in this so-called 'developed' continent (and disabled people are very likely to be found in the most impoverished sectors of the population). On the other hand, war is – in an obscene way – a great leveller. Some newly arrived aid workers in Bosnia were shocked to see refugees wearing fashionable clothes, and intimated that these people, dressed like that, could not be 'real' refugees. But if those are the only clothes you have, what else are you supposed to wear? These people were still refugees: they had lost everything, apart from the one set of clothes they happened to be wearing when they were forced to leave their homes. You cannot eat fashionable clothes – you cannot even sell them at market to buy food, if (a) you can't get to the market for fear of being shot by snipers, (b) no one else has money to pay for them or wants to exchange anything useful for them, and (c) there is no food to buy or barter. And in sub-zero winter temperatures, one set of clothes, no matter how fancy they are, is not going to provide adequate warmth when there is no source of heating. In war-torn Bosnia, people died from hypothermia, pneumonia, and numerous other normally avoidable causes, irrespective of whether they lived in large houses or bombed-out high-rise flats or makeshift shacks. The lesson is that aid workers should avoid making instant value-judgements, and instead base their assessments on objective and informed criteria.

As with the experience of disability, the experience of being a refugee may differ in the details from country to country, but the fundamental experience of exposure to extremes of violence, fear, loss, trauma, and bereavement is very similar worldwide.

Navigating this manual

The manual begins with four narrative chapters. Chapter 1 presents the thesis and underlying principles of Oxfam's approach; to illustrate them, it offers an overview of the situation of disabled people and draws from Oxfam's programme experiences in Kosovo before and during a period of acute conflict. Chapter 2 outlines the principles of Disability Equality and illustrates its importance for development and relief agencies. Chapter 3 describes Oxfam-supported work with disabled people's organisations in Kosovo, and its outcomes. Chapter 4 provides a rationale for Disability Equality training and emphasises its importance for development and humanitarian agencies. Lessons learned in Kosovo and elsewhere are suggested as guidelines for good practice.

Part Two of the manual consists of a description and analysis of the Disability Equality Training of Trainers Course run in 1997 in Kosovo, the materials for which form the basis for the materials presented in this manual. This is followed by an introduction to the training materials, and the materials themselves – workshop activities, facilitator's notes, and handouts. The two central themes are 'Acquiring Facilitation Skills' (commonly known as 'training of trainers') and 'Disability Equality'. Other training sections cover preparations, introductions, energisers, and forming the group; action planning; evaluations; and useful quotations.

The manual ends with some sample workshop agendas and a brief list of useful resources. The conclusion offers some final thoughts on the impact of initiatives to promote the rights of disabled people.

Parts One and Two form a whole text which aims to start from a Disability Equality perspective, to include (but not focus exclusively on) gender issues, to be applicable to work in emergency-response and development situations, to make learning accessible and empowering, and to fill the gap in the literature and avoid further duplication of effort.

Who can use this manual, and for what purpose?

The manual is designed to be used by two distinct sets of readers:

- Local or national disabled people's organisations, seeking to raise awareness and put Disability Equality into action among their membership and the broader community.
- The humanitarian and development community (from donors to implementers) and government staff, seeking to promote Disability Equality, whether internally within their own organisations or externally with programmes and beneficiaries.

The narrative and theoretical chapters, the training materials, and the background reading materials may be used by disabled and non-disabled people, and international and national staff, in the following ways: to inform and develop field work in emergency-relief or development situations; and to design courses, seminars, workshops, informal discussion groups, etc. The participants (or beneficiaries) could be disabled and/or non-disabled people; national and/or international staff, volunteers, members, or activists; members or staff of grassroots organisations, or national and international NGOs and agencies; local and national community leaders, educators, medical staff, civil servants, and so on.

The materials may be used to introduce or increase awareness of Disability Equality and support its practical implementation; to help disabled people to (re)gain self-esteem and confidence; to train disabled and non-disabled disability-rights activists; to encourage NGOs to consider disability in relation to the work of a group of women survivors of violence, or the work of reconstruction engineers, public-health workers, and other sectoral staff; and to teach others how to facilitate Disability Equality workshops or discussion groups. The development of local networks of facilitators is important in countries where there is a lack of Disability Equality trainers, especially those who are disabled. Beyond the contexts listed above, Part One of the manual may be read by individuals who want to find out more about Disability Equality and its relevance to their lives and work.

The manual may be read in its entirety, but we appreciate that busy readers will select certain sections that seem most relevant to their work. We have tried to write with this in mind, repeating some information where it seems necessary, and directing readers to additional information in other sections of the manual.

A frequent problem with relief and development publications is that, while usually much attention is paid to the abstract theory, the principles applied, and the conclusions to be drawn, the reader is often left thinking: 'Yes, I understand all the theory and principles, but what did you actually do? How does that work out in practice? What was the actual process that you went through in order to reach these conclusions?' Therefore, one of the aims of this manual is to present the theory and principles of Disability Equality, which are universally applicable, but also to relate the theory and principles back to specific settings and real examples – from Kosovo, Ghana, Cambodia, Bosnia, and elsewhere. Not in order to say 'this is the way to do it' (because there is no one 'right' way), but as a reference point, or a stimulus for comparison, analysis, and application to different settings.

Finally, we hope that this manual will provide an example of how, when social change is on the agenda, it does not matter that there never seems to be an optimum time to get started, or a perfect way of doing things. Whoever we work for – DPO, NGO, donor agency, etc. – the problems are the same. Very often the planning and practicalities are all wrong: there is too little money, not enough time, not enough staff, too much external interference. Maybe we know in advance that the results are not going to be spectacular (how can one adequately measure how someone feels about being alive, and the changes that result in his or her life?). But if we wait until all the conditions are perfect, we will be waiting for ever. Doing the best we can, whatever the circumstances, and focusing on the principles and process, as much as on the end product, is enough to make a start. And once the start has been made, who knows where the process will lead us?

A note on language

Language carries intent: how we think about someone or something is reflected in the language that we use, and this is translated into action. In addition there is a huge difference between attaching a label to another person and choosing how to describe and name oneself. One action disempowers, the other empowers. Across geographical borders which share a common language, and within a country, there may be differences in the terms that people choose as appropriate for themselves. For these three reasons we have consciously used and not used specific words related to disability in this manual, according to prevailing opinion within the disability movement in the UK.

We hope that this will not be confusing to readers from other countries, and for clarification we recommend reading the sections in the training materials on language and definitions of disability (section 9.5). Briefly, we use the word '*impairment*' when we want to talk about someone's physical, sensory, or developmental limitations, and '*disabled*' and '*disability*' to talk about the dis-abling experience that constitutes everyday life for people with impairments, due to society's prejudices and discrimination. North American readers, please note that we have used the following UK-accepted terms:

- '*disabled people*', in place of the US term '*people with disabilities*';
- '*learning difficulties*' as it is understood in the UK, which is a broader definition than in the USA and includes all types of developmental impairments such as Downs Syndrome and 'retardation' (a term that is still surprisingly and commonly used in the USA), in addition to impairments like dyslexia, Attention Deficit Disorder, etc;
- and '*disability rights*' in the broadest sense of rights – encompassing human rights and basic rights, as well as legislation and social security.

One area where there is no wish to show intent through the choice of language is the spelling of 'Kosovo' (as opposed to the Albanian-language Kosova or Kosovë), used throughout this book. With the polarisation brought about by the political crisis, the way in which one spells and pronounces the word can be interpreted as a statement of one's allegiance to one side and an insult to the other. This is not the intention. We use 'Kosovo' with no political intent in any sense, and purely because it is the commonly accepted English-language spelling of the word.

Hopes and fears

This introduction would not be complete without some provisos about the manual. Firstly, in order to try to say anything at all about such complex issues, which no two people, in a variety of complex circumstances, will experience identically, we have had to make some generalisations. We have tried to make them as accurate and representative as they possibly can be; but in the knowledge that generalisations always end up excluding or offending some people, we ask for tolerance and understanding.

A significant shortcoming of this manual is that it is not written in such a way as to be accessible to many people with learning difficulties for their direct use. As a start, what the manual can and does try to do is to include consideration about how the issues of rights and equality relate to people with learning difficulties, and to prompt non-disabled people and people with physical and sensory impairments to think about this. The experience of the disability movement shows that change will come most effectively from disabled people themselves. This process can start with people with physical and sensory impairments becoming politicised, working together across the spectrum of impairments, and supporting people with learning difficulties to become actively involved. But it does not always happen this way, and there is also a need to support groups of people with learning difficulties to organise, speak, and act on their own behalf.

Many people contributed to this book in various capacities: as relief and development workers, as members of disabled people's organisations, and as disabled and non-disabled individuals. This made it hard to find a consistent voice in which to write: who is 'us' and who is 'them'? Using the first person would have made the text more immediate and accessible in tone, but might also have confused the reader. So in the end 'we' wrote it all in the third person (with the exception of this introduction). We apologise if this results in a certain dryness.

Lastly, we see this manual as a starting point, not the final product. We believe that it constitutes a powerful tool for change, even though it is shaped from a relatively limited range of experiences. We hope that readers will be inspired to use it and, with broader application and adaptation, improve it.

Part One

The principles of Disability Equality training

1 Disability and development:
an overview of the issues

Defining disability

What is disability? Trying to define it is a complex and controversial matter. It is important to consider the preferences of disabled people themselves, and to bear in mind that acceptable terminology changes over time, and from one culture to another. Two key terms – 'impairment' and 'disability' – are often used synonymously. However, their meanings are different, and it is important to make a distinction between them. **Impairment** has been defined as *'lacking all or part of a limb; having a defective limb, organ or mechanism of the body'.*[1] Some disabled campaigners question the use of this term, because of its negative implications; they prefer the more neutral term 'condition'. A condition may or may not be perceived as an impairment and may or may not restrict one's ability to function.

In contrast, the term **disability**, as used by disabled people's organisations (DPOs), emphasises society's denial of the human rights of the person with the impairment. In the words of Disabled Peoples' International: *'Disability is the disadvantage or restriction of activity caused by contemporary social organisation, which takes little or no account of people who have impairments, and thus excludes them from the mainstream of social activities.'*[2]

The distinction between the two terms is neatly summarised in a discussion paper issued by the UK government's Department for International Development: *'Disabled people have long-term impairments that lead to social and economic disadvantages, denial of rights, and limited opportunities to play an equal part in the life of the community.'*[3]

Societies may differ in their treatment of disabled people or in the way in which discrimination is expressed, but in general the marginalisation of disabled people is international and irrespective of social class.

Three major types of discrimination have been identified: **attitudinal, environmental,** and **institutional.** Disabled people may be socially excluded by attitudes of fear and ignorance on the part of non-disabled people, who may use negative and pejorative language about them; or they may be excluded from society because of generally low expectations of what disabled people can achieve. Environmental discrimination occurs where public services, buildings, and transport are not designed with access for disabled citizens in mind. Institutional discrimination occurs where the law discriminates (explicitly or by omission) against the rights of disabled people, making them in some way second-class citizens – without the right to vote, to own land, to attend school, to marry and have children.

'Disabled people want to be treated as normal citizens, with rights. They want to be treated equally and participate as equal citizens in their own communities. To achieve this, you need political and social action to change society.'[4]

The prevalence of impairment

The United Nations Development Programme (UNDP) estimates that in 1990 one in 20 of the world's population had a moderate to severe impairment (either physical or mental); the proportions ranged from 4.5 per cent in 'developing' areas to 7.7 per cent in 'developed' countries. The World Health Organisation, surveying the whole range of impairments, from mild to severe, estimates that between 10 and 15 per cent of the population of 'developing' areas are affected, with higher levels in affluent countries.[5] Detailed surveys indicate wide variations in the prevalence of impairments within and between countries, depending on a range of factors. For example, endemic river-blindness may affect many people within a particular area; in populations with large numbers of older people, conditions caused by the normal process of ageing are more prevalent; where armed conflict has included use of anti-personnel mines in rural areas, exceptionally high numbers of amputees may be found.

High mortality rates among children and young people with disabilities reduce the recorded incidence of impairment; yet, even if those who have died prematurely are excluded from the estimates, disabled people form a substantial minority of any population. If, in addition, we consider the families of disabled people, their carers, and others who are seriously affected by disability, then in some parts of the world the majority of the population may be affected by disability.

Disability, gender, and poverty

There exists a vicious cycle that links poverty and disability. Poverty frequently causes disability, or makes its effects worse, by virtue of factors such as malnutrition, inadequate housing, dangerous work in hazardous conditions, poor-quality medical treatment, and inadequate access to services. Disabled people are likely to face barriers to their inclusion in society, to educational opportunities, and to their access to health care and employment, which in turn will perpetuate their poverty. Families with a disabled member also face barriers and are likely to experience a greater degree of poverty than similar families without disabled members.

The need to care for a disabled family member makes demands upon other members and reduces the time available to them for economic activity or skills development. Disability has a disproportionate impact on males and females: in developing countries, most of the caring, as well as much of the production, is done by women, and girls are frequently withdrawn from school to look after a disabled brother or sister. Although in global terms 51 per cent of disabled people are women, disabled girls and women have even less access to education, health care, and employment than disabled boys and men have. Disabled women are doubly discriminated against: as women, and as people with impairments. They are often invisible to the providers of health care, and particularly reproductive-health care, yet they are also the frequent victims of sexual abuse.

While it is true that poverty is the cause of many impairments, disability affects rich and poor people alike. In Kosovo, there is a myth that people who are educated, wealthy, or professionally qualified take better care of disabled family members than people who are poorer or less educated. In reality there may be more pressure on a wealthy family to hide a disabled relative, so as not to damage the family's social status. Oxfam found that disabled people and their families who were wealthy or belonged to the social elite were less likely to become involved in disabled people's organisations, whereas people who were really struggling to survive became very active, both as contributors and beneficiaries.

Discrimination against disabled people is compounded if they belong to an ethnic minority or other marginalised group. But irrespective of their social class, or their religious or ethnic identity, disabled people around the world are likely to be poorer in terms of money, power, and rights, than non-disabled citizens of the same group.

Organisations *for* disabled people and organisations *of* disabled people

Throughout Eastern Europe, under the socialist system, State-funded associations based on types of impairment (blindness, paraplegia, etc.) catered for disabled people. They gave people access to orthopaedic equipment, State welfare benefits, and occupational therapy, but they resulted in the segregation of services for disabled people and did nothing at all to empower them to claim their rights. Once the socialist system collapsed, even welfare benefits were lost, with nothing to replace them.

In the absence of a strong civil society, there was no mechanism for disabled people to participate in and lobby for changes that would improve their conditions. On a fundamental level they were not represented in forums where they might have claimed their rights and expressed their needs, and as such they were disenfranchised from the State process. In Kosovo the problem was compounded by prevailing attitudes of rejection or shame, which meant that disabled people were either hidden away and left to die, or cosseted and over-protected, deprived of any opportunity to live independently. The net result was that disabled people were virtually invisible and lacked mobility, opportunity, and confidence. Disabled women experienced these problems even more keenly than disabled men.

In all societies, many families respond to disability by being over-protective. They rarely allow disabled family members to go outside the home, in case they get hurt or ridiculed. Everything is done for the disabled person, including things that he or she would be perfectly able to do independently. The effect of this over-protectiveness, usually motivated by love, is to render the disabled person passive and inactive, and to feel helpless and patronised. Denied the freedom to take risks and responsibility or to learn from mistakes, he or she is permanently treated as a child, and not allowed to grow up.

None of these problems is unique to Kosovo, but in a highly politicised environment it is particularly difficult for disabled people to articulate their specific needs, as distinct from the needs of the whole community. Throughout the 1980s and 1990s, tensions grew between the Kosovo Albanians and the Belgrade government. This evolved into a full-blown conflict in 1998. The prevailing view in Kosovo was that the situation of disabled people would automatically improve if and when the political problems were resolved for the whole population. The needs of the minority were subjugated to those of the majority – but many of the problems that disabled people faced were not at all dependent on a resolution of the macro-political problems.

Well-meaning professionals and carers have for many years decided what opportunities and services are offered to disabled people. Organisations for various disability sub-groups have tried to complement State provision by running additional services, such as organisations for blind people, or deaf people, or those with limited mobility. Whether run by the State or by the voluntary sector, both these approaches have been based on addressing the special needs of disabled people, particularly those closely relating to their impairment.

In recent decades, disabled people have reviewed the progress made towards meeting their needs via this model of service provision, controlled and organised by non-disabled staff with little room for the inclusion of the end-users. Since the International Year of the Disabled Person, 1981, and the ensuing Decade of Disabled People (1982–1992), disabled people and their own organisations have played a critical role in speaking out in international forums about the specific needs of disabled people, and in developing a rights-based approach to disability. This approach assumes that disabled people have diverse needs, like those of non-disabled people, which should be met as part of the general provision for the whole population: education services should meet the needs of all students, whether disabled or not; health services should be open and accessible to all.

The global, cross-disability movement called Disabled Peoples' International (DPI), to which most national organisations belong, describes itself as 'the last civil rights movement'. Its motto is *Nothing about us without us*. This is a call to disabled people and their organisations for action, involvement, and commitment. It urges disabled people not to allow others to ignore or forget about them, but to consult and listen to them, and to take their needs and rights into account. It encourages disabled people to make their presence felt and their opinions known, and to be actively involved in making decisions about all the issues affecting them.

Three models of disability

A major contribution made by disabled people to an understanding of disability has been the description and development of 'the three models of disability'. These are frameworks which help to explain the ways in which society responds to disability and to review the appropriateness of its responses.

The medical model of disability

The medical model tends to view disabled people first and foremost as having physical problems to be cured. The disabled person is relegated to the passive role of patient, with medical personnel and care professionals making many decisions – even about issues unrelated to impairment, such as how the individual should dress or what he or she may eat. This model is problematic because of its excessive focus on the desirability of fixing the disabled person's impairment. The quest for a cure is often protracted, painful, and unnecessary; it means that the rest of life is put on hold while professionals strive to return the body to a more 'normal' level of functioning. Corrective surgery is used to extend and straighten limbs, callipers are applied, and people are encouraged to try to walk, rather than use wheeled mobility appliances; deaf people are taught to speak and lip-read. Health-care professionals may refuse to tell disabled patients and their families that there is no cure for their condition, in the mistaken belief that this will sustain hope that they one day might be 'normal'. But if it happens that the impairment cannot be fixed, the disabled person is regarded as being beyond hope: his or her life is seen as worthless. By this stage, such a negative assessment may well become internalised by the person concerned.

There are clear cases where relatively simple levels of medical intervention can reduce the impact of impairments substantively; examples would be a surgical operation to correct a cataract or a club foot. It is also the case that some disabled people have a medical condition which requires support and intervention. Preventive measures to reduce the incidence of impairment and to promote its early detection are also valuable means of reducing the level and impact of disability. Disabled people do not reject medical intervention, but they stress that the impact of disability on the individual is much greater than its medical implications, and that it is misleading to focus on the search for a cure, rather than helping individuals to manage their own lives.

The medical model perceives disability as a problem located in the disabled individual, and assumes that working on the individual can solve it (or not, as the case may be, in which case the person concerned might as well give up all hope of a full and satisfying life). The disabled person becomes defined solely in terms of his or her diagnosis, as a patient with medical needs and no longer as a person with a whole range of needs.

One young woman from Kosovo described the sense of liberation that she felt when, after many failed operations to lengthen one leg by 3 cm to make it the same length as her normal leg, she finally decided that this was unimportant. She and her leg were fine as they were. She turned her back on medical interventions and got on with the rest of her life: she became a hairdresser and beautician, building up a fine reputation, and now brides come from far away for her wedding make-up service. During the pre-war years of political and economic crisis in Kosovo, she supported her family from her own income.

The religious, or charitable, model of disability

In Kosovo, disability is traditionally interpreted according to religious beliefs: impairments are regarded as a punishment from God for a sin committed by oneself or one's family. Having a disabled relative is a source of shame, often for the whole family. Disability can damage the marriage chances of non-disabled siblings, especially sisters. Consequently, some families keep their disabled relatives hidden from neighbours, visitors, and even other family members. Some disabled people live out their existence, such as it is, isolated in one room, at times even chained up.

The religious, or charitable, model tends to view disabled people as victims of impairment and as the beneficiaries of charity, alms, and services – for which they should be grateful. Disabled people are viewed as tragic or suffering people, to be pitied and cared for. At the same time, disabled people may find that they have few choices, no means of accessing relevant advice, and no powers to decide how they could best be assisted. Services are designed for them and delivered to them, perhaps with the best of intentions, but with insufficient consultation. Carers may become unacceptably powerful, making decisions about what is best for those in their care. An extreme (though not uncommon) example of this is the enforced sterilisation, without consultation or consent, of disabled women.

It is not uncommon for disabled people to become dependent upon the source of help, and for the alms-givers to gain gratification and reward from the relationship. Charity is provided at the discretion of the giver, often on the basis of 'worthiness'. If the person providing charity or care decides that the disabled person is unworthy, bitter, or 'negative', help may be withdrawn on a whim. Disabled people are often caricatured as being tragic and passive, if they need high levels of support; as bitter, twisted, and aggressive, if they are beginning to question the *status quo*; and as courageous and inspirational if they have managed, against all the odds, to overcome the barriers that confront them.

Because disabled people are considered to be different from the norm, a range of different, or special, services to meet their needs has usually been provided for them: special transport; special buildings; special schools (where the courses are very often less challenging and academic than in mainstream schools, making it hard or impossible for disabled people to enter higher education and employment); special sports and recreational facilities; sheltered employment workshops. Extra resources are necessary in order to provide such special services, and in resource-poor economies the inability to provide adequate levels of service (in health care, education, production) for the whole population is frequently used as a justification for doing very little to provide special services for disabled people.

It cannot be claimed that either the medical or the religious/charitable approach has had much success in improving the lives of disabled people – as proved by the high levels of poverty, abuse, marginalisation, and discrimination that disabled people still face worldwide; yet for centuries these two models have determined disabled people's experience. Through what is known as the 'mirror effect', many disabled people (who, like others, see themselves reflected in the attitudes of the people around them) have come to believe that they are *unable*. In recent years the deliberate focus of the disability movement on abilities rather than inabilities has helped to develop a new understanding of disability. In order to create a society that includes disabled and non-disabled people equally, and thus achieves Disability Equality, we need a new way of perceiving and responding to disability.

The social model of disability

Such a concept and approach is described by disabled people themselves as 'the social model'. This refers to the way in which society organises itself, taking little account of people who have impairments and thus excluding them from participation in the mainstream of social activities. The social model identifies three major barriers that confront disable people who have impairments: physical (exclusion from the built environment), institutional (systematic exclusion or neglect in social, legal, educational, religious, and political institutions), and attitudinal (negative valuations of disabled people by non-disabled people). Removing these barriers is possible and has a hugely beneficial impact, both on the lives of disabled people and on the whole community.

Adopting the social model of disability does not mean rejecting any form of medical services, rehabilitation, or assistance from others; but it does change the way in which services and assistance should be given, placing them in the wider context of disabled people's lives. Disabled people's needs are basically the same as non-disabled people's: for life, love, education, employment, full participation in society, access to adequate services (including medical and rehabilitation services when necessary) as of right, and some choice and degree of control in their lives.

> 'We cannot give the blind person sight. We can give the sighted person the ability to enable the blind person to do what s/he wants.'[6]

The social model has allowed many disabled people to regain control of their own lives, becoming the experts on their own experience and changing their outlook in fundamental ways. An understanding of the social model provides a radically different framework with which to understand the discrimination that arises as a result of impairment. For many DPOs, the social model describes the true nature of the problem of disability. The problem is not in the individual, nor in his or her impairment. The impairment exists, but its significance is neutral – neither necessarily negative or necessarily positive. The problem of disability lies in society's response to the individual and the impairment, and in the physical environment, which is mainly designed (largely by non-disabled people) to meet the needs of non-disabled people. Disability takes on a social dimension and leads to social exclusion and the denial of human rights. The solution to the problems of disability must therefore come from change within the families, communities, and societies in which disabled people are living, rather than from changes in the impaired individual (as suggested by the medical model).

The social model is a helpful tool to enable disabled people and their allies to achieve positive changes in their lives, and for non-disabled people to understand more about disability. There are similarities between the claims made by disabled people and those made by other civil-rights movements, such as the campaigns for the rights of women, ethnic minorities, and people of different race. The disability movement has learned from other liberation movements that change has to start with action by the oppressed: in this case by disabled people themselves. They are the experts of their own experience, and they best understand how society is organised around the needs of its non-disabled members. Disabled people internationally are now gaining an increasing voice – articulating their own needs, taking an active part in meeting them and in lobbying for full inclusion in society. Non-disabled people share responsibility for changing attitudes, shifting positions, and making changes that will allow fuller inclusion of disabled people. Many non-disabled people play an important role as allies, understanding and supporting disabled people's struggle for equal rights and being prepared to make concessions in their own positions.

> When I adopted the social model as a lens through which to see my life, I realised it brought with it certain responsibilities. No longer could I claim victim status at the mercy of the non-disabled community. I had now found a way of dealing with society's treatment of me. I had a tool, which enabled me to redefine my experience. I now had a terminology and the language of oppressed people, which enabled me to belong and struggle against society's attitude towards me. At best we face society's ignorance and at worst we face their apathy towards the discrimination of disabled people in our daily lives. With others who think the same, and there are many, I now had the responsibility to try and do something about it. (Liz Crow, quoted in E. Boylan: *Women and Disability*, London: Zed Books, 1991)

Disability in the context of development

In the community-development field, the most common approach to disability emphasises rehabilitation, whether institutional or community-based. Integral to the medical model, rehabilitation frequently appears to address only a limited number of the needs of disabled people – in particular mobility aids, communication skills, and skills for daily living. No one would deny that these aids and skills can make an enormous difference to the quality of life and independence of disabled people, but their acquisition is not an end in itself: it is merely the first essential step towards enabling disabled people to gain access to all other services. The development community often fails to address the full range of disabled people's needs and rights, which are far more diverse than these most basic needs. For example, credit and income-generating schemes should not exclude disabled people by fixing criteria for inclusion – such as minimum land tenure or possession of fixed assets – that will automatically disqualify disabled people, who in general lack such resources.

The way in which rehabilitation services are delivered, predominantly by health-care and social-work professionals whose experience and outlook are strongly influenced by the medical model of disability, is problematic. Much has been made of so-called 'community-based rehabilitation' (CBR), which is an approach designed to deliver rehabilitation services through accessible and cost-effective mechanisms. But its implementation differs in almost every situation, and in its narrowest sense CBR is simply rehabilitation which has moved out of institutions, to be delivered in the community according to a template defined by the manual of the World Health Organisation. A more inclusive approach is evolving from a community-development approach to CBR, and some exceptional CBR programmes have been implemented with the full involvement of disabled people, their families, and their communities. The principles of rights, equal participation, and inclusion have now been recognised in some CBR programmes, but they still frequently appear as add-on extras, rather than as integral principles from which the whole approach is elaborated.

Current attitudes and approaches should be reversed to allow disabled people to participate in the definition of their needs and the design of projects to address those needs, and to include them in the management of systems to deliver benefits. Obvious parallels may be drawn with the inclusion of women as beneficiaries and as organisers of development activities to address the needs of women. The basic development principle of involving beneficiaries in identifying and prioritising needs, in influencing decisions about a range of possible solutions, and in managing and monitoring project activities (in other words, participation, consultation, and feedback) should be respected in all interventions intended to benefit disabled people.

Many agencies now argue for a twin-track approach to disability, suggesting that while it is still necessary to run development activities designed to address particular needs of disabled people through sector-specific projects, such as the provision of wheelchairs, hearing aids, and hygiene facilities, it is also vital to address disability as a cross-cutting theme, considering the needs of all sectors of a diverse population in generic development projects (for example, delivering good-quality health care and clean water to all). Ideally, all development staff should automatically consider the needs of disabled people within their target population – applying a Disability Equality dimension to the initial project analysis, so that disabled people are expressly included in the beneficiary group, rather than excluded by omission.

Mainstream development programmes may inadvertently discriminate against disabled people and exclude them if they do not apply a Disability Equality analysis. For example, in Uganda most micro-finance programmes set preconditions that are too onerous for disabled people to meet (since they are usually among the poorest in their communities). One livestock-distribution programme requires beneficiaries to own at least one acre of grazing land. According to local tradition, disabled people are not allowed to inherit land and are thus automatically ineligible for inclusion in the scheme. If staff responsible for identifying potential participants in any programme are not aware of the needs and capabilities of disabled people, they may bring their own prejudices into decision-making. If they focus on disability and not ability, they are likely to believe that disabled people are inadequate and assess them as a bad risk.

An approach to disability based on the social model is well illustrated by the 'Come To Work' programme in Bangladesh, as described by one of its participants.

'My name is Sufia. I am 52 years old. I live in a small village called Chak Krishnapur. My husband was a poor agricultural worker. He died about 12 years ago. I have seven daughters and one son, who are all married now. I started working as a day labourer in a rice-husking mill after my husband's death. My employer and colleagues said I was a sincere and hard worker. But one day an accident occurred: my sari (garment) got caught in the moving belt of the husking machine, and my life was changed. I lost my left hand and became disabled. I lost my job and became unemployed. I saw everything dark around me and became dependent on others. People were sympathetic, but I did not like their attitudes. I cried every night, could not sleep, and could not see how I would survive.

One morning a woman from Come to Work (CTW) came to meet me and described their activities. She suggested I join the CTW women's group, and said that my disability was not a barrier to joining the group. I started dreaming again after talking to her. I joined the nearest women's group, called Chak Krishnapur Mahila Samity, and started to generate savings. The other members accepted me and were very co-operative, helping me to learn a lot, including the rules and regulations of the credit scheme.

Within six months of joining the group, I got Tk. 500 credit from CTW for income-generating activities. I bought a goat, which produced two kids, and I made a profit. I repaid the credit to CTW and received Tk. 1500 to buy a cow. Gradually CTW increased my credit, and my income also increased. Now I own four cows, eight goats, 15 ducks, and five hens. I created all these assets from the profit on the credit-support provided by CTW. Now I have changed my life: I am not dependent on anybody.'

(As told to Shah Alam Liton, Oxfam GB, Bangladesh).

Disability in situations of disaster and conflict

In any crisis (whether it arises from war, or natural disaster, or political or economic upheaval), disabled people are likely to feel the negative impact of the crisis more keenly than other citizens. Their ability to cope and survive may be completely dependent upon others, and the capacity of any family to support its disabled members is keenly tested in a crisis. Anecdotal evidence from acute emergencies suggests that disabled people suffer particularly high rates of mortality and morbidity.

In conflict-ridden regions, there is always an increase in the incidence of impairment. In addition to those who were disabled before the onset of the crisis, many more become disabled as a result of a range of factors:

- combat injury and poor medical care behind the lines;
- mutilation used as a tool of war (for example, amputation of the hands of suspected government sympathisers by the Revolutionary United Forces rebels in Sierra Leone)
- land-mine injuries to civilians
- deterioration in medical services within a country in conflict
- interruption of preventative health-care programmes.

Within displaced and refugee populations, disabled people are frequently abandoned and left behind, to be killed by the enemy or to face starvation.

- They get left behind because they have no transport, because they cannot travel on foot over mountains, or because their families are unable to carry them.
- They get left behind because priority is given to the survival of non-disabled family members. (This is frequently the case for people with learning difficulties, for whom mobility is not even an issue.)
- They become more dependent, even totally dependent, on others, for food, water, assistance with basic bodily functions, and information.

Disabled people have additional and specific needs for protection. Anecdotal evidence from refugees indicates that in Sierra Leone soldiers would shoot dead on the spot any disabled people they came across, 'to put them out of their suffering'. Oxfam programme staff in Bosnia heard how disabled people became trapped in institutions during the war and starved or froze to death. An institution housing physically disabled people became caught between military front lines; staff fled, and the disabled residents all died.

In the words of Myrvete, a disabled woman activist from Kosovo: 'If a non-disabled person has one problem, a disabled person's problems are twice as big. For example, during the recent conflict, I've been working with disabled people from areas directly involved and I can't imagine how they escaped. I imagine them being carried by a family member and friends away from the shelling. Some were not so lucky: we know of a disabled woman who was killed because she couldn't move herself.'

People with impaired mobility who are able to flee may subsequently become more dependent because wheelchairs and other aids were left behind for reasons of space, or are not usable in the new environment. Visually impaired people may not be able to rely on their usual strategies for orienting themselves, both as they flee and when they arrive in places of temporary refuge. People with learning difficulties are known to be particularly exposed to risk, despite the fact that they have no direct mobility problem. For a disabled person who has never been allowed outside the family compound, fleeing may cause enormous physical and psychological trauma, and at the outset disabled people may be unable to assess the risks or make a choice about whether to flee or to stay.

Lack of understanding of the problems of people with learning difficulties (whose needs are often the last on the list of priorities, even among DPOs) often means that their need for psychosocial support and protection is overlooked. During the Krajina emergency in 1995/96, when Croatian troops displaced nearly 300,000 Croatian Serbs into Bosnia, Oxfam staff found people with learning difficulties left to fend for themselves, while others who were less vulnerable benefited from the whole range of available assistance. During the crisis in Kosovo, disabled people told Oxfam of their wish to leave their villages for a safer location, which was frustrated by their families' reluctance to move. Because disabled people in this environment were heavily dependent on their family, they were left with no choice over their own immediate future. At the other end of the spectrum, some disabled people were used against their own wishes by their families, who got permission to leave Macedonia on humanitarian grounds and seek asylum in other countries.

The vulnerability of the population as a whole is increased in a crisis; and, given the scarcity of resources, people's needs have to be prioritised. Those whose value to society is not recognised are given lower priority. In registering for assistance, displaced families may fail to indicate that they have a disabled member, which results in that person's general and specific needs remaining unmet. The disabled person may have to wait until everyone else in the family has been fed before he or she is provided for. Frequently the breakdown of support structures within a disaster-affected population further endangers the position of disabled people; they may lose their ability to function independently – and with it their dignity.

During the emergency in 1995 in Krajina, Croatia, a man with muscular dystrophy reached a temporary refugee reception centre. Before the conflict this man had lived in his own accessible apartment with his wife (who was also physically disabled). He had his own electrical repairs business and supported his ailing elderly mother and seven-year-old son. Since fleeing from home and arriving at the centre, this man virtually fasted – eating and drinking the bare minimum in order not to use a toilet very often. Because the toilet at the reception centre was completely inaccessible to him unaided, and it was very hard to find someone willing to help him, the indignity of his need was causing him to place himself at risk. If this man had become sick or died, the human loss and the care of his three dependents would have cost his community and those providing aid far more than the provision of a simple accessible toilet or toilet chair.

Disability within a relief context

The effects of an emergency, while significant for everyone concerned, are not equally felt. Long-held attitudes and established cultural norms determine who is valued in society, who deserves what, and who has access to power, decision-making, assets, and money. In emergencies this results in inequitable access to resources and services that should be basic rights, in favour of those with higher status. People who are accorded lower status are therefore usually very vulnerable and exposed to a higher risk of suffering. It is widely accepted that in complex political emergencies the denial of human rights is very often at the heart of the crisis. It must also be recognised that the inequitable effects of the crisis – the fact that the impacts are harsher for marginalised groups than for other groups – are also primarily a matter of human rights. Relief and development workers are now recognising the disproportionate vulnerability and suffering of women and girls, but most have yet to recognise the particular problems of disabled people.

Disabled people tend to be invisible to emergency registration systems. They are frequently left unregistered, which means that they fail to receive their basic entitlements to food, water, and clothing, and their specific needs are not met either. Disabled people may lack the necessary documents which would give them refugee status and rights as returnees. This problem was particularly acute in Kosovo, where for ten years many children had not been registered (as part of the Albanian refusal to participate in structures that they perceived as part of the Serbian State). Disabled children were even less likely to be registered, which made it hard to prove their right of return.

Emergencies compound the dependence of some disabled people on their primary carers. For others, used to living independently, lack of appropriate responses in a crisis can create a situation in which they are forced into becoming more dependent on others. This was acutely obvious in the refugee camps in Macedonia in the late 1990s, where initially there was no provision at all for disabled people. They were not recognised in the initial registration system, and they were not provided with any facilities that would make their lives easier (accessible latrines, water points, levelled terrain, alternative means of access to information, etc.). This was in direct contradiction of the Red Cross and Red Crescent Code of Conduct, which recognises the essential dignity of each human being, and the importance of providing assistance that enhances and promotes self-reliance.

In 1996 a survey organised by Oxfam in 13 municipalities in Bosnia identified more than 1000 disabled refugees and internally displaced people. The majority reported that the only aid they had received was very limited supplies of food, despite the existence at the time of a whole range of distribution and psychosocial support programmes. In addition, many were at increased risk of disease, due to the unhygienic conditions of their temporary accommodation (caused in large part by the inaccessibility of facilities) and their lack of access to medical attention.

It cannot be assumed that general distributions to the affected population will automatically reach the disabled members of that population, or that disabled people in a refugee camp will automatically have equitable access to whatever water is available. There are many reasons why disabled people are excluded, and unless agencies take specific action, things will not change. Common reasons why disabled people fail to receive their entitlements include the following.

- They are hidden by their families.
- They may not know there is a distribution, because they cannot attend community meetings or cannot hear radio announcements, and no provision has been made to inform them in any alternative way about their entitlements and the available services.
- Disabled people and their families may not consider themselves to be capable of participating in a micro-enterprise programme.
- Problems of access may be aggravated by poor terrain, or lack of mobility aids, or (for people with impaired sight) assistance with orientation.
- They may have become ill through not being able to keep clean, or through developing pressure sores in their difficult living circumstances, or lacking medication that they require.
- Emotional distress and/or mental illness, often caused by the trauma of the crisis, is another reason why people are prevented from gaining access to relief distributions for themselves and their families.

By including disability as a factor in assessments and using a variety of approaches to ensure that all people can obtain the relief to which they are entitled, it is possible to ensure that disabled people are included. Assessment and planning tools already commonly in use can be adapted to include disabled people; for example, participatory mapping processes should identify the locations of disabled people, and their particular resources and needs .

The post-crisis reconstruction phase

Major reconstruction often follows emergency relief work, but planners often miss opportunities to avoid recreating the inequitable *status quo* by adapting the design of the built environment to meet the needs of disabled people. For example, if schools are not rebuilt in a way that allows disabled children (both those who were previously disabled and the newly disabled) to attend school, this sends a damaging message to the disabled child and places limitations on his or her entire life. The long-term costs are high, since a disabled child who is prevented from going to school is far less likely to find employment and contribute directly to the national or local economy, and will thus require a lifetime of assistance from the State or his or her family.

It is often more cost-effective to modify the plans for a new building at the outset than to adapt an existing building retrospectively to make it accessible. Depending on the type of building, providing full access facilities from the outset costs an average additional 1.12 per cent (ranging from 0.1 per cent for public buildings to 3 per cent for individual family homes); for retrofits the additional cost has been calculated at 7.2 per cent (ranging from 0.12 per cent for public buildings to 21 per cent for individual family homes).[7] It is reasonable to expect that, as architects and builders become more experienced in incorporating elements to improve accessibility, costs will fall further.

To argue that accessibility is not cost-effective overlooks the fact that everyone, not just disabled people, will benefit from an accessible built environment. Older people, young parents with small children, those who are temporarily injured – a total of perhaps 40 per cent of the population – need the same sorts of access modification in the built environment. An accessible environment, designed to meet the needs of people with disabilities, is safer for everyone; it reduces the number of accidents, leading to long-term (but unrecognised) savings in health care and welfare costs, lost income, and so on.

The development of civil society

Post-war aid programmes which support the development of civil society and help people to exercise control over their lives and to have a voice in their community must guard against excluding disabled people from this stage of the reconstruction process. It is important to consider the place of disabled people in those programmes and in the civil society that they aim to create.

Uganda provides an impressive example of how disabled people can be fully included in community and civic development. Ten years of sensitisation, lobbying, advocacy, and organising by disabled people, working together as a united movement, led to their representation within decision-making bodies at all levels of government. At the time of writing, Uganda had five disabled Members of Parliament, and 46,210 disabled people serving as Councillors from village to district council levels. Achieving political representation is, however, a means rather than an end: Uganda's disabled people are now set to challenge institutionalised barriers to equality from within the decision-making institutions of their communities.

During the war in Bosnia, disabled people's organisations were the only local organisations to maintain their pre-war membership without prejudice based on members' ethnicity. Resisting enormous social and political pressure to discriminate according to ethnicity, disabled Muslims, Serbs, and Croats helped each other to survive. This type of cross-cultural co-operation should be recognised by agencies implementing civil-society projects and should be seized upon as an opportunity and entry point for fostering further dialogue and active co-existence between peoples who were previously at war. During and after the war in Kosovo, disabled people's organisations played a vital role in providing emotional support to traumatised and displaced disabled people: another key element in the process of healing and recovery, without which it is hard for civil society to develop.

Disability inequality: the consequences for the relief and development community

Despite the majority of UN member states being signatories to UN Standard Rules on the Equalization of Opportunities for Persons with Disabilities,[8] these standards, which provide targets and guidance for the inclusion of disabled people in society and provide for equal access to services and participation, are rarely put into practice. There remains an enormous amount of lobbying and advocacy work to be done to encourage governments to address these issues and to reach the standards set out in this and other conventions.

Many disabled people are excluded from relief and development programmes as beneficiaries, partners, and contributors. Their basic needs are simply not adequately met, and their human rights are at best ignored, at worst abused. The exclusion or omission of disabled people has a negative impact on the quality and effectiveness of programmes. Disabled people are among the poorest of the poor, the most disempowered, and the most in need; they are present in virtually every community in the world, as well as in all populations targeted by relief and development interventions. It follows that many agencies are currently failing to fulfil their mandates.

Most emergency, relief, and development organisations are mandated to address problems of poverty, marginalisation, powerlessness, vulnerability, and abuse of human rights. These issues form the basis of many disabled people's daily experience, and yet too often there is a disparity between the mandate and stated operational philosophies of agencies, and what they actually do in practice to support disabled people in their struggle for equality. It is still not uncommon for relief and development agencies and donor institutions to be blind to disability or to ignore its impact when analysing a given situation and the needs of those who are most affected by poverty or emergency. Whatever the type of programme (emergency relief, or development) under consideration, the target population will almost certainly include disabled people. Aid and development workers may not see them or know about them, but they will be there and they are likely to be among the most vulnerable or marginalised people within the target beneficiary group.

Relief and development agencies need to learn more about Disability Equality and use it as a tool to redress current imbalances, to put an end to practices which discriminate (unwittingly or otherwise) against disabled people. This will lead to fuller, more effective compliance with their mandates and their humanitarian obligations. Oxfam itself is not without fault in this respect, although, like many others, it is now seeking to develop its understanding, analysis, and practice to address the reality of full inclusion for disabled people in its programmes and in their communities. In part this strategy is grounded in the experience gained from working with disabled people in Kosovo.

Notes

1   K. Davis, *Re-Defining the Disabled Underclass*, Union of the Physically Impaired Against Segregation.

2   Disabled Peoples' International (DPI) www.dpi.org.

3   DFID Issues Paper, 'Disability, Poverty and Development', London, 2000.

4   Joshua Malinga, Chairperson of DPI, quoted in *Disability, Liberation, and Development* (written by Peter Coleridge, published by Oxfam, Oxford, 1993).

5   'Comprehensive Disability Policy Framework for Kosovo', Disability Task Force, Pristina, 2001.

6   Micheline Mason and Richard Reiser: *Disability Equality in the Classroom: A Human Rights Issue*, London: Disability Equality in Education, 1992.

7   A. Ratzka, Institute of Independent Living, 'A Brief Survey of Studies on Costs and Benefits of Non-handicapping Environments', 1994.

8   Adopted by the UN General Assembly in December 1993 and available at www.un.org/ecoscodev/geninfo/dpi

2 What is 'Disability Equality'?

Fundamental principles

The concept of Disability Equality is grounded in two fundamental principles.

Principle 1: Redefining disability according to the social model

Our understanding and interpretation of disability should be guided by the social model and recognise the three forms of discrimination – attitudinal, environmental, institutional – that prevent full inclusion of disabled citizens. (See Chapter 1.) Through applying this analysis, one comes to see that disabled people are handicapped by the barriers that society, and non-disabled members of that society, have erected around them. One gains a better understanding of disability – not as a medical condition, but as a product of the way in which society is organised, making insufficient allowance for the needs of all its members. Understanding the social model has been a turning point for many disabled people, and also for their allies.

Principle 2: Disability is a human-rights issue

Disability must also be understood within the context of human rights. The rights of disabled citizens are the same as those of non-disabled citizens. All people should have equal access to opportunity and services, as of right, be they women, older people, disabled people, or members of ethnic minorities. Many disabled people are isolated socially and/or physically, and learning about their human rights, including that most basic right to have some say and control over their own lives, has been the first step towards self-liberation.

The Universal Declaration of Human Rights (UDHR) has been signed by virtually every country in the world and underpins the philosophy and mission of many relief and development agencies. But disability has largely been ignored when human rights are under scrutiny. The physical and psychological discrimination that many disabled people suffer is not typically considered in the same manner as other violations of human rights. Most people associate human-rights abuse with politically or ethnically motivated killing, imprisonment, torture, and restrictions on freedom of movement and freedom of expression; they overlook the fact that every day disabled people are denied the right to express themselves, to make choices, and to obtain access to education, employment, and health care.

A rights-based approach to disability recognises that disabled people have the same rights as other citizens, although their entitlements may frequently be denied to them. The needs of disabled people are not different from those of other people. They have basic needs (for food, clean water, shelter, health care, education, and income); psycho-social needs (for friends, relationships, reproductive rights, equal access to services, and inclusion in the community); and political needs (to be able to organise, to associate freely, to be represented, and to have legal and voting rights). In addition, disabled people have fundamental needs in terms of communication and mobility that must first be addressed in order for them to be able to claim their other strategic rights as equal citizens. Meeting these practical needs is only a pre-condition, albeit a vital one, to enable disabled people to achieve inclusion in all other aspects of life.

Tools for change: Disability Equality training

Disability Equality training is the process of raising awareness of the causes and consequences of disability, and helping disabled people to claim their full and equal rights as citizens. Within the UK disability movement, Disability Equality has been promoted by disabled trainers as a tool to sensitise and mobilise disabled people to take action to lobby for rights and services. In Kosovo, Oxfam's Disability Equality training work was led by a staff member who as it happened was not disabled. There is no one way of carrying out Disability Equality training. Its aim is to bring about action that will lead to greater inclusion, equality, and rights for disabled people; this requires both action on the part of disabled people, and a change in attitude on the part of the rest of society. Thus both disabled people and their non-disabled allies are promoting and encouraging Disability Equality as a framework around which to construct an approach to disability that is based on the principle of equality of access to full services and rights as citizens.

Despite the deep poverty and discrimination experienced by many disabled people, Disability Equality training can be effective – because it begins by changing disabled people's perceptions of themselves. It focuses on what people *can* do, rather than what they cannot do, and it deals with feelings of powerlessness and the lack of self-confidence which might otherwise cause programmes to fail. Disability Equality training helps everyone to review their attitudes to disability, and their understanding of it, and to assess what changes they each might make towards overcoming the barriers that exclude disabled people from full participation in society. An approach based on a commitment to Disability Equality is equally valid for disabled and non-disabled trainees. It is about starting with what is possible, in terms of dismantling barriers to inclusion (be these in our own minds, or in the environment over which we have some influence). It helps disabled and non-disabled people to find practical, workable ways of putting principles into action. It identifies ways in which non-disabled people can support disabled people in their struggle for equal access and inclusion – not because this is a worthy thing to do, but because it is the right of all citizens to be included in society, on equal terms. These are some of the specific aims of the training:

- To empower disabled people.
- To encourage everyone to value the lives and contributions of *all* members of society.

- To create an enabling environment which gives each individual an equal opportunity to develop his or her potential and to participate and contribute in whatever way he or she chooses.
- To identify the particular needs of disabled people which must be met if they are to make the most of the opportunities open to them.
- To provide equal access to necessary resources.
- To encourage respect for differences and diversity, while celebrating our common humanity.
- To gain equal rights and responsibilities for disabled and non-disabled people, in law and in practice.

'Impairments can be endured, but the lack of human rights, the marginalisation and exclusion, the deprivation of equal opportunities and the institutional discrimination that disabled people face cannot be endured and can no longer be tolerated.'

(Maria Rantho, Deputy Chair, Disabled Peoples' International, speaking at the World Conference on Women, Beijing, 1995)

Myths and unconscious attitudes

As part of Oxfam's Disability Equality Training project in Kosovo, humanitarian-relief and development workers were encouraged to talk about disability, in order to uncover common assumptions, most based on misconceptions and ignorance, which helped to explain some of the inadequate programmatic responses to the situation of disabled people, and to validate the need for a Disability Equality approach. If NGOs are to meet the challenges posed by the exclusion of disabled people from society, and their invisibility in their own programmes, these attitudinal barriers must be identified, challenged, and changed.

Unconscious – or half-conscious – prejudice against disabled people was expressed in statements such as the following:
- *'We need to sort out the problems of "normal" people first.'*
- *'It's not cost-effective to include disabled people. ...Disability access is a luxury that we can't afford back home, let alone here.'*
- *'I feel sorry for them, but there aren't many disabled people here anyway, so it's not really an issue.'*
- *'It's not in our mandate – we don't "do" disability.'*
- *'We don't have the skills to work with disabled people.'*
- *'We should create a special programme for them.'*

Below we examine some of these misconceptions and offer a different perspective.

'We need to sort out the problems of "normal" people first.'

But disability *is* normal: disabled people are present in every community across the globe; it is just one expression of the diversity of the human race. Our perceptions of reality are distorted by social norms which keep disabled people out of the public arena, and by the narrow vision of beauty/perfection that is frequently presented in media images. The aid and development community works to counter conditions which would allow only for the survival of the fittest. It should recognise its obligation to work equally hard to improve the life chances and quality of life for disabled people.

'It's not cost-effective to include disabled people.'

Including disabled people is still all too frequently seen as something extra which happens only in an ideal world: it is a luxury, rather than an essential. The statement that 'we only have enough money for the basics, so we can't afford to include disabled people' denies the reality that disabled people's basic needs *are* the basics. While increasingly it is standard practice to assess the particular needs of specific population groups – women, men, children, older people – there is still little recognition that this applies equally to the needs of disabled people.

It does not necessarily cost a lot more to include disabled people in relief and development programmes. Billions of dollars of international aid were spent on reconstructing Bosnia after the civil war of the 1990s, but the opportunity to create once and for all an accessible built environment was not seized. Schools, hospitals, homes, and workplaces were rebuilt in a way that continues to exclude a significant part of the population. Accessibility is estimated to account for additional construction costs of between 0.1 and 3.0 per cent, yet the issue has not been tackled.

'There aren't many disabled people here anyway, so it's not really an issue.'

One reason why the issue of disability is treated as something too specialised for the ordinary NGO is the misconception that the number of disabled people within the target population is insignificant. This myth arises because many disabled people are invisible. For example, if aid-agency staff see very few disabled refugees at camp registration or food-distribution points, they may assume that there are very few disabled people in the refugee population. In reality, disabled people may be hidden away, unable to reach these points; or they may never even have reached the camp. Disability affects not only the individual but also his or her family, who may also become a target for discrimination and face increased poverty and hardship.

In cases where the aid community is aware of disabled people among the beneficiary population, if the numbers of people are small or considered to be insignificant, this fact may be used to justify a view that inclusion of disabled people would not be cost-effective. This position is unjustifiable, since vulnerable religious groups or ethnic-minority groups probably are included. The key issue is not the numbers of people involved, but whether marginalised groups are recognised as such.

'We don't "do" disability.'

A further factor that prevents relief and development programmes reaching all those most in need is that disabled people have traditionally been regarded as a distinct target group, rather than being recognised as present within all wider target populations. Thus some agencies specialise in disability, and others do not. One consequence is that both donors and implementing agencies may assume that the needs of disabled people are adequately catered for if one agency is implementing a disability-specific project. But in reality only a small proportion of the disabled population may participate in and benefit from such a limited programme, while the needs of the majority go unmet.

Omitting a disability component from all programmes is akin to failing to address the needs of a group of people who account for approximately 10 per cent of the overall population. All agencies should include the needs of the disabled minority in their programming, in response to the needs expressed by disabled people and their organisations.

'We don't have the skills to work with disabled people.'

Working with disabled people is in many ways not significantly different from working with any other sector of the population. Many needs are the same; sometimes the approach to meeting them is different. Disabled people themselves are the best experts and can often suggest modifications which would make things work for them. Doing nothing is not acceptable. We may lack the answers ourselves, but all we have to do is to *ask the people concerned*. If disabled people are unable to suggest solutions, answers are usually not hard to find. Staff should inform themselves about likely problems and remedies as part of their advance preparation for field-work; organisations should address such needs for information as a routine part of staff-induction programmes.

For example, a public-health worker taking on a new assignment would routinely find out what type of public-health issues s/he is likely face. The same should be true for others whose role will almost automatically relate to people with disabilities. It should be standard practice that engineers are conversant with the kinds of modification that will facilitate physical access. Site planners should automatically consider how to design facilities in ways that will make all aspects of camp life accessible to disabled people without ghettoising them. These blueprints can of course be modified on the ground, to take account of local circumstances and individuals' resources and needs.

Becoming disability-aware is largely about changing attitudes: looking for solutions, not just seeing problems. Sometimes low-tech simple solutions have a major impact on life for disabled people in emergency situations. For example, simple bench seats with holes can be fitted to latrines; temporary guidelines made of rope can help newly displaced blind people to learn the route from tented accommodation to food-distribution points; water taps should be made accessible and usable by disabled people.

'We should create a special programme for them.'

It is unrealistic to expect a single specialist intervention programme to address all the needs and rights of all disabled people. Many of these needs are anyway shared by other people and are not disability-specific, so they would be best addressed within the framework of the whole community. Just as relief and development agencies have been better able to address the needs of women by giving them particular attention, while ensuring that they have access to wider community services and structures (a process known as 'gender mainstreaming'), the same is desirable for disabled and/or ageing people.

Piecemeal approaches, for example addressing only the nutritional needs of refugees in a camp without also considering how other needs (for water, sanitation, shelter, health care, representation, and resettlement) are to be met would be poor practice in any population. All too frequently, disability programmes focus on the mobility and rehabilitation needs of disabled people, without ensuring that they have access to the support structures and services that should address their other needs.

Care must be taken to avoid a situation where any programme that does specifically address the needs of disabled people inadvertently perpetuates the *status quo* of marginalisation and unequal access to resources. An unrepresentative approach is still very common in disability programmes, particularly in emergency contexts. Assessments and decisions may be made exclusively by medical and rehabilitation professionals. Non-disabled people may implement special programmes, giving assistance directly to family members: items to be passed on to the disabled person. This approach reinforces the common perception of disabled people as passive recipients of aid and care and as the objects, rather than the subjects, of rehabilitation programmes. Special or separate programmes tend to be based on the medical or charity models, as described earlier. As a result, proposed actions are often inappropriate or address needs that are not the most urgent for disabled people. This is inappropriate for organisations which endorse rights-based approaches based upon the principle of equality: for example, one of Oxfam's core beliefs is that 'The lives of all human beings are of equal value.'

3 Working with disabled people's organisations

This chapter describes the work of a disabled people's organisation (DPO) in Kosovo. Although the details of the project are specific to the political and social context of Kosovo, the challenges confronting the DPO are typical of those encountered in many other countries, and its achievements show what can be done in an impoverished, conflict-ridden society, where disabled people and their concerns are not a priority on any official agenda.

The political context in Kosovo

Kosovo is a UN Protectorate, small, multi-ethnic, and predominantly rural, in southern Europe. It used to be an autonomous province within the Socialist Federal Republic of Yugoslavia, but in 1989 its political autonomy was removed, and direct rule from Belgrade, the Yugoslav capital, was imposed. A state of emergency was declared, and large numbers of security forces were deployed on a long-term basis. Kosovo had always been the poorest region of former Yugoslavia, and the crisis led to further impoverishment. The ethnic Albanian population, as part of their campaign of non-violent, mass non-compliance with the authorities in Belgrade, created parallel, unofficial systems of government, health services, and education. These functioned on meagre resources, and the impact of this long-term, low-key emergency on the poorest people of Kosovo – Albanian, Turk, Roma, and others – was enormously harmful. Many people in all ethnic groups faced hardship, abject material poverty, and an exhausting daily grind for survival. An estimated 80 per cent of the population became unemployed, one child in five was stunted by malnutrition, and the socio-economic situation resembled that of a less-developed country, rather than that of a province of a State on the continent of Europe. Feelings of fear, mistrust, and oppression dominated daily life, and there was no sense of security or confidence in the future. To live in Kosovo was to live in a state of permanent tension. In early 1998, the stresses finally erupted into open conflict between Serb and Albanian forces, and NATO intervention followed. In these circumstances, conditions for everyone, disabled and non-disabled people, deteriorated still further.

The situation of disabled people

It is estimated (by the Disability Task Force) that there are approximately 150,000 people with disabilities living in Kosovo. Before the civil war, most of them were physically and socially isolated. Having internalised their oppression, they had little opportunity or incentive to change the passive role to which they were assigned within their families and society. The social model was not well known as a tool with which to analyse the reasons for their oppression; few informal or formal opportunities to meet other disabled people existed; it was hard to share experiences, learn from each other, and gain encouragement and motivation to change the situation.

Associations for disabled people existed, but they were specific to particular impairments and isolated from each other. Even where disabled people played major roles in these associations, their scope for decision-making and involvement was limited: a reflection of the top–down approach that was adopted by the government and prevalent in society in general. The organisations were usually male-dominated; where women did have positions of power, they frequently put all their energy (as did their male colleagues) into retaining and increasing their own status, rather than empowering others.

The position of carers

Like the disabled people for whom they cared, carers in Kosovo had few opportunities for peer support and organisation at the grassroots level. Mothers were (and still are) often blamed for producing a disabled child, provoking in them feelings of guilt, shame, and low self-esteem. Women's work in the family home is time-consuming and labour-intensive; the additional demands of looking after a disabled child often add a significant burden. While many carers love their disabled children and try to do the best for them, they may face criticism from family and community for doing so, branded as bad mothers who should invest all their energy, resources (including food), and attention in their 'healthy' children, rather than 'waste' them on a disabled child. The social pressures were (and still are) enormous.

In Kosovo a significant number of fathers took on the role of main carer. Anecdotal evidence suggests that this may be due in part to very high levels of unemployment since the start of the political crisis in 1989. In some families it was due to the perception that a child with a disability is a special or particularly difficult problem, for which a man should take the responsibility. In other families it was simply a reflection of the close relationship between fathers and their children. Both male and female carers reported feelings of isolation, of having to cope alone, without information, resources, or assistance.

The Kosovo Association of People with Paraplegia (KAPP)

The KAPP was formed in 1983. In common with other disability organisations in former Yugoslavia, it functioned as a parastatal organisation, in receipt of official funding for its running costs and activities. Unlike many others, it survived the period of pre-war crisis (1989–98) and managed to avoid schism and closure, retaining its original mixed ethnic membership. During this difficult period it remained functional to a limited extent, severely restricted by economic, social, and political constraints.

Between 1993 and 1994, international non-government organisations (INGOs) arrived in Kosovo and began assistance programmes, mainly distributions of food, medicines, and winter items. KAPP was (and under its later name of Handikos still is) the only disabled people's organisation to have a network throughout Kosovo. Donors (who have included Handicap International – designated by the UN Mission in Kosovo as the international 'lead agency' on disability – and the Danish Council of Organisations of Disabled People, the World Health Organisation, and the Finnish Ministry of Foreign Affairs, as well as Oxfam) needed a local partner in order to avoid duplicating their efforts. Under the leadership of its original founder and President, Halit Ferizi, a wheelchair-user, KAPP became the main agent in the work of distributing supplies to disabled people.

Through the process of distributing aid, the KAPP became aware that its membership lists had become seriously outdated; an alarmingly high number of its members had died, very probably because of the lack of basic, essential, hygiene materials and medical assistance. Many others were seriously ill from causes that in more normal circumstances would have been avoidable. The KAPP came to realise that many people with types of impairment other than paraplegia, who now had no associations to represent them, were also in great need. It decided to strengthen its services, expanding its scope to include a cross-impairment membership, and restructuring its distribution mechanisms. It set about finding and re-registering former members and identifying other disabled people, regardless of their ethnicity and type of disability. Local sub-groups of the KAPP, known as Local Active Groups (LAGs), were established in approximately 20 places, covering both rural and urban populations. Many volunteers in the LAGs were medical staff employed by a local NGO, Mother Theresa Humanitarian Organisation (MT – unconnected other than by name and inspiration to Mother Theresa of Calcutta). MT had an established and growing network of 'health houses' throughout Kosovo, staffed by volunteer doctors, nurses, and medical technicians. Other LAG members were social workers, teachers, relatives or carers of disabled people, and (occasionally) disabled people themselves. The role of the LAGs was to identify and register disabled people in their community, establish their needs for medical and/or material assistance, and as far as possible provide for those needs, with their efforts co-ordinated through the central KAPP office. The KAPP's intention was to work towards a situation in which the LAGs would become independent from the KAPP; quite when and how this might happen depended both on the groups' own development and on external political considerations.

Oxfam's relationship with the KAPP

Oxfam's own relationship with KAPP dates from 1994, when it began work in Kosovo from its Belgrade base with distributions of winter clothing through local NGOs. The KAPP was one recipient organisation. Oxfam later opened an office in Pristina, the regional capital of Kosovo, and developed a programme which focused on building wells and latrines and the basic reconstruction of rural schools in one county, with a high level of involvement of the various ethnic communities. Complementary to this was the development of women's health-education courses in the county, and support for other rural women's organisations that were working to promote health, literacy, and girls' education.

Programme objectives

In a series of meetings with the President of the KAPP, Oxfam explained its broader mandate, beyond that of emergency-aid distribution. Staff raised the idea of using the principles of basic human rights as a starting point for effective work with disabled people. Both organisations agreed that *how* something is done, and the underlying philosophy, are as important as *what* is done, in terms of maximising the positive impact and sustainability of the project. Oxfam's key objectives in working with KAPP were as follows:

- to promote the social model of disability and to raise awareness of disability as a political and human-rights issue;
- to change attitudes to disability and introduce a Disability Equality perspective within the KAPP and LAGs, in order to make the groups' work (including distributions and home visits) more effective;
- to include disabled men and women in the groups, and support them to become active participants;
- to build a stronger, more representative organisation, which would have a more positive impact on its members' lives and on the broader community;
- to improve the self-esteem, status, and participation of disabled people – both men and women – inside and outside the organisation.

Both partners sought to promote understanding of what a disabled people's organisation could do to achieve real change, and to motivate people to take action to redress imbalances of power, both within the organisation and beyond it. A further aim of the group work was to offer support to family members and carers, to help to end the isolation that they experienced.

Development work with disabled people before the war

Work with individual groups

Oxfam began by developing relationships with four of the LAGs, to begin introducing the ideas and approach of Disability Equality, and to assess their relevance to the situation of disabled and non-disabled members of the KAPP. With each of the four groups, Oxfam staff began by attending group meetings and by accompanying members on home visits to disabled people and their families. Each group had its own particular composition and motivation; over time, the work with each group evolved differently, in response to the needs and personalities and interests of those involved. With some groups it was initially difficult to explain what Oxfam wanted to do – and why – in a meaningful way. In Kosovo most people associated humanitarian organisations (as relief and development organisations were collectively known) with aid-distribution and medical programmes. Although essential, these interventions frequently did not meet the medical or material needs of disabled people. They also led to the belief that an organisation which had nothing to distribute had nothing to offer.

In the context of the extreme material poverty of disabled people (and indeed of the general population) in Kosovo, words and ideas might have been seen as useless. Nonetheless, many programmes worldwide which seek to tackle poverty have discovered that responses to material needs, through income-generation or micro-enterprise projects, often fail unless the programme has first addressed the participants' lack of self-confidence and feelings of powerlessness. Unless people feel positive about themselves, they are unlikely to be able to bring about long-term changes in their lives. Campaigners for Disability Equality address this fact as a priority. In initial meetings with some groups, in order to be clear about their intentions, Oxfam staff apologised and admitted that they had mostly words to offer, because there was not much money for anything else. This explanation tended to be accepted by the disabled members of the groups. They were immediately interested enough at least to suspend scepticism, to listen and discuss. Some non-disabled people who had close personal relationships with disabled people in the groups were also very receptive and enthusiastic.

But there was a tension between tangible and intangible forms of aid, and it was reflected in an on-going debate within the KAPP about its own role. It pitted the organisation's President and other disabled members against others, mostly non-disabled people. At issue was whether LAG activists should visit disabled people only when there was something to distribute or they needed medical attention, or whether the role of the organisation was broader than this. Disabled people (and their allies) felt strongly that social interaction and other intangible forms of support were as important as the provision of aid and medical care, especially to people who were psychologically or geographically isolated. This notion was disputed, and sometimes even ridiculed, by some non-disabled LAG members. By providing information about the experiences of disabled people elsewhere, Oxfam staff were able to promote the broader role of the KAPP and LAGs, as well as highlighting the importance of peer support and role models in making positive changes to the lives of disabled people. They did this by arranging contacts and exchanges with DPOs elsewhere, and by providing the KAPP with disability-related materials in English and in translation, and with access to other sources of information over the Internet.

With one group the focus remained on attending group meetings and home visits, while trying to encourage links and information-sharing with the local women's group, which had activists in villages throughout the LAG catchment area. Another group's membership was in decline, but after a few months it re-formed, with a new membership which included many more disabled people. Then Oxfam concentrated on supporting them to set up a multi-activity children's community centre, run by disabled adults and relatives of disabled children. The centre's ethos was based on principles of human rights.

With the remaining two groups, the focus shifted to workshop-style activities and facilitated discussions, often held in the homes of activists or disabled people, for want of any other location. These sessions were very informal; each lasted for two to three hours, with activities which emphasised equal rights, models of disability, barriers to inclusion, concepts of independent living, and increased awareness of the experiences of people with varying types of impairments and disabilities, in order to support the development of a cross-impairment approach in the LAGs.

The opportunity for social interaction and making friends was also important, and there would be time for singing and chatting. On occasion, the effects of the political repression and crisis would somehow suddenly catch up with the participants: people would feel utterly worn down and unable to focus their attention on the topic under discussion. The groups were able to offer support to family members and carers who felt isolated. Oxfam wanted to encourage carers and other non-disabled members of the groups to think of disabled people in a different way: to look at the whole person, not just his or her impairment; to identify the positive things in the lives of disabled people, which were often unrecognised and buried under the burden of shame and tragedy, and to build from them. Disabled adult activists can be invaluable as role models and a source of information and support for disabled children and their parents, but this potential was often overlooked in the LAGs.

Regional workshops

The KAPP wanted to take the Disability Equality work out to reach more members in more LAGs; so, having tested some workshop materials, assessed their relevance to the first groups, and modified them as necessary, Oxfam staff agreed to hold more formal regional workshops with participants from each LAG within the six regions of Kosovo. The first regional workshop was designed with and co-facilitated by the President of the KAPP. Oxfam was concerned that most participants had had no previous exposure to participative workshop methods, nor any experience of dealing immediately with issues of Disability Equality. At subsequent workshops, two disabled LAG activists were included as co-facilitators, and a few people from the original groups were included as participants. Lessons from the initial work with groups were applied to later sessions, timings were adapted, and particular activities or issues were modified.

At each of the regional workshops there was demonstrable goodwill and openness on the part of most participants, who entered actively into participation and discussion. A small number of people who had been exposed to conventional styles of education felt threatened or alienated by the informal, interactive approach, and it was necessary to take this into account. They had been expecting the 'banking' style of learning, described by Paulo Freire in *Pedagogy of the Oppressed*, whereby a 'knowledgeable' teacher dispenses information to 'unknowledgable' students, who are supposed to passively 'bank' or store the information that they acquire. On the whole, however, participants' reactions affirmed the reason for adopting an interactive approach: it was more enjoyable, and it helped people to relax, to participate actively, and to open up to learning.

Peer support

Sharing experience and gaining information through direct contact with other disabled people and their organisations, both locally and internationally, is a particularly significant way for disabled people to start making positive changes in their lives. Oxfam secured funding from various sources over a two-year period to support several such initiatives. A disabled woman was enabled to attend a short series of workshops on disabled women's issues in Belgrade, organised by the Autonomous Women's Centre. Another disabled woman attended the International

Conference on Self-Determined Living for Disabled Women, held in Germany in 1996. Disabled people were funded by Oxfam to visit Albania, to meet and learn about and exchange experiences with DPOs and the Oxfam Disability Unit there. And disabled people from Kosovo, together with disabled people from Belgrade, paid a visit to the Independent Living Centre in Dublin, Ireland. The Oxfam Regional Disability Adviser in Belgrade arranged a meeting between the KAPP and the President of Disabled Peoples' International (DPI), thus bringing the KAPP into contact with the global disability movement. KAPP representatives attended a regional disability conference for Oxfam staff and partner organisations. Links were established with Oxfam's programme and partners in Lebanon, and a visit was made there in August 1998.

The value of direct contact and peer support cannot be over-emphasised. People return from study visits with increased confidence and motivation, new ideas, a commitment to human rights, and renewed strength of purpose. Seeing experienced, successful organisations run by other disabled people can make a huge impact on those who are otherwise inclined to think that this would be impossible or impractical in their own situations. Sometimes the effects are immediately obvious, and sometimes they begin to emerge much later: it can take time to assimilate new experiences. Sometimes it will not be one single event, but a combination of several factors, that leads people to make positive changes. Contacts with groups in countries where similar cultural, economic, and/or political conditions prevail are obviously helpful, but the value of contacts with groups in the rest of the world, including more developed countries, should not be dismissed. As we have already argued, many of the factors that shape disabled people's experiences have little to do with the specifics of their cultural, political, or economic conditions, and more to do with globally negative attitudes, which result in the inequitable distribution of resources and power. Learning at first hand about the situation and the continuing struggle of disabled people in countries viewed as rich and stable can help to dispel myths and motivate people to take appropriate actions now.

Disability Equality Training of Trainers

Over an 18-month period, Oxfam's work with individual groups and the regional workshops and other activities had gone a considerable way towards creating a general understanding and acceptance of the relevance of Disability Equality principles to the KAPP's work and the lives of disabled people; and it had helped to build the confidence and abilities of certain individual members. The programme then moved on to the next stage: the Disability Equality Training of Trainers (DETOT) course. This was more structured training, which aimed to give LAG members the skills, knowledge, and attitudes to facilitate workshops about disability awareness themselves, and to raise awareness of the need for gender equality. In all, twenty LAG members completed the DETOT course and were able to share their learning with other LAG members and put it into practice in their everyday work and lives. The contents and methodology of the course form the bulk of this manual.

Work with women

For some disabled women in the LAGs, the discrimination they had faced – as women, as disabled people, and as disabled women – had left them feeling inadequate in social or group situations, believing that they had nothing to contribute, or too afraid to say anything in case it was not intelligent or correct. One woman apologised for not expressing herself clearly, saying she wasn't used to having the opportunity to express herself. Another woman could not remember ever having been asked for her opinion before. It was gradually possible to dismantle these barriers, by encouraging women to believe that what they had to say was valuable, interesting, and important (it truly was), by creating safe situations – like work in pairs or small groups – where it was easier to talk and gain confidence, and by not pushing women to speak when they felt uncomfortable.

Even after some time, when women (disabled and non-disabled) had begun to participate more broadly in the KAPP structures, their acceptance remained at times fairly tokenistic: often they would attend meetings but say virtually nothing. Or there would be an unspoken assumption that women could make a useful contribution only on issues that were specific to women. However, as some women gained strength and found their voice, their contribution did come to be recognised and valued; progress was slow but visible. Disabled men and women eventually began meeting to discuss personal matters and other issues, in private, without the involvement of non-disabled people.

Work with children

The KAPP organised a campaign of visits to disabled children and their families, with the aim of encouraging parents to take a 'whole child' approach and provide children with opportunities for play, social interaction, and education. This was followed up by a series of meetings with parents of disabled children, to encourage their involvement with the LAG. Seven community centres were set up throughout Kosovo, with disabled people and parents of disabled children organising activities and playing key co-ordination roles. Events for children in the community were organised: for example, picnics in the park, and a Christmas party in a café with a visit and gifts from Father Christmas, paid for by a local donor. To be out in the community having fun was a new experience for disabled children and their families, and it was important for parents to share their children's happiness and excitement. Such small things can have a big impact, changing families' perception of disability, improving relationships, and vastly improving disabled children's quality of life. Birthdays and traditional holidays were celebrated with parties in community centres, when disabled and non-disabled people danced until the small hours. Such banal, normal interactions played a great part in overcoming barriers between disabled and non-disabled people.

Using the media

An audiocassette of children's stories featuring disabled children was produced and broadcast on radio. For the first time, disabled children in Kosovo heard their own experiences reflected in stories, and were exposed to the discussion of ideas which they themselves might use in order to overcome some of the barriers that confronted them in society.

The public profile of disability was raised by the use of other media too. A magazine for rural women published poetry written by a disabled member of a LAG. She had never previously shown her writings to anyone, because her family had made her believe she was worthless. The magazine also published stories about disabled children and included images of disabled people. The same rural women's group worked with women from one of the LAGs to set up a literacy group for disabled and non-disabled women.

In Mitrovica, the local theatre contacted the LAG for advice on staging a play featuring a young woman who used a wheelchair. This was in itself without precedent: a wheelchair had never before been seen on stage. The non-disabled actress playing the role came to learn from disabled women about their experiences. However, there was uproar when the play ended with the disabled woman's husband killing her. Disabled women in the audience decided to write their own play, to counter this negative message and demonstrate to audiences that the suffering associated with disability is caused less by their impairments than by the attitudes of other people.

The KAPP and LAGs marked the International Day of Disabled People with round-table discussions in which disabled people could share their experiences and discuss their rights and their ideas for the future with members and leaders of the local community. Mixed groups of children sang songs and recited poems and produced an awareness-raising poster, portraying disabled people as integral members of society.

Education

Local Active Groups lobbied the authorities for access to mainstream education. They engaged in dialogue with families who resisted sending their disabled children to school, and with schools which were blocking willing parents from gaining a place for their disabled children.

A local English-language school provided a number of places on its courses, free of charge to LAG members who otherwise could not have afforded the course. This increased the visibility of disabled people within the community, encouraged interaction between disabled and non-disabled peers, and improved students' employment prospects. The opportunity to acquire language skills was particularly important, because English was fast becoming the only common language among Kosovo's various ethnic groups.

Institutional development

While all these initiatives were going on, Oxfam was helping the KAPP and the LAGs to build their own institutional capacity. This work took the following forms.

- Providing training in organisation management, including how to write funding proposals, how to manage financial accounts, and computer skills.
- Holding regular meetings with the KAPP President, to ensure inclusive, transparent decision-making between Oxfam and the KAPP in matters of fund-raising, planning, budgeting, and implementation.

- Developing the skills of a KAPP member who worked voluntarily in the Oxfam office, in order to gain experience in administration and finances that she could take back to the KAPP.

- Enabling the LAGs to make contact with other DPOs and thus to share experiences and support each other.

The KAPP successfully broadened its financial support-base, in order to reduce its dependency on any one donor. Gradually the KAPP and LAGs increased their skills and organisational capacity, which made them better prepared to act effectively in the escalating crisis.

Relief work with disabled people during the war

With the onset of war in early 1998, the KAPP remained active, despite very difficult operating conditions. Although by this stage it was fully committed to the social model of disability, strongly believing that service provision is the responsibility of the State, the KAPP recognised that in war-time there were gaps that had to be filled. It concentrated its energies on the following initiatives:

- Tracing disabled people displaced by the conflict.

- Helping displaced disabled people to find family members from whom they were separated.

- Helping displaced disabled people and their families to find suitable accommodation.

- Distributing emergency relief to displaced disabled people and their families (both general relief items and disability-specific items such as mobility aids and hygiene materials).

- Providing emotional support to disabled people who had been traumatised by the conflict.

- Continuing the work of raising awareness about the rights of disabled people.

- Continuing to run the seven community centres that were a focal point for LAGs and disabled people, as well as a resource for disabled children for physiotherapy, play, and education.

The KAPP worked through its extensive grassroots network to identify the problems of disabled people, and it lobbied Oxfam and other international NGOs for assistance. At that time many distributions (of food and other items) relied on people presenting themselves at warehouses in inaccessible locations, which was impossible for disabled people. As a result of KAPP's lobbying, Oxfam took the unusual step of providing sanitary items to 2500 disabled people who were at risk of serious health problems because this specific need was unmet.

Oxfam was able to make distributions of non-food items, such as clothes and shoes, through the networks of KAPP and rural women's groups. It was nevertheless difficult for the KAPP to reach its members: the front lines of the conflict were constantly moving, such that areas which were safe one day were not safe the next. It was hard to make plans, even where the location of members was known;

transport was difficult to secure, and the scattered locations of disabled people within the population meant that distribution was relatively expensive and difficult. Oxfam paid transport costs for the local distribution of supplies and delivered the goods as far as possible along the line, reducing the distances that the KAPP would then have to travel.

This type of distribution is time-consuming and labour-intensive, especially in a context of insecurity, but the KAPP was able to provide volunteer labour. Seventy per cent of these distributions were successful – a significant achievement, given all the difficulties, which reflects the pre-conflict strengths and skills within the KAPP. Individual local groups which were strong and active prior to the conflict were able to respond creatively and effectively during it; groups which had struggled prior to the emergency were less effective in the crisis. The joint efforts of KAPP and Oxfam enabled at least some of the needs of disabled people to be met, and their right to aid was not wholly neglected. In other aspects of its general response to the emergency, Oxfam attempted to meet the needs of disabled people: household-equipment kits included commodes, and accessible latrines were designed. In Macedonia an area within the refugee camps was established for disabled people, with accessible facilities and levelled ground. This type of work was carried out by the refugees themselves, both disabled and non-disabled.

Oxfam was also able to identify, with support from disability-aware field workers who were now in Macedonia following their own expulsion or flight, what problems would confront displaced disabled people when they returned to Kosovo. Oxfam then supported the KAPP to use its community centres as accommodation and support bases for disabled returnees, giving them the opportunity to assess what would be needed to enable them to return to their villages.

Before the emergency, Oxfam had supplied materials for the development of a disabled people's community centre in Pristina, and provided disability-awareness training in this and other centres established by the KAPP and Handicap International. Thus these centres had been helped to develop inclusive, rights-based principles and methods of working. During the emergency, the centres became important bases where displaced disabled people could find practical assistance and emotional support. Many disabled people learned about the work of the KAPP for the first time through these centres. For staff in the centres (disabled people and their non-disabled supporters), particular problems were caused by the lack of information about the current locations of disabled people and what had happened to them in the chaos of displacement. At the request of the staff, Oxfam funded transport to enable them to drive to areas where returnees had newly arrived, identify disabled people among the population, and link them into the available support networks. Through this process, more than one thousand displaced disabled people were identified and provided with assistance. Although these figures may seem small in relation to the scale of the emergency, they are significant in two ways. The effort invested by the KAPP and centre staff to produce these results was remarkable, and the identification process and follow-up support made a considerable impact on the lives of disabled people and their families, and in less immediately visible ways on the lives of the broader community.

Rehabilitation, reconstruction, and advocacy work after the war

Handikos (the new name for the KAPP) still works on the charitable and medical levels – not because it wants to, but because it has found itself obliged to do so. Despite its strong commitment to the social model, it recognises that some degree of service provision will be necessary for the next five to ten years. Its objective is to involve beneficiaries in the design of service provision, and this work is on-going.

The membership of Handikos has grown from fewer than 5000 members before the war to 18,000 now. However, Handikos staff and activists believe that there are still more disabled people who have not been reached yet, so they continue their activities of identification and registration. All who register by completing a questionnaire are considered members, even if they are not active, and they are given information on current projects so that they can choose whether or not to be involved. New questionnaires have been designed to include more information on people's abilities and the particular barriers that prevent their participation in society. Staff making home visits continue to inform disabled people about their rights and give them information about their entitlements. Some members have gone on to become trainers and have gained skills in setting up meetings, lobbying donors and authorities, and expressing their ideas.

The development of the Local Active Groups

Decisions within Handikos are made on the basis of needs expressed by its members and beneficiaries. The LAGs act as a medium for making grassroots voices heard, thus influencing the strategies and the future direction of Handikos.

There are now 25 LAG offices, each with three workers. They carry out field visits to obtain direct information on the situation of disabled people, and they are the first point of contact for new and existing members. All the field activities of Handikos are carried out through the LAGs, which are now organised into eight regions, each with a co-ordinator responsible for the running of the offices and community centres, writing proposals, and identifying training needs. (However, Handikos will shortly begin a programme of restructuring, and the number of staff will be reduced.) Most LAG staff are disabled, and overall approximately 60 per cent of the Handikos staff members are disabled. The groups vary greatly in the democratic nature of their decision making, which largely depends on the personalities involved.

Community centres

Handikos now runs ten community centres, where disabled children receive physiotherapy and group/play therapy. Before the war, everyone at the centres worked voluntarily, but now each centre has five paid staff members. Therapists have been trained, although they are not professionally qualified.

The centre at Peja, which serves 800 disabled people, illustrates the work of these institutions. It has the capacity to work with 60 children at a time, and the groups change every three months. There is good support for the centre from the local community: the local municipality pays all the utility costs, and members of the community respond quickly to requests for help if there are problems with electricity or heating. This indication of support has prompted the centre to begin to look for local donors. Regular meetings are held with parents, to offer them advice: about the benefits of education; about new legislation to guarantee the rights of disabled people; about the dangers of over-protecting their children. The benefits of bringing parents together have been very noticeable: staff report that there has been a change in attitudes, and children are brought to the centre more often. Staff cite themselves as examples (all are disabled in some way) and teach parents to appreciate their children's abilities. When they first arrive at the centre with their children, parents tend to be seeking a cure; they need support to accept the fact that there will probably be no cure, and encouragement to believe that the situation will improve, and their children will be able to live fulfilled, independent lives. It is a slow process, but parents who gradually see their children benefiting from the centre's approach act as advocates of the social model to other members of the parents' group.

To further its work of raising awareness of Disability Equality in the wider community, the Peja centre has a good relationship with the two local radio stations and also has contact with the local TV station. Staff have held meetings with the three main political parties. They lobby local employers who discriminate against disabled people when recruiting workers, and head-teachers who have tried to block the registration of children in mainstream schools.

The centre is also home to a disabled women's group, which has 30–40 active members who meet weekly to discuss their needs and learn how to claim their rights. Their families tried to prevent the women from attending the meetings at first, but they have gradually become more supportive. The women learn handicrafts skills at the centre and teach each other to produce items for sale at a shop in town, which takes orders for their products. The income-generation groups give their members a degree of independence, although the amount of money earned is small. A local donor has provided materials for the craft work and helps with marketing. The women hope to open their own crafts shop in Peja, which would employ three field workers to sell products and look for outlets. They are confident that local wedding customs would guarantee a demand for their products.

The community centre also runs literacy courses for disabled women and girls, who have tended to be kept at home by their families. One 60-year-old participant from a village outside Peja wept when she joined a class, because it was the first time she had ever been to school. Computer courses have been very successful and have given the women employment skills.

Women's groups

Initially Handikos encouraged disabled women to join existing women's groups, but the hoped-for integration did not happen: the disabled women felt reluctant to participate in discussions with non-disabled members. It was therefore decided to offer them training in capacity-building skills in their own groups. With Oxfam's support, Handikos established sub-groups for disabled women within each LAG during 1999–2000. The groups are now managing themselves; they influence other women's organisations on topics such as legal rights, and they visit officials of the United Nations Mission in Kosovo (UNMIK) to represent their own interests. Handikos has a shop in Mitrovica, selling handicrafts made by disabled women, and the shop is completely managed by the women themselves. However, the situation of the women's groups varies greatly from place to place, depending largely on the leadership skills of the members. Some are very strong, but others ceased to function after Oxfam funding came to an end in 2001, in accordance with a decision to cease the support of projects specifically and exclusively concerned with disability, in favour of incorporating awareness of the needs and potential of disabled people into the whole Oxfam programme in Kosovo.

Although the women's groups have made impressive progress in some respects, they face some serious challenges. For one thing, there does not appear to be a clear strategy for their future development; no other international donors seem interested in supporting this kind of project. For another, the activities of the groups are determined by cultural considerations: although on the surface Kosovo seems to be an open society, the lives of many women are still constrained, whether they are disabled or not. For example, although it is common for women to work, they are also responsible for maintaining the home, and in practice they cannot work over-time or travel overseas. Although in statistical terms women are well represented within Handikos, most of them are young and are likely to leave the organisation when they marry. Another problem is the considerable difference in levels of education between those born disabled and those who became disabled later: all the members of the Handikos executive were disabled as adults and have been educated in the regular school system. This means that at the decision-making levels of the organisation there is a preponderance of disabled women (and men) who lack first-hand experience of the problems of people who have been disabled all their lives.

Public education and media work

To a certain degree, the war changed public attitudes towards disabled people, forcing them to become visible when they were forced to flee with their families. Since the war, the disability movement has worked hard to keep its concerns in the public domain, and to raise awareness of the positive achievements of disabled people. A typical campaign slogan is '*Discover abilities to build opportunities*'. Television programmes, concerts, and sports events now feature disabled people. For example, in 2001 TV coverage of a basketball match between Kosovo and Albania was preceded by the live screening of a match involving the national wheelchair teams.

Influencing government policy

Handikos has made good progress in influencing the post-war policies of government (both UNMIK – the transitional administration – and municipal structures). It was a key member of the Disability Task Force, established by UNMIK in December 2000, with the primary task of developing a comprehensive strategy on disability for Kosovo, in line with UN Standard Rules on the Equalisation of Opportunities for People with Disabilities. The Task Force includes representatives of Handikos, other disability groups, and Handicap International. Its report, published in December 2001, presents a radical vision of a society in which 'all citizens, regardless of their diverse origins and abilities, are able to exercise their rights and responsibilities'. Its proposed strategy is based on the following principles:

- the right to self-representation
- the full integration of disability into all government programmes
- the need for sustainable funding.

The proposed policy objectives cover (among other matters) the State's obligations to prevent avoidable incidences of disability; to develop comprehensive health-care services for disabled people; to include disabled people in the planning and implementation of rehabilitation services; to create a barrier-free society; to develop an accessible system of public transport; to guarantee equal access for all to a single system of education 'that will cater for the needs of all learners within an inclusive environment'; to create conditions to broaden the range of employment options for disabled people; to ensure equitable access to goods, services, and facilities; and to ensure that disabled people are able to play a full part in political life.

The Task Force has proposed the establishment of a Disability Office in the Office of the Prime Minister, with the task of implementing the Comprehensive Disability Policy Framework at all levels of government in Kosovo. It is intended that the Task Force should be transformed into a Disability Council, to serve as a consultative, advisory, and monitoring structure on disability-related matters.

Livelihoods and education

Two particular areas of concern are livelihoods and education. Currently Handikos is the only organisation in Kosovo which systematically employs disabled people – a situation which needs to change, not only to increase opportunities but to counteract the idea that disability-related work is the only type of employment of which disabled people are capable. The general unemployment rate is 70 per cent – and the rate is higher still for disabled people. Proposals for the employment of disabled people have been made in the Comprehensive Disability Policy Framework, but progress will largely depend on political will and the economic situation of the country. Recruitment procedures do not automatically offer equal opportunities to disabled candidates, and physical accessibility is still a big problem in public buildings: although it is a legal requirement of reconstruction programmes (thanks to the influence of Handikos), it is not always ensured.

Handikos is working towards a fully integrated education system. In 2001 it ran literacy courses, funded and supported by Oxfam, to motivate disabled children and to make them and their parents aware of their abilities. Around 30 of the 200 participants now attend school and are completely integrated into the mainstream system. Through dialogue with teachers, individually and in seminars, Handikos also promotes the acceptance of disabled children in mainstream schools. More work still needs to be done with parents, to promote awareness of their children's abilities. Over-protection is common, and many parents choose to keep their children at home. Primary education is compulsory by law, but this requirement does not apply to disabled children. Illiteracy is a problem among disabled people, especially women and those living in rural areas, and (as noted above) there is a significant difference in educational standards between those with congenital impairments and those who became disabled later in life.

The impact of international NGOs

Another challenge confronting Handikos is to recapture the spirit of solidarity and voluntarism that existed before the war. The presence of international donors and agencies has created inequality and unrealistic wages (a security guard employed by a foreign NGO may be paid five times more than a locally employed doctor, for example), and fewer people are now willing to work on a voluntary basis. But the international community will eventually withdraw from Kosovo, and it will be increasingly difficult for local NGOs like Handikos to obtain international funding.

Handikos has secure funding for 2002 and 2003, and will use the money to develop its sustainable social work. It would like to be able to work purely on the social model, handing responsibility for distributing medical supplies and services to the Department of Health. But the government is likely to take at least three–five years to develop this capacity, and it is doubtful whether international funding will remain for so long.

Mainstreaming disability issues within Oxfam

The Oxfam office in Pristina was totally inaccessible for anybody with mobility impairments when it was first established, and initially disability was considered to be an issue that was separate from the main programme. Despite its developing relationship with the KAPP, Oxfam at first made no attempt in its other projects to assess or meet the needs of disabled people within the beneficiary populations. In 1996 there began a slow and rather unfocused attempt (by Alison Harris) to encourage staff (and to a lesser extent Oxfam's project partners) in the main sectors of the programme to think about disability issues in relation to their work, and to develop a consistent approach which would integrate disabled people and their concerns into all aspects of Oxfam's activities in Kosovo.

Two one-day workshops were held for staff and partners (one addressing general Disability Equality issues, the second dealing with disability and gender). The lessons learned were reinforced through informal discussions and team meetings, and gradually there was a significant shift in the approach of Oxfam's management team in Kosovo. Disability issues were included in the strategic and programme-planning processes, and some of the reconstruction projects included the provision of ramps, handrails, and accessible toilets. Oxfam-supported women's groups planned and implemented basic strategies for including local disabled women in health-education work, literacy groups, and other activities. Other international NGOs which were engaged in reconstruction programmes were lobbied successfully to provide access for disabled people. The Oxfam office itself moved to accessible premises. Making the office accessible allowed more interactions, both formal and informal, among Oxfam staff (irrespective of their roles) and disabled people from KAPP. This helped to break through attitudinal barriers and contributed to a better understanding of disability. The benefit of this then began to percolate through to all of Oxfam's work in the region.

4 Guidelines for good practice

Even in the earliest stages of an emergency, agencies should plan for disability-specific provision at a later date. They can do this by including estimates based on overall numbers when drafting their proposals and budgets, and including the identification of disabled people in the registration process. Such steps provide a basis for on-going contact, and future consultation and service provision as the situation allows. Before the crisis in Kosovo, Oxfam had a dedicated staff member working there on disability issues, and a team who had undergone training in disability rights and gender rights and who were therefore disability-aware, committed to the core principles, and willing to voice them; this proved to be very important for the effectiveness of Oxfam's response in the crisis. But when the conflict escalated, it was necessary to ensure that disability issues were mainstreamed, and awareness of disability raised, throughout the programme and among everyone concerned. Donors, policy makers, and implementing staff – engineers, nutritionists, hygiene promoters, emergency programme managers, and so on – all need to develop a disability analysis, along with a clear perspective on gender: hence the publication of this manual.

Although much of the work in Kosovo took place in a context of crisis or protracted emergency, many of the principles and ways of working which led to the positive outcomes noted in the previous chapter are equally applicable to a more stable development context – as comparisons with other Oxfam programmes operating in distinctly different environments in Bangladesh, Uganda, Sierra Leone, and Bosnia have shown. It is therefore suggested that the following principles of good practice would in many circumstances lead to greater impact and more effective programming, to the benefit of disabled members of any target population.

A disability dimension in development

Disabled people are daily confronted by negative attitudes, pejorative terminology, and visible and invisible barriers which discourage their equal and active participation in the lives of their communities. They are seeking equal opportunities for inclusion, and the resources that are necessary to achieve this, as of right. Organisations mandated to deliver relief and support development must consider their responses to crisis and poverty from the perspective of disabled people and their needs, as well as those of other members of the community. The assumption that support for general populations will automatically benefit disabled people within them is false: disabled people do not have equal access to resources and opportunities, and specific measures are necessary to ensure their full inclusion and participation.

Agencies should incorporate disability into their current programmes as a high priority. Experience shows that it is vital to refer explicitly and distinctly to the needs of disabled people, and that failure to do so almost always results in their being overlooked. In the short term, therefore, it is important to develop a disability perspective that is applied deliberately and consciously to all aspects of relief and development work. In the long term it is desirable for disability to be included automatically in all elements of an organisation's work – in much the same way as situations are automatically analysed with reference to a poverty analysis and a gender analysis – by asking questions such as: *How can disabled people be included in this programme? What are their particular needs? How will they be affected by the programme? How can they be involved in decision-making?*

Many agencies now adopt a twin-track approach which allows for separate programmes to meet disabled people's specific needs in terms of communication, mobility, and information, as of right, but also attempts to include disabled people on an equal basis in all programme activities. For this, adequate resources are required.

Applying the social model of disability

Many disabled people are still unaware of their human rights and the social model of disability, since their own analysis has been shaped by the medical or charity models, and they have not been exposed to the ideas of the disability-rights movement. Raising awareness among disabled people themselves, and among agency staff, whether they work in development, conflict, or disasters, is essential. As a priority, disabled people should be supported to become activists, advocates, and facilitators. The lifelong discrimination that they have experienced and the resulting internalisation of their oppression mean that many disabled people lack the necessary self-confidence, information, or skills to do these things, but they have a wealth of ability and experience to draw on.

Aid and development agencies have an important role to play to support disabled people's struggle for equality by applying a social model of disability and principles of Disability Equality. These are the key challenges:

- Agencies and individuals need to become more aware of how their current practice, directly or by omission, contributes to discrimination against disabled people.
- Agencies and individuals need to engage actively with disabled people and their organisations, to learn from them, and to work together with them to overcome the barriers to equal participation.
- Agencies should adopt positive approaches to participation, and ultimately to recruitment, which allow disabled people to become colleagues and programme partners, not just beneficiaries.

Reviewing mandates and policies

Organisational mandates, policies, strategic plans, and programmes should be reviewed and revised, in the light of the UN Rules and the principles of disabled people's equal rights and need for participation. Such a review should be based on an understanding of Disability Equality, using input from experienced disabled people

– otherwise the quality of conclusions and decisions will be weak. Disability Equality training might therefore be the starting point for such a review, with further reviews of plans and programmes made possible once this has been accomplished. The process of inclusion, review, learning, and change does not have to be a top–down process; individual initiatives which respond to local needs can lead to change that is driven from the grassroots and they may become an effective catalyst for learning and broader application throughout an organisation. However, at some point such a policy shift must be clearly endorsed and fully supported by senior managers, who otherwise might block progress because of their lack of awareness and understanding.

Organisations should recognise disability as a key factor in their poverty analysis and methods of needs/assets assessment. Disability should be seen as a cross-cutting theme that underlies all relief and development work. Organisations should establish a disability policy which considers both relief and development issues, and covers all stages of programme funding and planning, implementation, monitoring, and evaluation, in order that disability is fully integrated into the project cycle. Oxfam addresses disability through its corporate policy on social diversity (see Appendix).

Disability Equality training

Disability-inclusive programmes can be given a kick start with short sessions of Disability Equality training for staff. In the long term it is desirable that all programme staff should share responsibility for the inclusion of disabled people in their work, but in practice in the short term the input of specialist disability staff has proved essential, providing specific support to programme staff and maintaining the profile and resources for inclusive work. In the early stages their role in influencing policy making and resource allocation has been fundamental to maintaining Disability Equality as a priority and encouraging non-specialist staff to create time to consider it. Ultimately a point should be reached where disability is integral to all programme work, and the inclusion of disabled people within beneficiary communities is automatic; then there would be no further need for designated staff.

Initial training should start with general Disability Equality issues and move on to focus on participants' specific areas of work. Disability awareness should be included in all briefings, debriefings, terms of reference, job descriptions, and person specifications for all staff (even those on short-term assignments). All staff directed to work in emergency contexts should be given Disability Equality training before leaving for the field, ideally as part of their induction or orientation when first hired. Wherever possible this training should be carried out by disabled people. Where the lack of suitably skilled disabled people or certain security situations make it impossible to use national trainers, expatriate staff may play a role in knowledge transfer and skill building. Headquarters-based training should use experienced Disability Equality trainers who have had some exposure to operating conditions and cultural differences in the countries where relief and development work is undertaken.

Consulting and involving disabled people

Disabled people have invaluable expertise and should be involved in all stages of programme planning, policy making, and implementation. Working together with non-disabled allies who are disability-aware, participants in even small projects can make an enormous impact on the lives of many disabled beneficiaries. Consultation must take place with representatives of disabled people's groups. This is vital, although it is important to remember that these groups may also reflect the unequal power relationships that exist in the broader community. If so, they may not necessarily represent all types of impairment, or poorer disabled people, or disabled women.

One of the more significant ways for disabled people to make positive changes in their lives is through peer support: sharing experience and gaining information through direct contact with other disabled people and their organisations, both locally and internationally. This should be encouraged and resourced. Organisational learning and exchange of experience should be supported, and media and advocacy strategies should be developed, to raise the issue of disability, and to support disabled people and their organisations in making their own voices heard, at local, national, and international levels. The UN International Day of Disabled People (3 December) is an annual opportunity for advocacy work.

Longer-term partnerships with local NGOs concerned with disability should be developed, and capacity-building programmes targeting local organisations and civil society should include disabled people and their organisations. The quality and effectiveness of disability-specific programmes (such as community-based rehabilitation, the distribution of orthopaedic equipment, and micro-enterprise and employment programmes) should be improved by prioritising the full and equal participation of disabled people. Since the 1970s, the disability movement and DPOs have been gathering strength, organising and taking action for political and systematic change. Disabled people are the leaders and active participants in this process; they have valuable experience and insights which can only improve the response of relief and development agencies.

Where disability programmes are implemented, the organisations running them rarely employ significant numbers of disabled staff. Disabled people should be offered employment opportunities within agencies, especially at levels of decision-making and influence. Opportunities in the Head Office are as important as those in Field Programmes: disability should not be seen as something that merely involves beneficiaries in the field. Disabled people should not be restricted to posts within disability programmes, although disabled staff with an understanding of a rights-based approach will make a great impact. Assumptions about a candidate's ability or inability should be avoided: the work experience and skills of disabled people are diverse, and disabled people, with appropriate arrangements for access and support, have become public-health specialists, interpreters, funding officers, project managers, evaluation officers, and more. Attracting and employing disabled staff will significantly improve the work of relief and development agencies, which will involve extra costs – but these should not be allowed to hinder recruitment. The resources that non-disabled staff need are already provided, and opportunities for disabled people should not be prejudiced by failing to provide the resources that they need. Care must be taken to avoid inadvertently setting up disabled staff members to fail, by not providing the information or resources that they need to do their jobs.

After two years in Kosovo, relatively small changes that were made to increase the inclusion of disabled people brought about real progress in ensuring that there was a disability perspective in all programme work. Significantly, this initial progress was made without any additional resources. Subsequently budgets included disability costs where necessary, although it should be stressed that these costs do not represent the provision of something extra for disabled people: they merely represent the cost of meeting the same basic needs for disabled people that are met without question for others. Disability-related costs should be factored into budgets as a standard element; all agency premises worldwide should be accessible. Information and communication should be accessible for all staff, project partners, and beneficiaries.

Disability and humanitarian work in emergencies

The examples of the emergencies in Kosovo, Krajina, and Macedonia show that successful responses include the following elements:

- distribution of relief items based on local knowledge and beneficiaries' definition of their own needs;
- lobbying and advocacy work directed at, or undertaken in conjunction with, other INGOs and NGOs;
- building on development foundations, where the situation allows; and
- linking disability organisations with women's groups, to ensure that the needs of disabled women are not neglected. In the case of Kosovo, rural women's groups carried out disability-inclusive work themselves, using links formed through disability-rights training before the conflict.

The paramount need for physical protection

In emergencies a range of responses is required to meet the various needs of disabled people – as is the case with other population groups. Yet the major lesson for Oxfam in the Kosovo conflict was the fact that the primary need of disabled people is for protection. This fact was largely unaddressed throughout the conflict – except, within its limited means, by the KAPP. Reviewing the direction of the programme after nine months of conflict, both Oxfam and KAPP felt that disabled people had been failed in this respect. While protection is difficult to achieve, having access to information is crucial if disabled people are to make informed decisions and locate sources of help. The availability of better, accessible information might have made a difference to the fate of many disabled people. It was not common practice to use the State-controlled media to advise people about options and services available, but the Albanian-language radio and press could have been exploited for this purpose.

The need for advance planning

Emergency responses must be set firmly within a human-rights framework, demonstrating a commitment to ensuring equitable and inclusive service delivery.

Oxfam was fortunate in Kosovo: having already established partnerships with disability groups and women's groups, this could be achieved with relative ease, although there were times when partners found Oxfam slow and bureaucratic in responding to the emergency. Where such partnerships do not already exist and staff or implementing agencies are not disability-aware, equity and inclusivity will be much less easy to achieve. Agencies should plan in advance and integrate disability-awareness into the various sectors of their emergency response; when the humanitarian imperative is such that thousands of people may die if they are not provided with water quickly, it is not the moment to start deliberating for the first time ever about access for disabled people. Programmes in Lebanon, Bangladesh, and Kosovo have shown how the presence of a relatively well-organised disabled community, combined with disability-aware programme staff and partner organisations, improves emergency preparedness and can make an enormous difference when disaster strikes. The pre-existing relationship with KAPP made Oxfam aware from an early stage of the difficulties that disabled people were facing in the crisis. Preparedness work must assess the capacity of local organisations and the potential for external support.

Monitoring impact

Impact measurement should include disability issues within the overall framework of assessment, indicator setting, and monitoring. The *quality of participation* matters as much as the *quantity of beneficiaries*. It is necessary to consider the process of consultation, levels of satisfaction, and the reported benefits that accrue. The Kosovo programme demonstrated that there is no one right way to change individual and institutional attitudes. What works in one situation might fail in another.

The Kosovo experience demonstrated the need for significant changes at an organisational level, as well as at the individual programme level. When the war started and large numbers of expatriate staff were taken on, most of them did not have Disability Equality training, and it became a struggle for the programme to maintain an appropriate level of focus on disability issues and apply a disability analysis to the emergencies work. This unsatisfactory situation is unlikely to improve unless organisations like Oxfam instigate institutional change, reviewing their corporate policies and introducing training for staff.

Respecting the dignity of disabled people

Many disabled people who have led very independent lives before an emergency suddenly find themselves dependent on others during it. This additional trauma can undermine their self-respect and their coping strategies. Aid agencies can help by providing opportunities for disabled people to play an active role in the relief process, thereby re-establishing some control over their lives, and by providing them with the physical means to regain their independence. The Sphere Project – the Humanitarian Charter and Minimum Standards in Disaster Response – calls for *'equity throughout the distribution process, the equitable allocation of water, and toilet facilities that are accessible and easy to use by all sections of the population including physically and mentally disabled people'*
(www.sphereproject.org).

Many of the items that disabled people need in emergencies are not different from other people's needs; but it is important to bear in mind that it can be harder for people with physical impairments to keep warm, due to lack of movement and poor circulation, so they may have increased need for warm clothing, blankets, firewood, etc. Exposed to crisis and trauma, people need to maintain their dignity and self-respect. In the absence of accessible toilet facilities, portable toilet chairs are cheap and simple pieces of equipment which can make an enormous difference to mobility-impaired disabled people. Pressure sores and urinary-tract infections can easily become fatal. It is essential that people with restricted mobility are able to change position, maintain hygiene standards, and be provided with catheters, barrier creams, and antiseptic creams. Enabling aids (hearing-aids and batteries, white sticks or the local equivalent, crutches, wheelchairs, portable toilet chairs, braille equipment) could be provided. While spectacles are already quite commonly provided in refugee camps to enable older people to participate in programme activities and daily life, it is less common for other aids to be recognised as essential.

Inter-agency co-operation

Agencies should address disability earlier than they currently do, given the existence of UN Conventions and Codes of Conduct which explicitly recognise and call for the inclusion of disabled people, and for their needs to be addressed on an equal basis with those of non-disabled people. As with all such texts, these conventions need to be applied in practice to make them effective, and personnel in the field must understand the issues in order to put the recommendations into practice. Raising disability issues at the interagency level in Kosovo helped to place them on the agenda at a time when agencies were busy responding generically and in so doing missing stark differences in needs and vulnerabilities. In later evaluations it became clear that in the early and middle stages of the conflict many disabled people were not reached and supported, and the structures that had been in place since the days before the conflict erupted were felt to be insufficient to overcome the problem. In reality, international agencies should have done more — and done it sooner. UNHCR, which is mandated to protect all refugees, should pay particular attention to the specific needs of disabled refugees, which in this case were not met.

The UNHCR Handbook for Emergencies recommends as good practice involving refugees in planning emergency responses, and promoting their self-reliance from the start. It also calls for the establishment of a system of refugee representation, which should be truly representative of all the various interests and sectors of the community and should be based on traditional leadership systems as far as possible – provided that they allow proper representation (for example, if the traditional leadership system excludes women, there should nevertheless be female representatives). These principles should be applied with respect to disabled refugees. There may be a need to provide information in a range of formats, to make it accessible to everyone. Camp committees should be encouraged to include disabled people – failing which, disabled people should be supported to organise themselves, to ensure that people are informed about and receive their relief entitlements.

Donor-driven agendas

Prioritisation of disability issues is also the responsibility of donors. Donor organisations, especially those who represent States signatories to the UN Standard Rules on the Equalisation of Opportunity for Disabled People, are well placed to encourage and fund projects which actively seek to include disabled people. Donors should consider the effectiveness of an applicant's Disability Equality policies and procedures; and, when analysing applications for funding, they should ask how the programme will affect disabled people within the target population. Budget lines to provide for Disability Equality should become standard. Donors can be most influential in the early stages, when fewer resources are available, and local and international NGOs are more receptive. They could therefore require a disability analysis, as many now incorporate a gender perspective, as a condition of all contracts. There is a particularly strong case for this to happen in the reconstruction phase after an emergency, since there is an opportunity for equal access facilities to be integrated from the very beginning, for example in the reconstruction of public buildings.

Lessons for disabled people's organisations

Experience in Kosovo has shown that the Disability Equality approach can be effective within disabled people's own organisations, especially in the following ways:

- in reaching out to the most marginalised and isolated disabled people;
- in achieving positive change in disabled people's lives;
- in helping the community's development;
- in being more effective in approaches to and collaboration with relief and development organisations;
- in developing an understanding of the rights and responsibilities of DPOs.

DPOs are encouraged from time to time to review their organisational mandate, policies, and practices in the light of the social model and Disability Equality. Organisations themselves need to guard against the risk of internalised oppression operating within their own structures. Does the organisation really represent the whole range of disabilities, the gender mix, and the socio-economic groups that it claims to represent? Accountability to the membership and access to transparent systems of decision making have proved important elements in building truly representative, community-based DPOs. Structures, membership lists, and programmes should be analysed, to identify the gender balance at all levels. Organisations should make conscious decisions about what to do to redress any imbalances between the sexes that may be found. Some associations have chosen in their early phases to focus separately on the needs and concerns of disabled women, and later to take positive action in an integrated way across the organisation.

Networking and developing contacts with other DPOs, both locally and internationally, can be vital for obtaining information, moral and technical support, links to donors, and experience. Other civil-rights movements may also provide useful examples, and DPOs are encouraged to share their knowledge and experience. DPOs should continue to lobby aid and development agencies for their support in building capacity and improving the impact of DPOs' own work. Through closer collaboration, DPOs may help such agencies to turn rhetoric into reality, by developing and influencing their understanding and response to disability.

DPOs have successfully worked with the media to change the way in which disabled people are represented, thus ensuring that disabled people are represented in all their diversity and human complexity. It is not useful to replace one set of stereotypes for another. The Universal Declaration of Human Rights, the UN Standard Rules, and the social model of disability should be used as tools for analysis and programme design, public education and media campaigns, lobbying, and other actions. In order to achieve equality of opportunity for disabled people, it is vital to work with both local and national structures (related to education, employment, government) to bring about changes in attitudes, policies, budgets, and practical procedures, as well as changes in legislation.

Conclusions

The experience of Oxfam and its partners is that disabled people are discriminated against and excluded from full participation in society not only because of the physical limitations of their impairment, but principally by the attitudes of non-disabled people, and by the way in which society organises itself. This is the basis of the social model of disability, which recognises the equal rights of disabled people.

Oxfam and other agencies must consider whether their style of operating and their organisational culture explicitly or by omission exclude disabled people. Disability awareness requires action and commitment, as well as a willingness to experiment, to reflect, and learn from mistakes, and to do this in partnership and consultation with the people who will benefit. Any organisation that claims a human rights basis for its work cannot really claim to uphold and respect those rights, or maintain its integrity, unless it is willing to adopt a disability analysis. As in other areas of development, if programmes are to be viable and effective, they will involve consulting beneficiaries; talking directly to beneficiaries; involving the community as well as direct beneficiaries; and making inputs and activities accessible. Working effectively to involve disabled people begins from these principles and does not necessarily require specialist input: respecting these basic good development principles in organisational practice is half the battle.

In addition, on the basis of the work conducted with disabled people's organisations in Kosovo, Disability Equality Training (DET) is suggested as one possible course of action. DET is relevant to both disabled and non-disabled people, although it should ideally be facilitated by trainers with personal experience of disability. The methods and outcomes presented in this manual are offered as a contribution to developing a way of working which will increase the awareness of disability and help to create an understanding of how and why disabled people are denied full participation and equal rights as citizens, and to develop realistic strategies to ensure their inclusion in society.

We conclude this section with the words of Myrvete, a disabled woman and activist from Kosovo: '*Just go for it. Never give up.*'

Part Two

The practice of Disability Equality training

5 The Disability Equality Training of Trainers (DETOT) course

This chapter describes the course of workshops devised and organised by Oxfam, entitled 'Disability Equality Training of Trainers'(DETOT). It took place in Kosovo between 1997 and 1998. It built on the 18 months of preparatory work described in Chapter 3, during which Oxfam staff, staff of its partner KAPP (Kosovo Association of People with Paraplegia, now known as Handikos), and community volunteers got to know and trust each other, through holding informal discussions, making home visits, attending group meetings, conducting group work, and running regional workshops. The course represented a more formalised stage in the Disability Equality programme, designed to give participants both the theoretical basis and the practical skills to take on the roles of Disability Equality activists and facilitators.

Aims, objectives, and methodology

The course was developed with support and advice from the President of KAPP. It was based largely on observation, experience, and feedback from participants during the various types of preparatory work described in Chapter 3. All the KAPP Regional Co-ordinators attended a planning meeting at which the basic idea and plans were presented for consultation, and practical details were discussed and agreed.

The overall aim was to develop the capacity of KAPP members to promote Disability Equality and raise awareness of disability in the wider community. In turn, local people, most of them disabled, would be able to educate others, and would reach more people (and do it better) than Oxfam could. The course was therefore designed for people who were already engaged, to some extent, in the activities of the KAPP's Local Active Groups (LAGs); it was hoped that they would apply the lessons that they learned from the course in their regional structures and individual groups, and draw in those LAG members who were still extremely isolated (physically or psychologically) within their own homes.

The DETOT course had the following specific objectives:
- to raise the participants' own awareness of human rights and Disability Equality;
- to increase their capacity to change attitudes within their communities, raising awareness of the needs and potential strengths of disabled people;
- to reach out to marginalised disabled people;
- to create a small core group of facilitators who, with further support and input, would be able to lead workshops and discussion groups on the rights of disabled people;

- to encourage discussion of gender-related issues and support the inclusion of women, particularly disabled women, in the LAGs;
- to develop the potential for the creation of a disabled women's support group.

The guiding methodological principle of the course was to create an environment in which participants and facilitators could share experiences and exchange ideas freely. The course was designed according to the principles of adult learning (explained in Chapter 8), to encourage the active involvement of all the participants. Because everybody learns in different ways, it provided a range of varied activities, including whole-group and small-group discussions and exercises, work in pairs and individual work, drawing, drama, posters, oral presentations, poetry, movement, stories, brainstorms, written handouts, and games.

Participants

Participants were chosen by the LAGs and regional structures of the KAPP. The only stipulation was that at least half of the course members should be disabled people. In the event, the final composition of the group was two non-disabled women, nine disabled women, four non-disabled men, and five disabled men. Most members had either participated in the regional introductory workshops or belonged to LAGs with whom Oxfam had done individual preparatory work. Two participants already had some personal experience of facilitating workshop activities.

In two regions of Kosovo it had not been possible to do any preparatory work with individual groups, so the DETOT participants from those regions came to the course with no previous direct involvement in Disability Equality or workshop methods. Overall, the course would probably have been more focused and more effective if the necessary preparatory work had been done with all the participants beforehand.

Initially, the facilitators set a limit of 15 participants (including one Oxfam staff member), in the hope that by the end five or six of them would become facilitators, and the others would apply their learning in other ways in their communities. But in fact the course began with 19 people and ended with 20, which reduced the time available for feedback and discussion, and meant that some issues were covered rather superficially.

Facilitators

The course employed three co-facilitators, working when possible in pairs; guest facilitators were invited to lead a couple of sessions. This exposed participants to various styles of facilitation. When workshops are being designed, two or more facilitators, working together and brainstorming ideas, often work more creatively than a single facilitator working alone. Facilitating activities in pairs also increases effectiveness during workshops: one person takes responsibility for the current activity, while the other is responsible for observing progress and keeping things on track; this is especially useful when a workshop lasts all day.

Scheduling and structure of the course contents

The course was held on one day a week for five months, with two two-week breaks. There were two modules: *Facilitation Skills* and *Disability Equality Issues*. However, to maximise the opportunities for learning, consideration of disability issues was included in activities that focused on facilitation, and vice versa. The idea was for participants to do an activity and learn from it of itself, and then to discuss and consider it from the point of view of a facilitator, answering questions such as: 'Why did we do that?', 'What would this type of activity be useful for?', 'Why?', and 'What would I do differently, to make it more effective in my own community?'

The first two sessions were devoted to forming the group, setting priorities, and developing agreed ways of working. Seven weeks of developing facilitation skills followed; then seven weeks were spent on exploring disability-related issues, one week on planning, and one week on evaluation, combined with a celebration of the course and of participants'contributions.

Language

We found that it was best, when possible, for workshops to be conducted in one language. Having to use an interpreter between facilitators and participants slows down communication and leaves less time for activities and discussion. However, it is more important that the participants should use their first language and communicate freely among themselves; so if the facilitator does not speak that language, the use of an interpreter is unavoidable, and more time should be allowed; and/or a more limited coverage of issues should be factored in.

If use is made of an interpreter, however skilled, the facilitator loses a lot of valuable feedback about the thoughts and feelings of the participants. Much of this comes from informal communication: incidental comments and casual conversation during group work, or during breaks. In partial compensation for this, the facilitator must pay close attention to the participants'body language and the interactions between them. In addition, the interpreter should translate any significant verbal exchange that takes place outside of the main conversation. However, this is asking the impossible of the interpreter: the level of concentration required for workshop interpreting is extremely hard to sustain, and regular breaks are needed. One suggested solution is to use two interpreters in an intensive situation such as a workshop.

Even with sufficient and experienced interpreters, some exercises, such as role plays, are hard to do through translation: the facilitator misses much of the significance of the verbal exchanges and cannot respond appropriately. This does not mean that role plays and improvised drama should necessarily be avoided; but the facilitator must be prepared to give up some control of the situation and trust the participants to manage the activity by themselves.

It is essential that the interpreters should understand the language and ideas of Disability Equality in order to translate the proceedings effectively. Linguistic fluency is less important than the interpreter's ability to comprehend and communicate the concepts that facilitators and participants are intending to convey. Time must be set aside in advance to brief the interpreter about the key concepts and vocabulary likely to be used during the course.

The situation in Kosovo was complicated by the fact that there was often no common language between the two main ethnic groups in the community – Serbs and Albanians – and even more so for disabled people and rural women, who had no schooling and therefore had never learned the language of the other community. But experience proved that working in three spoken languages is unsustainable for any large group situation for longer than a couple of hours. Participants lose too much of the main conversations, and the process becomes too time-consuming and tiring for all concerned. Partly for this reason, it was decided to use two languages, Albanian and English, for the DETOT course.

As for the use of sign language with hearing-impaired participants, it was found that interpreting between two spoken languages and sign language in workshops is feasible, as long as sufficient time is allowed, and the key information is made available in the form of written handouts, charts, and drawings on flipcharts.

Materials and activities

The materials and activities were designed specifically for the DETOT course, with much borrowing and adaptation from other sources. Handouts were produced in Albanian, in standard printed format. Materials and activities were designed to be accessible to participants, with the use of a partner for reading or drawing where necessary. Materials should also have been made available in large print or on cassette tape for visually impaired participants, but for logistical reasons they were not.

Some people on the course felt more comfortable having written information to study (alone or with a partner) at home, or to keep as an *aide memoire*, while others focused solely on what happened during the actual sessions and in their interaction with the other participants. The facilitators tried to strike a balance by providing plenty of handouts, but encouraging people to use them only if they found them helpful to their learning or for their future work.

Transport and funding

Transport is a particular problem for disabled people in Kosovo: many roads are impassable for those who use wheelchairs or crutches, and public transport is inaccessible to them. Long waits for buses and trains, especially in bad weather, the lack of public toilets en route, and the long journey-times, even over short distances, make travelling by public transport an ordeal for everyone. Most disabled people who owned cars before the start of the crisis had long since sold them in order to survive. Consequently, disabled people depended on friends and relatives for lifts every time they needed to go somewhere. Transport costs were therefore built into the budget for this project.

The British Embassy in Belgrade made a generous grant of £5000 to cover most of the costs of the course, and Oxfam supplied the remainder. The most significant budget line in any training scheme is likely to be staff costs, which should not be regarded (as they often are) as a negative sign of the value of the project.

Logistics and staff time

The DETOT course was held at the Oxfam office in Pristina. In many ways the whole office staff became involved: helping with transport; purchasing materials and refreshments; translating materials; and interpreting during the workshops. Two members of the regular staff acted as co-facilitators, together with an external consultant.

While it is true that the course was a drain on staff resources, there were great benefits for all concerned. Everybody looked forward to Wednesdays, when a large group of people took over part of the office, with all their energy, dynamism, and enthusiasm. In addition, the interaction between Oxfam staff (and other visitors to the office) and the DETOT participants helped to overcome some barriers and increase their understanding of each other.

Results of the DETOT course, and lessons learned from it

Feedback from participants and facilitators, gathered from the final evaluation questionnaire and from evaluation exercises, was very positive and encouraging.

Evaluation by the participants

Participants reported increased confidence in themselves and in their ability to express their feelings and ideas, to use their own experience, and to communicate with others. They felt more independent as a result of their involvement in the course, and reported improvements in their own listening and facilitating skills, and an increased tolerance of others. What they liked most about working as a group was being together often, exchanging opinions and experiences, and learning new things from each other. Sixteen out of the 17 respondents felt that they had been either 'involved' or 'very involved' in the work. The majority felt confident to apply their learning in their work with the LAGs, in workshops (as facilitators), in their everyday lives, and in informal group settings.

They identified the following ways in which they could to put into action their learning from the course:
- Organising and facilitating workshops on disability issues.
- Bringing people together, creating a space where all people have the right to express themselves.
- Working with people on Disability Equality in various contexts, such as with community representatives, at public events, and during home visits.
- Breaking the isolation of disabled people.
- Motivating other disabled people to be more active in the LAGs.
- Sharing information with others, especially about ways of removing barriers to disabled people's participation in society.

- Using their own experiences to support and enable others.
- Influencing public opinion and attitudes about disabled people.
- Using local and foreign examples to teach others about disabled people's rights, abilities, and contributions to society.

Well over the stipulated 50 per cent of participants who were selected to attend the course by their LAGs were disabled. This reflected a growing acceptance by KAPP of the crucial role that disabled people themselves should play in organisations that exist to represent their interests. Likewise, most participants were women, and although still more time was needed for a consideration of the particular needs of disabled women, and for consideration of the inter-relationships between disability and gender, by the end of the course these issues were more firmly and openly on people's own agenda than before, and some participants wanted to take things further by starting a women's group.

On a couple of occasions, when other arrangements broke down, two participants who use wheelchairs challenged physical and attitudinal barriers by taking a two-hour bus journey to and from the training centre, even though it meant being carried on and off the bus and being exposed to the prejudices of other travellers. The course provided a rare opportunity for people from different parts of Kosovo to meet together regularly, share experiences, work together, and get to know each other. Weekly attendance throughout the five months averaged 90–95 per cent, even during the final weeks, when the security situation was deteriorating.

Co-facilitators' evaluation

For the co-facilitators the course was a stimulating, energising experience, and the specific objectives were judged to have been met. Particular highlights included the high degree of interest and motivation shown by participants – passionate discussion of an issue would often continue through lunch and break times – and the evident increase in self-confidence as participants became aware of their own strengths.

The course helped to place disability at the heart of Oxfam's mainstream programme, and the whole staff team moved forwards in terms of their own awareness of, commitment to, and capacity to implement equal rights and opportunities for people with disabilities.

At the end of the course, the co-facilitators felt that about eight of the participants could immediately take on the role of workshop facilitator, with some further support and information. All the participants had shown that they were able to apply their learning to their roles within the LAGs and to their own lives. Their suggestions for future actions and plans were creative, relevant to their needs, and realistically achievable.

A particularly significant learning point for facilitators was that, although the course explored the nature of true participation with the group, and included work for small groups and pairs in order to create opportunities for everyone to participate, some individuals tended to dominate whole-group discussions and feedback sessions.

Facilitators eventually realised, however, that when these discussions were allowed to continue for a long time, a natural sequence of contributions seemed to be established, and everyone eventually got a turn to speak. Often the most interesting things were said by those who spoke last, prompting much further comment and discussion. Maintaining a brisk pace was not as important to the group as allowing plenty of time for the expression of ideas. It also helped if each person was encouraged to contribute to general discussions in turn, without interruption, which helped to break the pattern imposed by the dominant speakers.

With the benefit of hindsight, facilitators reported that they would make the following revisions to the course:

- Plan fewer activities each day and allow more time for each topic, so that each could be covered in greater depth.

- Strictly limit the size of the group to 16 people.

- Create more opportunities for participants to practise facilitation, including a period of one or two months in which there were no workshops, during which time participants would design and work on a Disability Equality awareness-raising project in their own communities and then report back on their experiences.

- Move the session on designing workshop activities towards the end of the whole course, rather than include it in the first 'facilitation skills' section, so that all participants would have more experience and ideas with which to work when creating their own activities.

- Define each co-facilitator's role and responsibilities clearly and in writing, before the start of the course.

- From the beginning, introduce the idea of inviting each participant to speak in turn, without interruption, on the subject under discussion, before allowing unmediated general debate.

Facilitators agreed that some important matters were beyond the scope of the DETOT course and would have been better dealt with in a different forum. These topics are identified here for the benefit of readers who might be considering designing a Disability Equality course or a course to train trainers:

- Safe and constructive ways for disabled people to express feelings of anger and frustration; and the role of facilitators in this.

- Dealing with conflicts within groups.

- Personal issues, including sexuality and reproductive rights.

- Discrimination against people with learning difficulties; accessibility of information and self-advocacy for people with learning difficulties.

- Physical and sexual abuse experienced by disabled people.

- The practicalities of inclusive education and employment of disabled people.

Conclusion

The completion of the course was the appropriate time for the expatriate Disability Programme Support Manager (Alison Harris) to depart from the programme. Twenty members of the Kosovo Association of People with Paraplegia (KAPP), most of them disabled, would continue the promotion of Disability Equality within KAPP and the wider community. The DETOT course strengthened the capacity of both individual members and the KAPP as an institution to improve the living conditions of disabled people, working within a clearly articulated framework of human rights and Disability Equality. It is perhaps not unreasonable to believe that when Kosovo subsequently descended into conflict and chaos, the knowledge, skills, and understanding that the participants on the DETOT course had gained (especially from each other) increased their determination and ability to fight for their right – and the right of other disabled people – to survive.

6 Outline of the training materials

To provide a coherent structure, the training materials are presented in an order and format similar to those used in the Disability Equality Training of Trainers programme in Kosovo in 1997. Most of the activities had been used previously in other contexts, for example in Disability Equality or capacity-building workshops with aid-agency staff, women's groups, community groups, and other disabled people's organisations. Some of the activities were used only in those contexts, and not in the DETOT course, but they are included in this manual in order to broaden out the scope and choice of activities. It is intended that users of this manual will pick and choose activities to suit their own needs and circumstances, rather than follow the complete agenda. The workshop activities are organised in the following way.

Chapter 7 Preparing for the workshop and forming the group

7.1   Practical considerations 76
7.1.1   *Make the workshop fit the participants, not vice versa 76*
7.1.2   *Access! Access! Access! 79*

7.2   Introductions, icebreakers, and energising exercises 84
7.2.1   *'Find someone who ...' 84*
7.2.2   *'Open the day' 86*
7.2.3   *Paired interviews and introductions 87*
7.2.4   *Name game 88*
7.2.5   *Guessing game 89*
7.2.6   *'Darling' game 90*
7.2.7   *What I like about you 91*
7.2.8   *What I am proud of myself for 92*
7.2.9   *Positive feedback 93*
7.2.10 *Name-badge exercise 94*
7.2.11 *My life pie-chart 95*
7.2.12 *Wallpaper exercise 96*
7.2.13 *Gesture energiser 97*

7.3   Expectations and priorities 98
7.3.1   *Hopes, concerns, contributions, and needs 98*
7.3.2   *Setting priorities 99*
7.3.3   *Agreeing guidelines for working together as a group 101*

7.4   Working together: establishing group guidelines; communication; respect; participation 104

7.4.1   *Mapping for Mars 104*

7.4.2   *Listening exercise (1) 107*

7.4.3   *I respect you/You respect me 110*

Chapter 8 Facilitation skills

8.1   How adults learn 112

8.1.1   *The 'process of learning' exercise 112*

8.1.2   *Creating a positive learning environment 115*

8.1.3   *Stages of learning 118*

8.1.4   *Rates of learning 119*

8.1.5   *Components of training 121*

8.1.6   *Whole-group activity 123*

8.2   Facilitating adult learning 124

8.2.1   *Facilitation: brainstorm and discussion 125*

8.2.2   *Listening exercise (2) 129*

8.2.3   *Discussion of good and bad listening 129*

8.2.4   *Open the day 131*

8.2.5   *Guessing game 131*

8.2.6   *Observation exercise 131*

8.2.7   *Mapping for Mars 134*

8.2.8   *Know your apple 134*

8.2.9   *Whole-group discussion of room layout 134*

8.2.10   *Whole-group discussion of timing and pacing 134*

8.2.11   *Line-drawing exercise 138*

8.2.12   *Facilitation checklists 142*

8.3   Planning workshops 144

8.3.1   *The eight sunrays of planning 144*

8.3.2   *Organising the workshop: a two-part exercise 147*

8.3.3   *Planning the agenda and contents of a workshop 151*

8.4   Handling difficult topics 153

8.4.1   *Prevention of impairment: presentation and discussion 157*

8.4.2   *Prevention of impairment: small-group discussion 161*

8.4.3   *Prevention in the home: picture-based exercise 162*

8.4.4   *Fishbowl exercise 165*

Chapter 9 Disability Equality in practice

9.1   Models of disability 167

9.1.1.   *Introducing the topic 167*

9.1 2   *Presentation of the three models 169*

9.1.3   *Discussion of the three models of disability 173*

9.1.4   *Life stories: activity based on the models of disability 174*

9.1.5   *How can I help? 175*

9.2   Barriers to equal participation 177

9.2.1   *Identifying barriers: the wall exercise 177*

9.2.2   *Problem-tree exercise 183*

9.2.3   *Action-planning to overcome barriers: for DPOs and local community members 188*

9.2.4   *Action planning to overcome barriers: for aid-agency staff 189*

9.2.5   *Barriers: a case study 191*

9.3   Disabled people's rights: human rights 192

9.3.1   *Fairness and rights: camouflage energiser 194*

9.3.2   *What rights do we have? The calendar game 196*

9.3.3   *The imaginary country 200*

9.3.4   *Rights and responsibilities 202*

9.3.5   *'Choosing' rights 203*

9.3.6   *Stereotyping and discrimination: Know your apple 205*

9.3.7   *Global and local discrimination 208*

9.3.8   *The evolution of documented rights for disabled people 211*

9.3.9   *Applying the UN Standard Rules to real life 213*

9.3.10   *Interviews in pairs 220*

9.3.11   *Improvised drama about disabled people's rights 222*

9.3.12   *Identifying allies 224*

9.3.13   *The right to education: whole-group discussion 226*

9.3.14   *Puppets exercise 231*

9.3.15   *Two ways to cross a river 233*

9.4   Gender and disability 235

9.4.1   *Who am I? 236*

9.4.2   *The gender quiz 238*

9.4.3   *Sex and gender 240*

9.4.4   *Restrictive gender roles 241*

9.4.5   *Gender roles: whole-group discussion 242*

9.4.6   *The game of life 243*

9.4.7   *Disabled women's voices: diamond-ranking exercise 247*

9.5   Images and language of disability 251

9.5.1   *Media search 251*

9.5.2   *Using positive and non-stereotypical images of disability 253*

9.5.3   *Posters exercise 255*

9.5.4   *The impact of language: Mr Biswas photo exercise 256*

9.5.5   *Word-list exercise 258*

9.6   **Definitions of disability** 263
9.6.1   *'Our definitions' exercise* 264

9.7   **Self-determined living** 266
9.7.1   *In/ter/dependence drawings* 268
9.7.2   *My contribution* 270
9.7.3   *Independent (Self-Determined) Living: presentation and discussion* 271
9.7.4   *Putting Independent (Self-determined) Living into practice* 276

Chapter 10 Action planning

10.1   **Short and half-day activities** 277
10.1.1   *Individual reflection* 277
10.1.2   *Objective setting* 278
10.1.3   *Eight sunrays of planning* 279
10.1.4   *'Nothing about us without us'* 280
10.1.5   *More planning exercises* 280

10.2   **Half-day or whole-day session on action planning** 281
10.2.1   *Immediate action* 281
10.2.2   *Future actions: a competition* 282
10.2.3   *Future actions exercise: diamond ranking* 283

Chapter 11 Evaluation

11.1   **Quick evaluations in the round** 284

11.2   **Small-group and whole-group evaluation activities** 285
11.2.1   *Sketch/mime* 285
11.2.2   *Throw out or keep* 285
11.2.3   *Song* 285

11.3   **Mid-way evaluations** 286
11.3.1   *Reflecting on facilitation* 287
11.3.2   *Writing and drawing* 288
11.3.3   *Collage* 289

11.4   **Questionnaires** 290
11.4.1   *Questionnaire for general use at the end of a day's workshop* 290
11.4.2   *To end a facilitation-practice session* 291
11.4.3   *Detailed questionnaire for a final evaluation* 292

Chapter 12 Case studies

12.1   Individual case studies 300
12.1.1   *Shapla, Bangladesh 301*
12.1.2   *Mamadou, Mali 302*
12.1.3   *Lao Sonn, Cambodia 303*
12.1.4   *Françoise, Burkina Faso 304*
12.1.5   *Annya – Abkhazia 305*

12.2   Disabled refugees and internally displaced people: case studies with
         questions 306
12.2.1   *Hassan 307*
12.2.2   *Suada 308*
12.2.3   *Milica 309*
12.2.4   *Flora 310*

12.3   Case studies of social and political action by disabled people 312
12.3.1   *Grassroots representation in Cambodia 312*
12.3.2   *The Soroti Agricultural and Craft Association of the Blind, Uganda 314*
12.3.3. *Election monitoring and the right to vote in Ghana, Bangladesh, and Zambia 316*

Chapter 13 Some useful quotations 318

Chapter 14 Sample workshop agendas

14.1   One-day general introductory workshop for local and international NGOs
         and agencies 320
14.2   One-day workshop on disability and gender for local staff of NGOs
         and agencies 322
14.3   Two-day workshop for members of local DPOs 323
14.4   Five-month training course for disability-awareness trainers 324

From this range of activities it should be possible to construct workshops, seminars, discussion groups, and so on for a variety of participants – expatriate and local staff of international NGOs and agencies, staff of national or local organisations, government representatives, members of disabled people's organisations (DPOs), members of the community, etc. Most activities are applicable (with some modification) to all these potential participants. Some specifically focus on one particular group: where this is the case, we make it clear and we offer alternatives for other groups.

The materials cover the main issues relevant to the twin topics of facilitation skills and Disability Equality. But they are not exhaustive: many other interesting topics could be added. And of course the approach that was adopted is only one way to do training. It is important for facilitators to bear in mind, and to stress with participants, that there is no single 'right' way. It is vital for the facilitator to find the approach that she or he is comfortable with and that is suitable for the group.

Each activity in the manual is presented step by step, together with its objectives and/or learning points and notes for facilitators. We suggest how much time to allow for each activity, but of course the duration will vary, depending on the size of the group and whether or not an interpreter is used. We have tried to make the materials as self-explanatory as possible, so that facilitators with a broad range of experience will find them easy to use.

Some topics are presented in the form of a discrete and self-contained session, with a specific structure and logic which could be followed without modification. Other topics are more loosely structured, and it is not intended that all the activities will be done in one workshop, nor that they will necessarily be done in the order presented. In some sections we have suggested links between particular sessions or activities, to show inexperienced facilitators how to lead from one to the next. This helps to reinforce the learning process and keep people engaged.

Chapter 8, 'Facilitation skills', is designed with a particular focus on members of disabled people's organisations, because in the long term they are ultimately best qualified to take on the role of training others in disability awareness and rights-based work. However, this chapter should be of use to other facilitators too, whatever their level of experience, and many of the activities are suitable for various group-work situations, not just the training of trainers.

The activities in the manual vary considerably in their levels of complexity, in terms both of the concepts and issues covered, and the facilitation methods involved. Again, the idea is that facilitators should choose the activities that are most appropriate for their participant group and their particular circumstances (including the availability of materials), and adapt them where necessary.

Most of the activities can be used with a broad range of participants, irrespective of their levels of education. Facilitators should beware of oversimplifying concepts – especially when participants lack formal education – because this is patronising and risks reinforcing negative assumptions. It may be necessary to find an appropriate way to explain jargon and specialist terminology, to avoid or modify it, but don't underestimate participants' ability to understand and apply the underlying concepts.

Some of the activities require a certain level of literacy, but facilitators might be able to substitute symbols or objects for words in these cases. Other activities which require reading, writing, or drawing can be done with the help of partners or an appointed person in each small group. The activities are generally suitable for groups of people with a broad range of physical and sensory impairments, but they may require further adaptation, depending on the needs of individual participants. For some of the activities we suggest specific alternatives to take into account additional or different impairment-related (or literacy-related) access needs. In addition, general guidelines for making the workshop environment and activities accessible are given in the next chapter (*7.12 Access! Access! Access!*).

Note that none of the activities features the simulation of impairments or disability, in which for example non-disabled people wear a blindfold, or have their hearing blocked, or are required to spend time using a wheelchair; nor are disabled people required to simulate an impairment different from their own. The reason for this deliberate omission is that such simulation activities give a very unrealistically negative impression, which can reinforce prejudices and stereotypes. With blindfolds, for example, people crash into things and feel disoriented and helpless, but this is not the reality for most people with impaired vision. DPOs recommend that if participants need to know what it is like to have a particular impairment or to experience disablement by society, it is best for a workshop facilitator (or a guest speaker) who has experience of that impairment to talk and answer questions about it.

This manual makes considerable use of handouts, flipcharts, and verbal presentations, but these are suggestions, not prescriptions: if they are not appropriate, you should devise your own alternatives. Different people learn differently: even within an apparently cohesive participant group, there will be some people who depend on handouts and some who don't find them helpful at all. It is good to have handouts available, but they are not essential. On the other hand, for courses designed to train trainers, handouts can be very useful to jog the memories of participants after the session, and as the basis for activities or discussions in future group-work that they will themselves facilitate.

Wherever possible, use locally available objects, equipment, and stationery. For example, for writing on flipcharts in Kosovo we used very cheap, locally available packaging paper, but in most cases a blackboard and chalks would have been just as good.

The DETOT course relied heavily on participative learning methods. Participants in your groups may be resistant to them, perhaps because of cultural or traditional assumptions about the best methods of teaching and learning, or because of the participants' status within their community. The only way to find out how they will react is to try! However, you can take measures beforehand to maximise the applicability and appropriateness of the workshop: get to know at least some of the participants, let them get to know you, and see how they respond to some of your ideas; seek out the opinions of others who have done group-work in the region; or consult people who have a better understanding or a different perspective on the local culture. But be prepared to take risks and to learn from your mistakes.

7 Preparing for the workshop and forming the group

7.1 Practical considerations

When preparing to facilitate a disability-awareness workshop, there are two key principles to bear in mind:

• The workshop must be relevant to the participants' needs and interests.

• The environment, the materials, and the activities must be accessible to all the participants.

7.1.1 Make the workshop fit the participants, not vice versa

Find out as much as possible about the participants before the workshop begins, and adapt the contents and approach to suit them. You have only a limited time, and disability awareness touches on all areas of life and human activity, so focusing on what is most immediately relevant to your particular participant group will help to ensure maximum participation and optimal learning. No matter how much you may want to, you can't do everything in a day, or two, or even twenty; it is better to be specific, make a few clear points, and get participants engaged and interested, so that they will transfer something from the workshop into real life.

Try to think yourself into the minds and motivation of participants. What is likely to be each one's particular starting-point and perspective on disability? Here are some general suggestions, based on our own experience, to start you thinking.

Health-care/ medical staff For health and medical staff, the main motivators are often compassion and a desire to find a cure, to make people 'better', or to prevent them from becoming ill. But in their dealings with disabled people, medical and health-care staff need to understand that such attitudes, whether conscious or unconscious, may be very harmful. They also need to be aware that, by virtue of their professional training and privileged access to information, they may be perceived by disabled people as wielding power over them – a perception which may lead to a lack of trust and poor communications. When health professionals have understood these potential problems, they are usually keen to explore appropriate ways of working.

Engineers   Engineers are trained to be problem-solvers. They approach a structure by asking questions such as 'How can we make the best use of this structure, and what resources do we need to make it work?' If they understand that they can make significantly better use of a structure or facility by taking account of the needs of disabled people, they can then set about 'solving the problem' of making it accessible to all.

Accessibility is an investment that pays off for society in many ways. It allows disabled people to go where everyone else goes – and the more that disabled people are visible and participate in society, the more easily they cease to be 'the unknown', and attitudes towards them will change. For people with visual impairments, an accessible built environment means not having to depend on someone else to take them where they need to go. If the only person who can accompany them also happens to be the family breadwinner, an accessible environment can make all the difference between the family eating or not eating that day.

Although engineers sometimes complain that ramps for wheelchair users require more cement than steps do and therefore cost more, they usually appreciate the argument that steps cause far more accidents than ramps do, and that the cost of treating the injuries may be far higher than the cost of the extra cement. But while cost is a significant factor, there is a more fundamental issue: buildings are built to be used, and we all have the same right to use them. Choosing to make a building accessible to only part of the population (the non-disabled) is an arbitrary and discriminatory decision. Thus, a one-day introductory workshop to raise awareness of disability among NGO engineers (most of whom might be men and non-disabled) could start with the concept of equal rights (illustrated with statistics about the numbers of disabled people), before proceeding to consider the three 'models of disability' and then examining barriers to access, using relevant examples, to help the engineers to understand why disability is relevant to their work – whether they specialise in the provision of water and sanitation, or building and reconstruction.

Real-life situation studies, or working through actual building plans, are a good way of getting engineers to start applying their skills to the needs of disabled people; to examine myths, such as the 'huge extra costs' of ensuring accessibility; and to challenge the notion that accessibility is something 'Western' and not relevant in the context of emergency aid or community development in poor countries. It is important to include a consideration of gender: getting engineers to think about the access needs of disabled women as well as those of disabled men.

Distribution staff of humanitarian agencies

For staff of aid-distribution programmes, the main question is 'How can we make sure that these supplies reach those most in need?' Workshops should emphasise the rights of disabled people to receive aid; consider how to identify disabled people within target beneficiary populations, and how to assess their needs (some of which will be the same as those of non-disabled people, and some of which may be different); discuss how disabled people can be enabled to claim their entitlements and participate in relief programmes; explore how they might be represented at all stages of the programme; identify the barriers to equal access and discuss how they can be removed; and assess the potential role of DPOs in distribution programmes: how might national and international organisations learn from, work with, and support local DPOs?

Women refugees

A workshop for the women's committee of a camp for refugees or displaced people (most, perhaps all, of whom will be non-disabled) might also start with a consideration of rights, models, and barriers, but should focus on the problems confronting disabled women, disabled children, and carers in the camp, finding out their views and needs, and making sure that they are involved in everyday activities and decision making.

DPO staff and members

A workshop with staff and members of a local DPO (all, most, or some of whom would be disabled, and most of whom might be men) again might include rights, models, and barriers, but should be based on activities which help to raise participants' self-esteem or explore their own experience of impairment and disability, and move on to consider how they might raise awareness among the disabled and non-disabled public. It might also include discussion of gender-related aspects of disability.

7.1.2 Access! Access! Access!

If at all possible, workshop facilitators should contact participants in advance, to enquire about their access needs. If this is not possible, you should make sure that the physical environment is generally accessible, and be ready to adapt activities on the day. Check with the participants, either individually as they arrive, or as a group at the start of the workshop. The point is that all participants should be given the opportunity to participate and learn on an equal basis, and it is the facilitator's job is to create the conditions for this to happen.

Accessibility of the physical environment

Here is a list of basic considerations. Environmental barriers vary from place to place, so it is always worth checking with disabled people what the most frequently encountered barriers in their community are. If in doubt, ask someone who is disabled to check out the space. For technical information, check the ISO Building Construction Guidelines (details in the Resources section at the end of this book). This list could be made into a handout for workshop participants.

Steps
- If there are a lot of steps, can a ramp be made (of wood or concrete)?
- The angle of any ramp should follow ISO guidelines (or at the very least should not be dangerously steep).
- Paint a white line at the edge of each step to improve visibility.
- Add a handrail along steps or ramp, to assist people with impaired mobility or sight.

Lift/elevator
- Is there one? Does it work? Is the electricity supply reliable?
- Can a wheelchair fit inside the lift, with all the doors closed?
- Buttons should be reachable from a wheelchair, and/or there should be room for someone who can reach the buttons.
- Differentiate buttons by the use of Braille or by numbers drawn with a raised line.

Doorways
- Check that doorways are wide enough for wheelchairs to pass through them.
- Check to see if the floor under the doorway is flat.

Toilet
- Is there space for a wheelchair to enter and turn? And for the door to be opened and closed while the person is inside?
- Does the door open outwards?
- Does the toilet have a seat? Enough space in front and beside it for transfer?
- Are there handrails?
- Are the toilet-flush mechanism, hand-basin, mirror, and door-lock at a level where they can be reached by someone sitting in a wheelchair?

General
- Put tactile or Braille labels at the entrance to each room.
- Signs should be in large print.
- Any visual information should also be provided verbally, and vice versa.
- Check to see if parking space is available close to the building, and if the route from the car park to the building is obstructed in any way.
- Paths leading to the building should be cleared of snow, ice, and mud.
- Arrange for blind or visually impaired people to become familiar with the layout of rooms and facilities.

Accessibility of activities and materials

For people with physical impairments
- Focus on what people can do; for example, use an energiser that uses facial gestures or words, instead of a physically demanding game like Musical Chairs (which involves running from one chair to another).
- Be aware that for some people any movement, or certain movements, can cause pain. Find out if this is so for any participants in the group and modify the activity if that is the case.
- Don't assume that an active, interactive workshop necessarily requires a lot of movement, variety of pace, and noise. For many people, action and movement are totally unrelated concepts, and speed or noise (or lack of either) do not necessarily indicate levels of energy or vibrancy.
- Provide chairs, mattresses, tables, or work surfaces so that as far as possible all participants, facilitators, and interpreters work and communicate at the same height. For example, wheelchair-users tend to feel distanced and excluded from any activity that requires participants to draw on the ground. Instead, you might provide a table for everyone to use, or (if they are comfortable about it) wheelchair-users might transfer to a cushion or mattress on the ground.
- Ask if any participants need to lie down for part of the time, or transfer to different seating (to help to prevent muscle pain, or to prevent pressure sores).
- People with impaired mobility often feel the cold acutely. Check that the room temperature is comfortable for them.

For people with hearing impairments
- Use a sign-language interpreter (where applicable), and allow time for interpretation. Provide short breaks for the interpreter to rest.
- Speak clearly (do not shout).
- Assist lip reading: do not cover your mouth with your hands, or turn your face away so that your mouth cannot be seen.
- People should not pass in between the interpreter and deaf participants.

- Written displays and handouts, and other visual aids, should be used to reinforce what is said by facilitator and participants.
- If you show a video, use subtitles or provide an accompanying text that participants can read for themselves or have signed for them.

For people with visual impairments

- Always read out what is written and verbally describe what is drawn on flipcharts, handouts, diagrams, etc.
- Provide reading partners, to read out handouts used in the workshop and at home.
- Depending on the technology available locally, consider also the use of Braille, cassette tapes, and raised-line drawings.
- Use shapes, textures, and sounds in activities, instead of colours and other visual markers.
- Avoid games and exercises requiring visual co-ordination, such as catching a ball; use exercises involving verbal skills, music, and texture instead.
- Repeat readings as often as necessary (for example, you may need to keep repeating a list of questions to be discussed by small groups, or criteria to be prioritised in a diamond-ranking exercise).
- Include everyone in exercises that involve drawing or writing, by appointing one person in the small or whole group to draw or write for everyone else (including themselves).
- When dividing the large group into smaller units, make sure that visually impaired people are not left unsure of where to move to.

For people with speech impairments

- Allow as much time as the person needs for an activity. Encourage the group to respect each person's particular needs – as of right.
- Focus on what the person is saying, not his or her impairment.
- Consider using an interpreter, but it must be someone who understands the speaker(s) and will not 'put words into their mouths' by saying what the interpreter thinks the speaker should say.
- Encourage speech-impaired participants to write or draw their contributions on the flipchart, or to use a spelling board.

Preparatory questionnaire

If you do not know much about participants as individuals before the workshop starts (and even if you do), it is helpful to use a questionnaire to find out more about their interests and any access-related needs. If possible, you should distribute the forms before the first workshop.

HANDOUT 1
Preparatory questionnaire

Name of workshop:

If you are helping someone to fill in this questionnaire (because they cannot see, or do not write, etc.), please consult them and write down what they say.

1.   Name:

Name of group/organisation:

Region:

2   Where and how can we contact you between sessions?

3.   What is your role in the group/organisation?

4.   Have you knowledge or experience of training or workshops? (If so, what?)

5.   What do you hope to gain from the workshop?

6.   Would you like to be a trainer in future?

Yes   No   Not sure

7. Which aspects of training are you most interested in?
   (Please tick as many or as few as you want.)

   Section 1

   Facilitation   Planning

   How people learn   Motivating other people

   Listening skills   Theory

   Communication   Practice

   Developing self-confidence   Others (please specify)

   Section 2

   Human rights   Prevention of disability

   General disability issues   Independent living

   Disabled women's issues   The language of disability

   Disabled children's issues   Others (please specify)

   Attitudes to disability

   Barriers to disabled people's
   participation in society

8. Do you have any special requirements in order to participate fully in this
   workshop? Please tick as appropiate:

   wheelchair access?

   sign-language interpreter?

   diet (diabetic, vegetarian, etc.)?

   crèche?

   other (please describe)?

9. What is your first language?

   Other languages?

10. Additional information/comments?

    Thank you completing this questionnaire. It will help us to prepare a
    workshop better suited to you.

    Please return the form to {name and address} by {date}.

7.2   Introductions, icebreakers, and energising exercises

Some of the following exercises are for use at the start of the day, to introduce facilitators and participants to one another and to create a positive atmosphere. Others may be used at the start of the next day, or after lunch, or at any point where the group seems to have lost its energy and needs to be refreshed. Many of the exercises can be used directly or indirectly to help to raise participants' self-esteem.

7.2.1   'Find someone who ...'

Time   10–15 minutes

Preparation   Prepare a list of numbered statements, or make up your own.

Write them on a sheet of paper, with spaces for the answers, as in Handout 2, and make copies for each participant.

Process   Give each person a copy of the handout, but also read out the statements to the whole group.

Ask them to go around the room and find, for each of the statements, one person who matches the statement.

They should write down the person's name against the number of the relevant statement. If someone cannot read and/or write, they can work with a partner who is literate.

They should find a different person for each statement.

Allow five minutes for this stage. It doesn't matter if they can't find a match for each statement in the time allowed: they can finish the activity during the break.

Once back in the whole group, ask people to name a few examples of new things that they had learned about other members of the group.

Facilitator's notes   This is good for using with a group of people who do not know each other at all, or know each other just a little. It is a good icebreaker, which starts people talking to each other and makes them feel more comfortable to talk/participate in the whole group. By limiting the time allowed and inviting participants to finish the exercise in the break, you give them something to talk about outside the session, which is especially helpful for people who are shy or who do not know each other at all before the workshop.

Option   For people who are not literate, you could use drawings instead of written statements to represent each point that you want them to find out about.

HANDOUT 2
Find someone who ...

1   likes the music of [a popular local artist or group]

2   has attended a workshop before

3   would rather listen than speak

4   had a bad dream last night

5   likes vegetables better than meat

6   has a skill or knowledge which you want to have

7   wants to change the situation of disabled people

8   likes communicating to large groups

9   believes that disabled people need rights not charity

7.2.2   'Open the day'

Time   30 minutes

Process   Ask participants to work in pairs.

Each participant has to show his/her partner how s/he is feeling today, using a sound or a facial expression or a gesture, but no actual words.

They have five minutes to do this, and then they will have to rejoin the whole group, where each person in turn will show the rest of the group his/her partner's sound or gesture (NOT his/her own).

Ask people to demonstrate to the whole group what their partners are feeling.

Facilitator's notes   This activity is a lively way to start a session, but it is also good for getting people to start thinking about feelings – other people's feelings as well as their own. It can be used as an introduction to a session about non-verbal communication or about responding to feelings. Or in a session concerned with people's right/need to express themselves/speak for themselves, it can be used to lead into a discussion of when it is OK and when it is not OK to speak on someone else's behalf, instead of allowing them to represent themselves.

7.2.3 **Paired interviews and introductions**

Time   30 minutes

Process   Ask participants to work in pairs. They have five minutes to interview each other and find out the following information: their partner's name, where s/he comes from, and the nicest thing that has happened to him/her in the last month.

Back in the whole group, they introduce their partner to the rest of the group, and share the information that they have learned about him/her.

Facilitator's notes   This is good for use with participants who do not know each other (and whom you do not know). It can start the day on a positive note, and it can start people thinking about others (not just themselves). If someone introduces himself or herself and not their partner during the feedback, this will indicate to you that this person is maybe not used to listening and/or following instructions, or maybe s/he is very self-absorbed and not used to working as part of a group. Extra support for this person may therefore be necessary.

Option   Change the questions to fit the group better, or to form an appropriate lead-in to the next activity that you have planned. But don't require them to ask too many questions, because the introductory exercise is supposed to be a quick, energising way of getting people to be comfortable together. If it is too long, it becomes slow and boring.

7.2.4 Name game

Time	30 minutes

Objectives To help participants (and you) to remember everyone's name. (It is good to use with people who know each other at least a little, but if this is the first time they've met, and if it's a big group, it will be too difficult)

To create energy in the group (after lunch, for example).

Process Ask everyone to sit in a circle, so that they can see each other (and you).

The first person in the circle (you can start, or choose someone else) has to say their first name and a word that describes them (an adjective). The word they choose should start with the same letter as their first name (for example, 'Jolly Jeton').

The next person has to do the same for him/herself and then say also the first person's name and word. The third person then has to do it for him/herself, and for the second person, and the first person.

This continues with each new person in the circle saying his/her own name and word, plus those of the people who were before him/her.

Options The word that a person chooses to describe him/herself does not need to start with the same letter. It could be any word that they like or one that they feel suits them. This variation is especially suitable if there are people in the group who are not literate.

The word that people choose can be the animal that they think is most like themselves. (This variation works well with people who know each other and can laugh together, but not with people who are likely to be offended easily.)

7.2.5 Guessing game

Time 30 minutes

Preparation Write up on a flipchart or a board a list of things to guess (see below).

Give out one blank sheet of paper and one pen per participant.

Process Ask participants to get into pairs (ideally with someone whom they don't know well).

Without talking to each other, they have five minutes to look at their partner and guess the following about him/her: favourite food; favourite film star; age; one unfulfilled ambition.

They should write down their guesses on a piece of paper. (If anyone in the group cannot write, they can do this exercise verbally.)

After five minutes, they reveal their answers and check how accurate they were.

Back in the whole group, ask for general feedback from participants: how accurate were they? Was it easy to guess? Or hard? Why?

Option You can use this game as a lead-in to work on non-verbal communication and assumptions. After the general feedback from participants, ask them what they think this game showed them. Someone will probably say (or you can if necessary) that it shows how we all make assumptions about people, just from looking at them and through non-verbal communication. We do this all the time, and some of our assumptions might be correct; but many will be wrong, and this is not a reliable method of making judgements or communicating. The activity is especially relevant for non-disabled people, who may be tempted to make automatic assumptions about people with impairments, their capacities and their needs, rather than taking the trouble to find out directly from the disabled person.

You can change the things that participants have to guess, and/or make the list longer.

7.2.6 'Darling' game

Time   30 minutes

Objectives   To re-energise a group (for example, after lunch or after an exercise which required a lot of intellectual energy). It generates laughter and so helps people to relax. But don't try it with groups for whom it would be culturally inappropriate, or with people who do not know each other well enough to feel comfortable.

Process   Ask participants to sit in a circle so that they can all see each other. Tell them that the purpose of this game is just to have fun.

The first person says to the second, '*Darling, I love you. Do you love me?*'. The second person turns to the third and says the same thing, and so on around the whole group.

The only rule is that they are not allowed to laugh. If anyone laughs, then the whole game has to start from the beginning again. (Don't apply this rule too strictly after the first few times!)

No specific feedback is required.

7.2.7   What I like about you

Time   30 minutes

Objectives   To create a good spirit of support and solidarity.

To build individuals' self-esteem.

Preparation   For each participant, have ready one blank sheet of A4 paper, one safety pin, and some coloured pens.

Process   Give each participant a sheet of blank paper, a safety pin, and coloured pens.

Each person should pin the sheet of paper to a partner's back.

Participants have 15 minutes to approach everyone in the group and write (or draw) on the paper on their back the thing that they like about that person.

When everyone has written/been written on, they take off their sheets and read what people have written/drawn about them.

If used on a capacity-building course or for the training of trainers, this can lead into discussion of the value of positive feedback.

7.2.8 **What I am proud of myself for**

Time   30 minutes

Objectives   To raise people's self-esteem. In many cultures, people are not encouraged to think or speak positively about themselves. Disabled people particularly can be influenced by the negative attitudes of others towards them. It can be helpful for people to have time and space to consider and express the good things about themselves.

To increase confidence and sharing within the group.

Process   Ask the participants to spend five minutes in quiet reflection, thinking about themselves and their reasons to be proud of themselves.

Before they start to do this, tell them that afterwards you want them to get into pairs, with someone they feel comfortable talking to, and share with their partner what they are proud about and why. They will not have to share this information with the whole group.

After they have thought for five minutes, they have ten minutes to share and discuss their feelings together.

Back in the whole group, if anyone really wants to share their own reason (not their partner's) for being proud about themselves, they can.

Otherwise, just ask for general feedback on the exercise: how did it feel? Was it difficult/strange to think about yourself in this way? Do you think it's good to do this? Why?

7.2.9 Positive feedback

This exercise leads on from the previous two, if you are trying to build up people's self-confidence and mutual trust over a period of time. Or it can be used separately.

Time   20 minutes

Objectives   To increase trust and understanding within the group.

To raise self-esteem and develop the ability to discuss positive feelings openly.

To introduce the idea that we all need positive feedback sometimes.

To illustrate the role that positive feedback plays in strengthening motivation (building people up, instead of knocking them down).

Process   Ask people to work in pairs and to say three things that they like about their partner.

There will be no specific feedback to the whole group, unless some people want to share with everyone, but this is purely optional.

They have ten minutes for this.

Back in the whole group, ask for general feedback: How did the exercise feel? Was it hard/easy to express positive things directly to their partner? Why is it important as group members (or facilitators) to be able to do this?

Option   This exercise can lead into a discussion or further activities about the need to recognise and value each person's contribution to society; and to illustrate that groups can be stronger if they consist of people with a range of strengths and skills – which should be seen as a bonus, not a threat.

7.2.10 Name-badge exercise

Time   20 minutes

Objectives   To learn each other's names.

To find out something about each other.

To focus on positive things.

Preparation   Provide blank sheets of paper, of various colour, coloured pens, and scissors; plus one safety-pin per participant.

Process   Ask each participant to take a sheet of coloured paper (whichever colour they like), some pens, and a safety pin.

The participants should make their own name badges, cutting the paper into any preferred shape, and surrounding their name with drawings of things that they like.

Reassure participants that this is not an art competition!

They have ten minutes to do this.

They pin on their badges and all go around looking at each other's badges.

Options   If you have more time, ask participants to share with a partner and explain why they chose what they drew.

Or each person can share his or her reasons with the whole group.

7.2.11 My life pie-chart

Time 20–30 minutes

Preparation Have ready one blank sheet of A4 paper per participant, plus coloured pens.

Process Tell participants that you want them to spend a couple of minutes thinking about themselves and their lives – who they are and what they do.

Their task is to represent the various parts of their life in a pie-chart, which they will then explain to a partner (not to the whole group).

They should choose as their partner someone in the group whom they don't know well, or haven't worked with very much so far.

Before they start that, draw a large pie-chart on a flipchart or chalkboard, with pieces of the pie labelled with different parts of your own life, as an example of what to do.

Give out the paper and pens, remind participants that they have a couple of minutes for thinking time, then five minutes for drawing, then five–ten minutes for sharing the results.

Back in the whole group, ask people what they thought or felt about the exercise? Did they learn something new about their partner? About themselves? (Seeing things about ourselves, represented in a visual form, can often be quite revealing.)

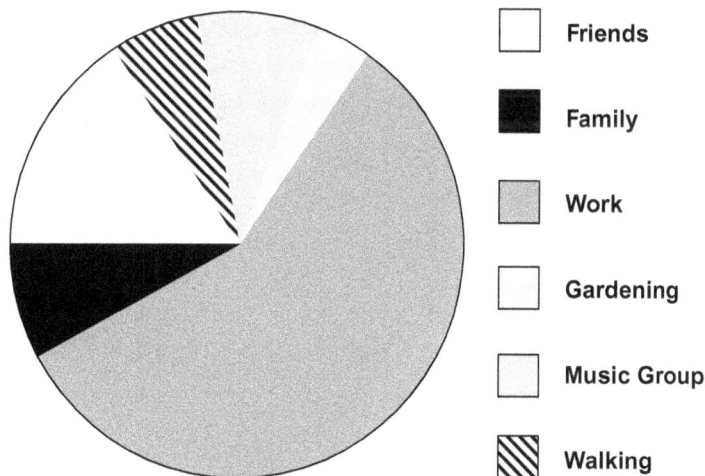

Friends

Family

Work

Gardening

Music Group

Walking

7.2.12 Wallpaper exercise

Time 30 minutes

Objectives To help participants to share something about themselves and to learn about the others in the group.

To encourage the group to focus on positive things about themselves.

Preparation Have ready a piece of paper and coloured pens for each participant.

Process Ask participants to spend 15 minutes drawing a picture of themselves doing something that they like to do.

Depending on the time available and the number of participants, feedback can take the form of sharing the drawing with a partner or with the whole group in the round.

Then display all the pictures as wallpaper.

7.2.13 Gesture energiser

Time 10 minutes for options (a) and (c); 30 minutes for option (b)

Process Divide participants into four groups.

Each group should choose one gesture or facial expression, such as a smile, a frown, a look of surprise, etc. Go around the room and make sure that no groups make the same choice.

Bring the whole group back together, sitting in a circle, but with small-group members next to one another.

When you say GO, all the groups should start performing their gestures or making their expressions simultaneously. But the point of the game is for everyone to end up doing the same thing, so they have to start gradually copying the gestures or facial expressions of other small groups.

The game ends when everyone in the whole group is doing the same gesture.

Options a. This can be done simply as an energiser, with no specific feedback.

b. Or it can be used to lead into discussion, considering issues related to difference and diversity, bringing out a variety of learning points, such as:

- the powerful effect of peer pressure, encouraging people to conform to group norms;

- the fact that sometimes it is not good to be, act, or think the same as everyone else;

- the contrary fact that it is sometimes hard to give up one's own ideas and accept other people's, especially if they belong to a different social group.

This could then lead into the '*Know Your Apple*' exercise (9.3.6), which develops these issues further.

c. If group members have impaired sight, the small groups could choose a sound to perform, instead of a gesture.

7.3   Expectations and priorities

This section includes workshop activities which can be done to increase your knowledge of the participants; to increase participants' understanding of what they may gain from the course; to help both you and the participants to understand the group's needs and priorities; and to help them to come together and form a group identity.

7.3.1   Hopes, concerns, contributions, and needs

Time   One hour

Objectives   For participants and facilitators to share their feelings – both positive and negative – about the workshop or course.

To help them to get to know and understand each other.

For facilitators to obtain information to help them to modify plans and adapt activities to match the participants' particular characteristics.

Process   Explain that you want to find out more from the start about participants' feelings and thoughts about the workshop, and to share with them your feelings and thoughts, so that you can make sure during the workshop that you respond as much as possible to what they want/need.

Divide them into groups of four and ask them to discuss their **hopes** and expectations: what do they want to gain from the workshop? And any **concerns** or anxieties they may have. And the **contributions** that they will make to the workshop. And the personal **needs** which will have to be met in order for the workshop to be successful for them. Write the four key words on a flipchart.

The facilitators and interpreters should also do the exercise, as a separate group.

After 30 minutes, bring the whole group back together and ask each small group to report back in turn.

Allow time for questions and comments. Conclude by explaining that during the workshop or course you will try to respond to all the points raised in the discussion – but be honest about any expectations and needs that you will not be able to meet. Write up their answers on a flipchart and keep them safe.

Return to the lists at the end of the workshop, as part of the evaluation process. Check which expectations have been met, and which were not; these may form the basis of a future workshop.

7.3.2 Setting priorities

Facilitator's notes

On a long course it is especially important for facilitators to understand participants' priorities, to enable the content to be adapted accordingly. Often, for reasons of geography or other factors, it is impossible to meet all the participants and discuss their priorities before the course begins. The pre-course questionnaire (Handout 1) includes a section on this topic, but it is worth also spending time on it in one of the first sessions. Facilitators constantly need to balance the needs of individuals with the needs of the group. Explaining this as part of the feedback on the exercise below can help the group both to understand the facilitator's role and to start thinking beyond their own needs to the needs of others in the group.

Time

One hour

Preparation

Make copies of Sections 1 and 2 from question 7 on the pre-course questionnaire (Handout 1).

Bring some sticky 'Post-it' notes in three different colours; or small pieces of paper in three different colours, plus drawing-pins or Blu-tack.

You will also need a blackboard and chalks, or some large sheets of paper.

Process

Introduce the activity by explaining that participants have already stated their individual priorities for the course (on the questionnaire), but you want to get an idea of the whole group's priorities.
This will give you and them a better understanding of what is important to the group as a whole.

Divide people into four groups. Give out some Post-it notes of each colour to each group, with pens and copies of sections 1 and 2 from question 7 on the questionnaire.

Ask them to work as a group, and decide as a group which of the topics in sections 1 and 2 they definitely want to cover (YES), which they definitely don't want to cover (NO), and which they are not sure about (UNSURE). They should discuss the reasons for these choices. There is no minimum or maximum number of topics that they are allowed to allocate to each category.

Put up three large sheets of paper (or divide the blackboard into three equal areas). Label one with a Post-it of one colour with YES written on it, another with a different-coloured Post-it with NO written on it, and another with a third coloured Post-it with UNSURE written on it.

Participants write the topics on Post-it notes of the relevant colours, to denote Yes, No, or Unsure. They have 20 minutes to do this.
One person from each group should be prepared to report back.

Bring the whole group back together. The representatives of each small group take turns to present their priorities, sticking all their 'Yes', 'No', and 'Unsure' labels on the corresponding sheet of paper or area of the board, reading out the topic as they go, and saying briefly why they chose to put it in one category rather than another.

Give time for comments or questions. You can develop a discussion with the following questions.

Discussion   Are there any surprises (for you or the participants)? If necessary, find out more about participants' choices.

How do people feel if their own priorities are not shared by the rest of their small group? Draw attention to the need to balance the needs and priorities of groups and individuals. How do participants feel about that?

Describe briefly how you intend to use the information from this exercise to plan the rest of the course. If you aim to spend most time on high priorities and less time on low priorities, be clear about this, otherwise you will cause confusion, and participants will think that you are not keeping your word. If there is a topic that as the facilitator you feel is important to include, but the group does not (or vice versa), you need to discuss this and negotiate what to do.

Sum up.

7.3.3   Agreeing guidelines for working together as a group

The following exercise is designed for participants who are new to workshops (or other types of facilitated group work) and need plenty of time to talk through the issues. For groups who are experienced workshop participants, the exercise may be shortened to a brainstorm, followed by a discussion of the suggestions leading to amendments, additions, and deletions by consensus.

Time   10 minutes – one hour

Objectives   For the group to decide what guidelines to set for itself.

To gain collective understanding of the reason for each guideline.

Preparation   Draw up a rough list of elements that you consider necessary for working together as a group.

Process   Explain that you want participants to agree on a set of guidelines, to help you all to work together productively and harmoniously. Guidelines can help people to work better together, in a way that is fair and respects everyone's needs and contributions. Guidelines can help people to feel safe within the group, to establish boundaries, and to remind the members how they want to be or act (which is especially useful during difficult times).

Divide people up into groups of four or five, and ask them to make a list of all the things they think should be included in the guidelines.

After 15 minutes bring everyone back together, and ask each small group in turn to share their suggestions.

Write up their suggestions on flipchart paper or a blackboard. Each time another group makes the same suggestion, indicate this with a tick.

Check your own list, to see if there are any items that the groups have not identified, but that you want them to consider. Consult the participants: should these suggestions be included in the final list, or not?

Discuss the guidelines, allowing time for questions and comments. Does anyone think that any of the guidelines should be amended, or removed from the list? How do other people feel about that?

Make changes to the list according to the consensus of opinion. It is not enough to take a vote and adopt the view of the majority: it is important (both for the formation of the group at this early stage and for later adherence to the guidelines) that all the guidelines are acceptable to everyone.

Discuss who is responsible for making sure that the group observes the guidelines (it should be everyone!) and how participants want to deal with situations where guidelines are not respected.

A final agreed list should be written up neatly on a large sheet of paper and permanently displayed in the workshop room, and/or the list should be typed up and copies given to participants in the next session. Or the group might want to start each workshop by reading their guidelines.

They might be interested to see copies of a set of guidelines drawn up by a disability-awareness workshop in Kosovo (Handout 3).

Facilitator's notes   Some groups/facilitators include 'having fun' as one of the rules or guidelines. Others do not – not because they don't think that workshops should be enjoyable, but because they think that this is something that one cannot make a rule about. This is a matter of personal choice.

HANDOUT 3
Group guidelines for a workshop in Kosovo

- Confidentiality: no personal information shared in the workshop should be repeated outside the workshop.

- Respect: respect and recognise differences of race, culture, sexuality, religion, etc. (and don't assume that they do not exist). Respect the opinions of others.

- Listening: everyone has a right to be heard.

- Personalised knowledge and feelings: speak in your own name; say 'I', not 'they/we/she'.

- Acknowledge emotion.

- Responsibility: we are all responsible for creating a safe environment; we are each responsible for our own learning.

- Avoid destructive criticism of others or oneself. Criticism or comments must be constructive, sensitive, and specific.

- Say when you don't understand.

- Take risks.

- Respect people's right to opt out of an activity. If it doesn't feel right for them, they shouldn't do it.

- Everybody should try to be punctual.

- Allow time for people with speech impairments to speak.

- There should be enough time for breaks and smoking.

- Language: use terms that everyone can understand. Speak as clearly as possible. Don't use abusive or offensive terms.

- Accessibility of information: always say aloud anything that you write down, and use large print on flipcharts, so that people who have impaired sight or hearing or are not literate can participate. Allow time for this.

- Allow time for interpretation (sign language, foreign language, personal assistance).

- Use reading/writing partners.

- Photographs may be taken if everyone agrees.

- No interruptions when people are speaking.

- Don't patronise others.

- Give of yourself.

7.4 Working together: establishing group guidelines; communication; respect; participation

The following exercises may be used in the following contexts and for the following purposes:

- with new groups, to develop understanding of and commitment to group processes, and equal participation of all members; and/or

- at any stage where participants are finding equitable communication and participation difficult; and/or

- to teach trainers or facilitators about group processes, and their responsibility to foster open communication and equitable participation; and/or

- to raise awareness of the disability and/or gender issues that are featured in the exercises.

7.4.1 Mapping for Mars

(adapted from *The Oxfam Gender Training Manual*)

Time   One hour

Objective   To appreciate the importance of acknowledging and encouraging expression of a diverse range of perspectives and views

Preparation   Sort out participants into groups (see facilitator's notes below).

Prepare large sheets of paper and pens.

Process   Explain to the group that you are a humanitarian/development worker from Mars. You have come to their region or country ('X') for the first time and you want to learn about X. You want them to tell you the most important facts about life in X.

Divide participants into small groups of four or five people, according to their geographical origins and other factors such as disability and gender, or other criteria that will ensure that the members of each small group have strong characteristics in common.

Ask each group to use flipchart paper and pens to draw a big map of X; they should all draw the same village, region, town, country, or continent.

Explain that each group is to draw on their map five–ten of the most important things about life in X for them: things that they want you to know, so that you can explain to people in Mars what life in X is like. Ask them not to use writing, because you do not read earthscript: they should use only symbols and drawings. They have 15 minutes.

Bring everyone together. Ask one member of each small group to present their map to the whole group, explaining what the symbols mean.

Then ask the whole group to decide which map is best. Explain that you will take the best one back to Mars. If the group cannot decide, choose the map of the most vocal small group.

Then ask those whose maps were not chosen how they felt about their maps being left out. Point out that the numbers of people in the room whose ideas are not represented are greater than the numbers of those whose ideas are represented on the chosen map.

How can this problem be resolved? Allow a discussion to develop.

Facilitator's notes This exercise can be done either as part of a workshop on any topic, to promote the participation of all members and respect for different ideas; or with people who are learning to be trainers, to help them to understand their responsibility to allow and encourage contributions from all the participants, and to value their different opinions.

If some or all of the participants are learning to train, during the drawing part of the exercise you should go around to the groups and point out:

- the importance of ensuring that everyone is at the same level – whether on the ground or on a table – so that, for example, wheelchair users or people working in a lying position are not distanced from the activity;

- the need to appoint one person to do the drawing for everyone else, if one or more participants is blind or partially sighted;

- for the same reason, the importance of making sure that all the drawings are described verbally, during the drawing time and during the presentations;

- the importance of using symbols, not words, in order to include people who are not literate;

- the importance of letting the participants do the discussion and analysis, while the facilitator observes;

- the opportunity that this gives the facilitator to observe group dynamics, including leadership, disputes, excluded individuals, etc.;

- the opportunity that this gives the facilitator to listen to people's process of analysis.

Emphasise to participants that the quality of the drawing is not important: it is what is portrayed that is significant. Once symbols are explained to us, we can remember and understand them.

Often one group's map will include information that is not on the other groups' maps. Women will highlight different things from men, disabled people will highlight different things from non-disabled people, etc. It is important in the feedback stage to emphasise that the wider the range of perspectives, the more the whole group learns, so everyone must have the space to contribute, rather than permitting a situation where certain individuals are vociferous and dominant. This principle applies to the contributions of individuals and of specific groups, such as rural/urban people, men/women, disabled/non disabled, young/elderly, etc.

Some groups may be resistant to being divided according to criteria of gender and/or disability. Or you may be concerned not to cause potential competition or division between certain groups of participants. If this is likely to be the case, consider carefully how you make up the small groups. For example, in Kosovo we sometimes grouped members by sex only, not by disability (even though the exclusion of disabled people and their opinions from discussion was the main point of the exercise), to avoid creating a divisive sense of 'us' and 'them'. The maps produced by the small groups of men (mixed disabled and non-disabled) generally did not show the existence of disabled people at all, and presented cultural, historical, and political concerns. The women's groups (mixed disabled and non-disabled) were more likely to include disabled people and things that were important to them, as well as practical elements of everyday life, hopes for the future, and political concerns.

If it seems best not to group people according to their disability or their lack of it, you can still bring out the main points that you want to communicate, by considering what participants did not put in their drawings, as well as what they did include. In the discussion you might ask the participants how complete an understanding they think that people in Mars will have of X, if the map does not contain information about disabled people or women. Keep emphasising the value of learning from the experience and ideas of each participant, not just those of a few vocal people.

One solution to the problem of partial information is to take all the maps back to Mars, so that all perspectives would be taken into account. Each one has its own story to tell, and, like pieces of a jigsaw, fills a fuller picture. There is no one best map: all are needed.

7.4.2 Listening exercise (1)

Time 30 minutes

Objectives For all participants to experience not being listened to.

To develop understanding of which people in society are likely not to be listened to.

Preparation Work out instructions for partners A and B. Suggested topics for A are given below and should be adapted to suit local circumstances.

You may need to write down the instructions and provide copies of them, for participants with impaired hearing.

Process Ask people to work in pairs. One person is A, the other is B.

Either bring all the As together and explain their role to them (where Bs can't hear), or give them written instructions. Do the same with all the Bs.

Partner A: Your role in this exercise is to talk to your partner and tell him/her all about what you did this weekend, or about your favourite music and why you like it.

Partner B: In this exercise your partner is going to start telling you about something. Your role is NOT to listen, and make it clear that you are not listening and not interested, by using any non-verbal (non-spoken) ways you can think of (such as yawning, fidgeting, looking away, etc.).

After five minutes, stop the exercise. Ask participants to exchange roles and repeat the exercise in their new roles.

Bring the whole group back together. Facilitate a discussion, using the following questions to draw out learning points:

- What did it feel like to be partner B, not listening to A?

- How did the As react? (Some may have got angry, others were perhaps intimidated and stopped talking.)

- How did Bs feel about that reaction?

- What did it feel like to be A and not to be listened to?

- Are there some (groups of) people in our community who are often not listened to? Who? Why? What impact does that have on them? And on the rest of the community?

- What can we do to make sure that we listen to (and learn from) each other? Suggested answers:

- Allow time for everyone to have their say; create different types of opportunity for people to contribute (through small-group work, work in pairs, drawings, role plays, etc., not just whole-group or round-table discussions).

- Say what you want to say, but realise your responsibility to respect other people's right to express themselves.

- Hear what the other person is saying: concentrate, focus on the speaker, do not fidget, do not think only about what you're going to say in response.

- Acknowledge what the speaker says, showing that you accept his or her viewpoint, or at least respect his/her right to hold it, if you disagree with it.

- Use body language to show that you are listening.

- Be aware that our ability to hear what is being said may be affected by our perceptions of the person who is talking, or the way they talk.

Finally, the exercise should be repeated, but this time the participants should practise good listening habits.

Facilitator's notes   We often have a false perception that certain people do 'all the talking'. (In an evaluation of a meeting held in New York, the men at the meeting felt that the women had done about 80 per cent of the talking, whereas the actual figure was 30 per cent.) A common reaction of listeners, either when they mistakenly perceive that someone is doing all the talking, or if someone really is dominating the discussion, is to switch off and stop listening.

Another common misconception is that people with speech impairments automatically also have learning difficulties and have nothing worth saying, which is a misconception in itself.

For group purposes, it is therefore helpful to check how our perceptions influence our listening, and to realise that if we are one of those who tends to talk a lot, we may be heard more if we talk less.

It also happens that, irrespective of how much they do or don't talk, when certain people start speaking, others stop paying attention and start up private discussions. Whether or not people pay attention is often determined by the speaker's sex, social status, or self-confidence and presentation skills. Either way, the group should commit themselves to supporting and hearing each other.

As the facilitator, you should quietly observe the group during several different discussions and activities and note down how many times each person contributes, whether he or she is listened to, and the identity of the speaker in each case: whether male non-disabled, male disabled, female non-disabled, or female disabled, etc. This can help you to build up a more accurate picture of actual communication patterns within the group, detect potential problems, and work out what kind of support to give to whom. If you do it at some stage before this listening exercise, it can also help you to decide how to focus the exercise.

However this exercise is adapted, it is important not to single out participants who either dominate or don't talk much, or aren't listened to when they do. For this reason, questions about who does/does not get listened to should refer to the community, not to the workshop group itself.

7.4.3   I respect you/You respect me

(adapted from *Learning to Listen* by Jane Vella, published by the University of Massachusetts, 1980)

Time   One hour

Objectives   To encourage participants to reflect on their feelings of respect and disrespect.

To differentiate between constructive and destructive group behaviours.

Process   Explain that the exercise offers an opportunity to think about the importance of respect in working together as a group (and as the facilitator of a group).

Participants take ten minutes to think and reflect about times in their lives when they have felt respected and not respected (slighted, insulted, put down). Tell them they can go outside, or to another room, but that they should be alone and quiet with their thoughts. Encourage them to reflect on their childhood and adulthood, their personal lives and their working lives.

Inform them before they start that they will not be expected to share personal information with the whole group.

After ten minutes, ask participants to form pairs and discuss their feelings. They should talk about the times when they felt they were not respected, and then about the times when they did feel respected. What happened? Why did it happen? How did they feel?

Back in the whole group, start a discussion by asking for the high points from the paired discussions. Do not require anyone to discuss anything too personal or embarrassing.

You can draw out learning points with the following questions.

Questions   What do you think this exercise shows us about respect?

What does respect have to do with being part of a group (or facilitating a group)?

Why?

How can we disagree with someone, or give them advice, but still maintain our mutual respect?

Facilitator's notes   To work together in a group to accomplish individual and group aims, it is necessary for all the participants to respect each other; and to take into account their own feelings and the feelings of others. Being respected is important to all of us – parent or child, woman or man, disabled or non-disabled person, urban or rural person, teacher or student – whatever our nationality or religion. We are all cheered or saddened by what others say (or don't say) to us or about us. We can be encouraged or discouraged to share our ideas, experiences, and knowledge with others, depending on whether we feel respected or not.

As group members (or facilitators) we can give criticism and advice or disagree with others in two ways: destructively – which causes pain and reduces people's self-respect; or constructively – which builds up people's self-confidence.

8 Facilitation skills

Most of the participants on the Oxfam course in Kosovo, if they had had any formal education at all, were used to being taught in classrooms where the teacher set the agenda for learning; where students were expected to absorb information passively, without questioning what they were told, or being invited to contribute insights from their own experience; where the learners sat in rows of desks, facing the teacher, with whom all the interaction took place. If these people were to become effective trainers of adults, they needed to unlearn many of the habits that they had acquired at school and learn new skills of communication and organisation, more appropriate to the needs and interests of disabled people's groups and the staff of aid organisations and official agencies. For a start, they needed to understand that adults learn in very different ways from young children.

8.1   How adults learn

8.1.1   The 'process of learning' exercise

Time 50 minutes

Objectives For participants to examine their own ways of learning.

To appreciate how other adults learn.

To understand the conditions that encourage adult learning to take place.

Preparation Write the questions listed below on a large sheet of paper, or on a blackboard.

Process Explain the purpose of the session. Then give each person a piece of paper and ask them to think about and write down two things that they have learned outside school, as an adult, that are important to them and that affect their daily life. These should be things that they can actually remember learning.

Then each person should choose one of their personal lessons and think through the whole process of how he or she learned it, using the following questions, written up on large letters, as a guide:

- Why did you learn it?

- Who helped you to learn it?

- What was the relationship between you and the person who helped you?

- What was the situation in which you learned it?

- In what way did you learn it?

- Can you remember anything that made your learning easier or more difficult?

Each person reflects or writes for 10 minutes. Then ask participants to share these points in pairs, or groups of three, for 10 minutes.

Bring the whole group back together and invite them to report their conclusions, which you (or a reporter) should record on separate pieces of flipchart paper under the following headings:

- **Content**: What was learned?

- **Situation**: In what context?

- **Method**: How was it learned?

- **People**: Who else was involved?

Summarise the points made by the group, and include the four major points about adult learning listed in Handout 4. They are based on the ideas of Malcolm Knowles, who pioneered new methods of adult education.

(This activity was adapted with permission from *Training for Transformation* Book 1, by Anne Hope and Sally Timmel. For details, see the 'Resources' section at the end of this book.)

HANDOUT 4
The psychology of adult learning

1. Adults have a wide experience of life and have learned much from it. They learn most from their peers. So facilitators should help them to share their own experience and create a situation where they are encouraged to engage in a dialogue with one another. Let them sit in a circle, where they can see each other's faces, so that speaking and learning can both be helped by making eye contact.

2. Adults are interested in and learn quickly about things that are relevant to their lives. So the facilitator needs to create a situation in which they can share in the planning, choose the topics, and participate in regular evaluation of what they are doing.

3. Adults have a sense of personal dignity. They must be treated with respect at all times and never made to feel humiliated or ridiculous in the presence of others.

4. As adults grow older, their memories may get weaker; but their powers of observation and reasoning often grow stronger.

(Adapted from *The Leader Looks at the Learning Climate*, by Malcolm S. Knowles, published by Leadership Resources Inc., Washington DC, 1965)

8.1.2 Creating a positive learning environment

Facilitator's notes This is especially valuable for new groups of disabled people, or those who need to review what they do and how. It may be helpful to refer also to activities in Chapter 10 ('Action planning').

Time 30 minutes

Objectives To give information about four factors which create a positive learning environment.

To encourage participants to consider the application of these factors to their own experiences.

Preparation Prepare copies of Handout 5 for each participant.

Process On a large sheet of paper or a blackboard, draw the central part of a flower, with the stem and leaves below it.

Tell participants that the flower represents the group. Label the central part of the flower 'Group'.

Draw on it one large petal, labelling it '*Acceptance*'; use Handout 5 to explain the significance of this.

Repeat the process for the remaining factors that create positive conditions for learning (*Sharing information and concerns; Setting goals; Organising for action*).

Allow time for comments and questions. You can lead into a discussion by asking participants how these four factors relate to their own experiences of learning. And to the ways in which learning happens in their community. And to the ways in which they work (or intend to work) as facilitators.

HANDOUT 5
Creating a learning environment: four needs of the group

1. ### Acceptance
   To begin with, people need assurance that they are truly accepted as they are – that it is safe to express what they really think and feel in the group or workshop. The unique value of each person, with his/her own experience and insights, needs to be recognised. People, like plants, need the right kind of 'climate' in order to grow, and the facilitator has a special responsibility for developing such a 'climate' in the group. Unless there is a spirit of respect and acceptance, people will not be free to learn, to rethink their old opinions, to change and grow, or to share their thoughts and feelings fully. The group will not grow into a real community.

2. ### Sharing information and concerns
   People working or learning in groups need information about each other: their experiences, ideas, values, and opinions; and about the issue that the group is considering, which they should perceive as relevant to their lives. They need to work out for themselves what they need to know, what to accept and use, what to set aside.

   The facilitator also needs an opportunity to share his/her information and concerns. But this should usually be done after the other members of the group have made their contributions, and should be offered for discussion, not imposed on the group.

3. ### Setting goals
   The third need of any group that is learning together is to set goals clearly. This applies to the framework of the workshop itself, and to any action-planning activities within the workshop. Unless the goals are created by the group, the participants will not be interested or committed to implementing. Unless the goals are clear to all, people become frustrated. The way in which decisions are made is directly related to the degree of commitment that people feel to them when carrying them out.

4. ### Organising for action, or putting learning into action
   Once goals have been set, the group needs to make definite plans to reach these goals and carry out decisions. Named people should take responsibility to do agreed, specific things, and they should be

accountable to the group to get these things done, where appropriate. That is why they should accept these responsibilities publicly, where possible. This implies the need for a structure which is appropriate for the group and which will ensure that one person will not assume all the responsibility or control all the actions.

It is essential to check how participants feel about a group or learning event, and the plans made; therefore an evaluation is needed immediately afterwards, and (where appropriate) again some time later, to make sure that plans are working effectively and that all are carrying out their self-chosen responsibilities. This second evaluation can be planned before the first meeting/workshop finishes.

These four needs should usually be met in this order in a meeting or workshop, but Gibbs points out that often they are not met once and for all. Any one of the needs can occur again at any point, and the best facilitators are those who are sensitive enough to recognise the need and find a way of meeting it.

(Adapted with permission from *Training for Transformation* Book 1, by Anne Hope and Sally Timmel, and *Basic Reading in Human Relations Training*, Book 1, by Jack Gibbs, published by the Episcopal Church, p.23.)

8.1.3 Stages of learning

Time   30 minutes

Process   Introduce the topic: 'We discussed in the previous exercise how we learn as adults. We are now going to consider some additional information about the process of learning. It will help you as group or workshop facilitators to support group members to learn.'

Explain that when we learn something new, we go through several stages. These have been described as follows:

1   **Unconscious ignorance:** this is the stage before actual learning starts, when you don't know what you don't know. Ignorance is bliss. For example, if you don't know any disabled people in your town, you are unaware of the difficulties that they encounter in daily life, and you assume that everything must be OK.

2   **Conscious ignorance:** now you become aware of what you don't know. This can be a difficult time, because knowing that you don't know something can damage your self-confidence, make you feel insecure, confused, even angry and defensive. These are normal reactions.

3   **Conscious knowledge:** by this stage you have learned enough to be conscious of what you know (like when you have just passed your driving test, but still have to make an effort to find the gears).

4   **Unconscious knowledge:** by now you have fully internalised what you have learned; it is in your subconscious mind, and you don't have to think consciously about what you're doing in order to do it.

As the facilitator working with a group of people, you will find that different people will be at different stages of this process at different times. If you can identify where people are, you can help them to move on to the next stage. The most difficult stage is that of conscious ignorance. If you can recognise what people are going through, you can help them to develop the confidence and motivation to keep going.

Also, as the facilitator, you will probably know your subject so well that you no longer have to break it down into steps, or think consciously about it. To be a good facilitator – to be able to communicate and share your knowledge with participants and help them to find their route to knowledge – you have to go back to stage 3, conscious knowledge, to think through what you know and how it is done. For example, if you want to teach someone to cut hair, you need to go back to the time when you had to think carefully about everything you did, and break down the process into steps – what to do first and how, what to do next and how, etc. – explaining and demonstrating each step.

8.1.4   **Rates of learning**

Time   20 minutes

Preparation   Make copies of Handout 6.

Process   Introduce the topic: 'Different people learn at different rates and different speeds. If you are the facilitator of a group or workshop, you can help participants better if you are aware of this.'

Copy the diagrams from Handout 6 on to a large sheet of paper or a blackboard, and explain the drawings:

1. Some people seem to learn a lot very fast, then they reach a peak and their learning levels out on to a plateau. They are often excited to learn at first, but they will probably need support to maintain their motivation after the initial enthusiasm.

2. Others seem to go more steadily, step by step, with many small plateaux between phases of progress. On the plateaux, learners may feel that they are making no progress, but these are in fact valuable opportunities to consolidate what has been learned so far and to prepare to move on to the next step.

3. Others seem to learn nothing for a long time, but suddenly, somehow, everything makes sense to them, and *Eureka!*: they have achieved their goal. The role of the facilitator is to help to maintain their motivation until they reach this point.

Allow time for questions and comments from participants. Can they identify their own typical learning rates?

HANDOUT 6
Different rates of learning

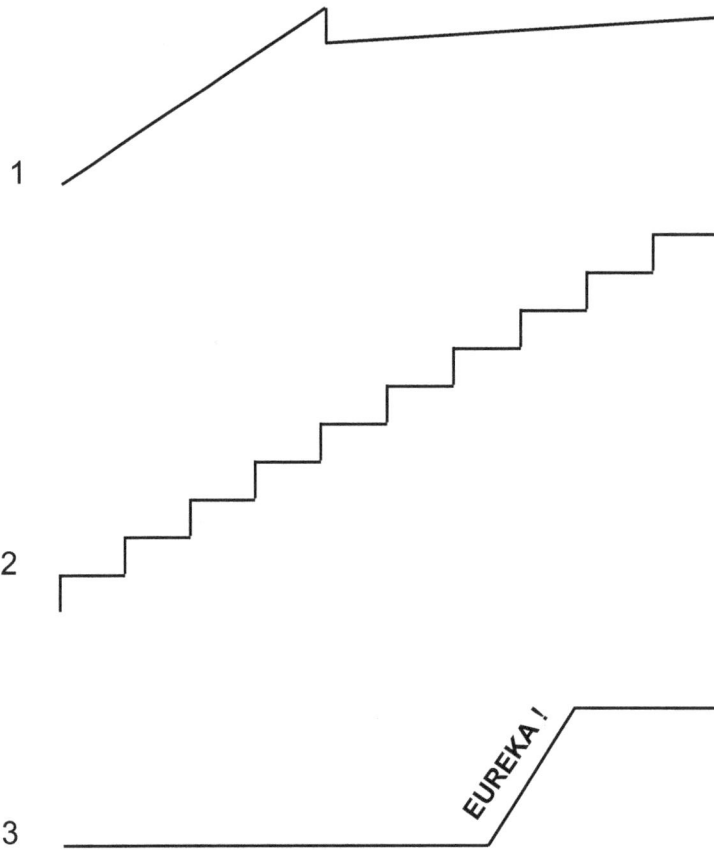

8.1.5 Components of training

Time 40 minutes

Objectives To review the elements that make up an activity or exercise.
To suggest a framework that facilitators can use when designing and/or facilitating learning activities.

For participants to analyse how the components fit together in an actual exercise.

Preparation Make copies of Handout 7.

Process Introduce the topic by explaining that all effective training involves certain processes, as follows:

1 **Setting objectives:** facilitators and participants together should agree why they are taking part in the training, and what they want to achieve.

2 **Presenting the content**, which consists of the following components (illustrated in Handout 7):

- *Skills:* how to do something; for example, how to listen to others, or how to motivate other disabled people to become activists.

- *Knowledge:* what we know about something, for example, legislation about human rights.

- *Attitudes:* how we think or feel about something, for example, a belief that disabled people are people, not cases for medical treatment or intervention by social services.

3 **Applying the methodology**, which should always be participative and should accommodate participants' different learning needs.

4 **Agreeing on further action:** what will happen as a result of the training – both in personal terms and in organisational/professional/political terms?

5 **Evaluation:** what was successful/OK/not successful? What did participants like/not like? Did we achieve our objectives? What will we do differently in future? What follow-up is necessary? What shall we do next?

(Based with permission on 'First Steps', published by Amnesty International)

HANDOUT 7
Components of training

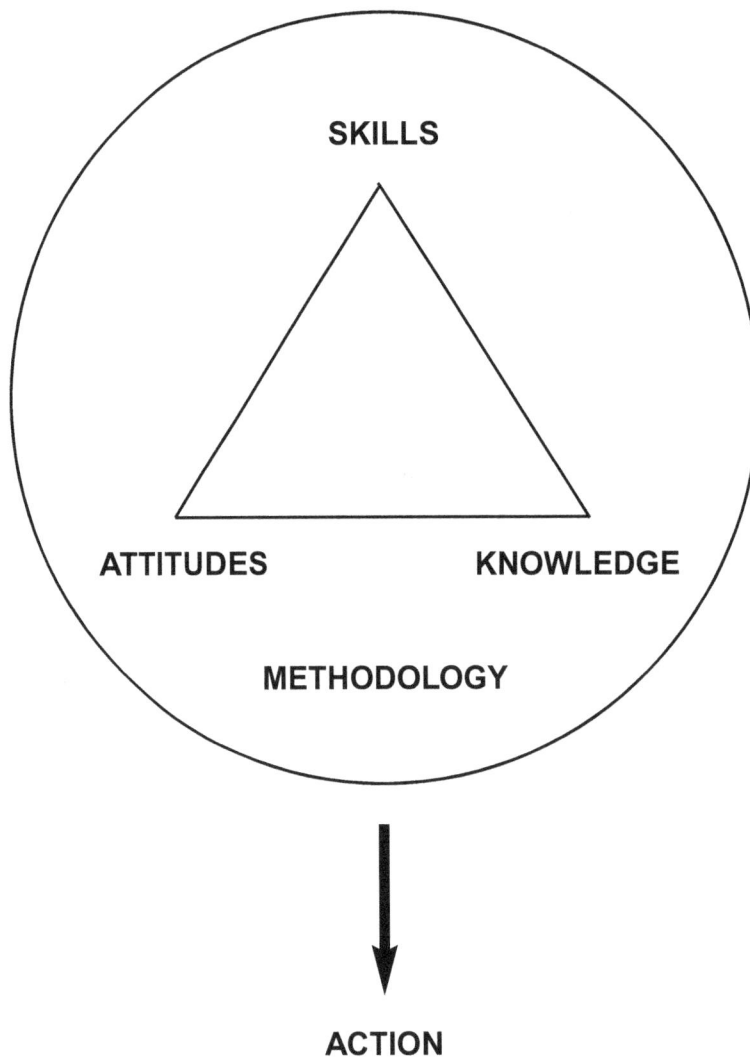

8.1.6 **Whole-group activity**

Time   30 minutes

Process   With the whole group, facilitate an analysis of an activity that you have done together – maybe the 'Process of learning' exercise (8.1.1 above). Ask participants to break down the activity into its constituent parts:

- What were the objectives?

- What was the content – skills, knowledge, attitudes?

- What change could the activity lead to (theory into action)?

- How effective was it, and how could it be improved (evaluation)?

8.2 Facilitating adult learning

We use the term 'facilitator' throughout the manual, but we recognise that in some circumstances other terms, such as 'animator' or 'moderator', might be more meaningful, or may be more easily translated. Whichever word is used, the purpose of the role is to facilitate adult learning, as described in the previous section: by supporting and motivating people to learn by reflecting on their own experience and that of others.

After an activity which will help the group to define facilitation (8.2.1), there is a section devoted to facilitation skills. The exercises, presentations, and discussions introduce some of the main skills required by facilitators. Within the structure of a workshop, these can either be treated as a separate section, or introduced at various stages throughout the course. Where possible, a variety of methods is given for each skill.

Listening skills
8.2.2   Listening exercise (2)
8.2.3   Discussion of good and bad listening

Communication and observation skills
8.2.4   Open the day
8.2.5   Guessing game
8.2.6   Observation exercise

Fostering participation and supporting diversity
Listening to the other members of the group and showing respect for them are vital ways to encourage people to take an active part in a workshop. To supplement the three activities presented here, you could also use exercise 7.4.3 (on respect), and 8.1.2 (on creating a positive learning environment), as well as exercises in section 7.2 that help to develop self-esteem.

8.2.7   Mapping for Mars
8.2.8   Know your apple
8.2.9   Whole-group discussion of room layout

Timing and pacing
8.2.10   Whole-group discussion of timing and pacing

Explaining and giving instructions
8.2.11   Line-drawing exercise

8.2.1   Facilitation: brainstorm and discussion

Time   One hour

Objectives   For participants to share their experiences and understanding of facilitation

Preparation   A large sheet of paper; copies of Handouts 8 and 9

Process   Write across the top of the flipchart: '*What is facilitation?*'

Ask people to spend a few minutes thinking about their experiences of facilitation – as a participant in a facilitated group and/or times when they themselves were the facilitators. From their own experience, how would they define facilitation? What is a facilitator meant to do?

Remind participants that in a brainstorm there are no right or wrong answers: they should say whatever they think, and not discuss the responses – there will be time for discussion later.

Brainstorm ideas for five–ten minutes, and write them on the flipchart. After the brainstorm, review the list: any comments or questions about any of the responses? Seek clarification if the meaning is not clear, either to you or to participants.

This may lead into a discussion, during which you can raise any points from Handout 8 that the group did not identify in the brainstorm: what do participants think about them, and why?

Highlight the elements on the group's list that relate to facilitating particular tasks, and those that relate to maintaining the well-being of the group and helping it to work effectively as a group.

Point out that usually it is best to have two facilitators working together, one leading an activity, the other focusing on group dynamics and time-keeping, and helping the other facilitator if problems occur.

Sum up by using Paulo Freire's comparison of 'banking education' (= teaching) and 'problem-posing education' (= facilitation). (See Handout 9.)

Options   For groups with whom brainstorms do not seem to be an effective method, either:

Divide into groups of four or five, and give participants 10–15 minutes to make a written or verbal list of responses to the question; then each small group should present their list; finally, lead into the discussion.

Or

In the round, ask each participant to say one thing that a facilitator is or does. Write up all suggestions as they are said. No one should say something that has already been said. Remind people of their right not to speak. Depending on the size of the group, do one, two, or three rounds. Then lead into the discussion.

HANDOUT 8
Facilitation of groups and workshops

The dual role of a facilitator (also sometimes known as an animator or moderator) consists of the following elements.

1. **Facilitating the group in tasks** (some or all of the following)
   - Ensure good communications.
   - Provide clear instructions.
   - Find the links between ideas and comments contributed by the participants.
   - Motivate group members to:
     - participate (on an equal basis)
     - think critically and constructively
     - identify problems
     - find new solutions.
   - Provide a learning or group environment in which people can:
     - feel accepted
     - exchange and discover concerns, information, ideas, experiences
     - develop skills, knowledge, or attitudes
     - set goals, make decisions
     - plan action.
   - Provide information, ideas, experience.
   - Provide materials.
   - Co-ordinate activities and keep time: ensure that group activities do not over-run the time available.
   - Summarise discussions.
   - Don't do all the talking!

2. **Group maintenance**
   - Understand the social and cultural background of the group, and plan activities accordingly.
   - Understand the emotional and psychological dynamics of the group.
   - Observe.
   - Listen.
   - Keep every member actively involved.
   - Co-ordinate the activities.
   - Mediate (identify any problem, help the group to understand and deal with it constructively).

HANDOUT 9
'Banking' education and 'problem-posing' education

The Brazilian educator Paulo Freire summarised the differences between the role of a teacher in conventional education, which he compared with 'banking', and the role of a facilitator in 'problem-posing' education.

Banking education

- The teacher talks, passing on information.

- The pupils sit and listen quietly, and act passively.

Problem-posing education

- The animator/facilitator poses a problem and asks questions.

- The participants are active, describe their experiences, share ideas, analyse, and plan together.

With banking education, the teacher 'owns' the knowledge and is the 'expert'. With problem-posing education, the facilitator draws out learning through debate, sharing, and action. The group uses each participant's contribution to gain a better understanding and find solutions to problems.

(Adapted with permission from *Training for Transformation*, Book 2, by Anne Hope and Sally Timmel)

8.2.2 Listening exercise (2)

Precede this exercise with *Listening exercise (1)*, section 7.4.2, if you have not already used it.

Time 30 minutes

Objective To give participants an opportunity to practise their listening skills

Preparation Work out a topic for participants to discuss. It may be related to disability, or to a controversial topical issue.

Process Participants will discuss the topic in pairs (A and B) for 15 minutes. Explain the rules: A starts, and B is not allowed to give an opinion until he or she has repeated back to A – to A's satisfaction – what A has said. Then B gives his or her opinion, and A must repeat it back to B satisfactorily before being allowed to respond.

Ask the whole group for feedback, based on the following questions.

What did you discover from this exercise?

Was it hard to repeat back satisfactorily what the other person had said? Why?

What can you do to make sure that you really hear what the other person is saying?

8.2.3 Discussion of good and bad listening

Facilitate a brainstorm in which participants identify things that prevent us from listening properly, and things that we can do to ensure that we listen well. Write up the responses on a large sheet of paper or a blackboard. Fill in gaps, using information from Handout 10.

HANDOUT 10
Good and bad listening

(Based on *The Oxfam Gender Training Manual*, p.469)

Blocks to good listening include the following:

- 'On-off' listening: the listener 'switches off' at times.
- 'Red-flag listening': certain words trigger a response which causes us to stop listening.
- 'Open-ears, closed mind' listening: we decide in advance that we know what will be said.
- 'Glassy-eyed listening': we appear to listen, while actually we are thinking about something else.
- 'Too-deep-for-me listening': we stop listening because we don't understand.
- 'Don't-rock-the-boat-listening': we deliberately don't listen to something that may challenge our opinions.

In listening we should try to do the following:

- Show interest.
- Understand the other person.
- Express sympathy.
- Identify the problem (if there is one).
- Listen for the causes of the problem.
- Help the speaker to associate the problem with the cause.
- Encourage the speaker to develop competence and motivation to solve his or her own problems.
- Cultivate the ability to be silent when silence is needed.

In listening, do not do the following:

- Argue.
- Interrupt.
- Pass judgement .
- Give advice (unless it is requested by the other person).
- Jump to conclusions.
- Become emotionally involved.

8.2.4   Open the day

See 7.2.2 for detailed instructions.

8.2.5   Guessing game

See 7.2.5 for detailed instructions.

8.2.6   Observation exercise

This activity can be used to assess levels and types of participation within a group and to observe patterns which might indicate the need to do some work on fostering participation and supporting diversity within a group.

Process   Divide the whole group into three small groups. Two of the small groups will watch the third group discuss the proposition that *'Disabled people need jobs as much as non-disabled people do'*. The discussion group will consist of six people, each of whom plays one of the following roles in the discussion:

- bored

- dismissive (s/he thinks s/he knows everything already, so regards the discussion as a waste of time)

- the joker

- dominating (s/he likes to talk more than listen)

- supportive (s/he likes to hear what other people have to say and supports what they say)

- uncomfortable (s/he does not feel at ease in this group)

The two observation groups should watch the discussion and try to see what is going on in the group: how each person is feeling, thinking, speaking, etc., and what role they are playing in the group, how much they talk, etc.

After the role play, the two observation groups should separately discuss what they have seen, write their conclusions on a flipchart or blackboard, then come back as a whole group. Each observation group should share its conclusions, then everyone can comment and discuss. Here are some learning points to draw out (see also Handout 11: 'What to observe in a group'):

- Facilitators should closely observe participants' expressions and non-verbal communication, and intervene when necessary.

–   Some appropriate interventions might be changing the pace; taking a break; directly addressing an apparent problem; asking a participant privately after the session about an apparent problem; refocusing the group; varying the format of activities (pairs, small group, whole group) so that more people get a chance to contribute; using a talking stick or other prop to limit the time taken by a very talkative person and give others the space to talk.

–   Sometimes it is hard to read a person's expression. For example, they may look annoyed, but it may have nothing to do with the workshop: maybe they have a problem at work or at home.

HANDOUT 11
What to observe in a group

We have all spent a good part of our lives in various sorts of groups, but we rarely take time to stop and observe what is going on, and why the members are behaving in a certain way. It is difficult to observe and participate at the same time, and the skill of doing both at the same time needs practice. We need to observe at three different levels:

A. **Content:** What is the group talking about? What is each person saying?

B. **Non-verbal expressions:** Apart from what they say, what indications are people giving of their feelings and reactions? For example, gestures, tone of voice, body language, facial expressions, order of speaking, etc.

C. **Feelings, attitudes, concerns, hidden agenda:** These factors have an important effect on the well-being of a group and must be taken into account. Sensitive observation of people's words and non-verbal expressions can give us clues about their feelings, but these clues may easily be misinterpreted; so if they seem important, they should be checked with the person concerned, for example: 'Do you feel uncomfortable about that decision, Paul?'

We can also observe the pattern of communication:

- Who talks? for how long? how often?
- Whom do people look at when they talk?
- Who talks first?
- Who interrupts whom?
- What style of communication is used?

This can give us clues to important things which may be going on in the group, such as who leads whom, or who influences whom.

(Adapted with permission from *Training for Transformation*, Book 1, by Anne Hope and Sally Timmel)

8.2.7 Mapping for Mars

See 7.4.1 for detailed instructions.

8.2.8 Know your apple

See 9.3.6 for detailed instructions.

8.2.9 Whole-group discussion of room layout

Objective   To understand the effect of room layout on people's participation, with input from facilitator (see Handout 12).

8.2.10 Whole-group discussion of timing and pacing

Initiate a discussion, involving the whole group, about the importance of keeping an overview of the time and varying the pace of activities. Use Handout 13 to prompt ideas.

HANDOUT 12
Room layout

Research has shown that the arrangement of a room has a strong effect on the level of participation in a discussion. For sighted participants, those who can see all the other faces are at an advantage, and those who cannot are at a disadvantage. If people are sitting in straight rows, it is very unlikely that a good discussion will develop between them, because they cannot see each other's faces. It is also harder to hear what someone is saying if he or she is sitting some rows behind, or in front of you.

Every effort should be made to enable the participants to sit in one circle, where everyone can see everyone else's face and hear what each other is saying. If the circle becomes so big that people cannot hear each other, it is better to have two concentric circles (or horseshoes, if they need to look at something displayed on the wall).

Whether participants are sighted or not, the circle or horseshoe arrangements help to create positive energy among the members, and a feeling of openness which encourages sharing and participation.

In cultures where people are used to sitting behind desks in rows, whether for education or political gatherings, it can take time for people to adapt to more open and participative seating arrangements. Discussing the advantages and disadvantages, for the participants and the facilitator, may help the process of adjustment; games and small-group activities may also help to overcome inhibitions. In some circumstances it may also help if participants sit around small tables in a circular formation. Some suggested layouts are shown overleaf.

If an interpreter (of sign language or any other language) is used, ensure that s/he is placed so as to see/hear everyone and to be seen/heard by those directly using the interpretation.

(Adapted with permission from *Training for Transformation*, Book 2, by Anne Hope and Sally Timmel)

(continued)

Not this

But this

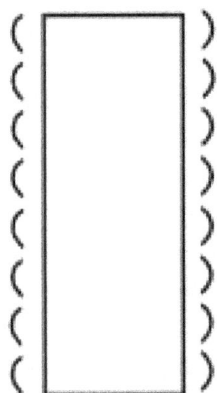

HANDOUT 13
Timing and pacing

One of the most important skills for successful facilitation is accurate timing and appropriate pacing. The facilitator should be very sensitive and watch for non-verbal cues to judge whether people are ready for a change of group, pace, or type of activity. Often in a big group, a few are still very interested when the majority have become bored or sleepy. The facilitator should check whether participants are getting a 'glazed stare' in their eyes, or starting to fidget, or looking at their watches, out of the window, or at the ceiling. All these are signs that it would be good to go into a small-group activity, change pace, or take a short break. It might be appropriate for those who are still involved in the original activity to continue, while others do something else.

The facilitator must constantly make judgements about when a discussion has gone on long enough, or when the allocated time should be extended because people are very much involved in something that is important to them.

People remain far more interested and involved if there is a variety of activities and a good balance between work in small groups and work in big groups. It is important to allow times for talking and times for listening, and times for being active and times for being thoughtful. It helps to change the pace from fast to slower work and vice versa.

Using any type of interpreter may slow down a discussion or activity. The facilitator should factor this in to the timing, and the group should be encouraged to allow extra time for translation, because this is an important aspect of making the workshop accessible to all participants. Whatever pace the facilitator initially sets for a discussion or activity, the interpreter should try to match the energy-level of the facilitator, because this will help to maintain the pace. Of course, participants themselves will often change the pace, consciously or not, and both facilitator and interpreter need to be responsive to this.

(Adapted with permission from *Training for Transformation*, Book 2, by Anne Hope and Sally Timmel)

8.2.11 Line-drawing exercise

Time   20 minutes

Objectives   For participants to experience how their instructions may be interpreted differently by listeners.

To consider what constitutes clear, easily followed instructions.

Preparation   Copies of Handout 14, blank papers, and pens.

Process   Put participants in pairs, A and B.

Give partner A a copy of the line-drawing (Handout 14), which partner B is not allowed to see.

Partner A must give instructions to partner B, telling him/her what to draw, on a separate sheet of paper, in order to replicate the line-drawing that A has been given.

Partner B is not allowed to ask questions about the object to be drawn.

When they have finished, they should compare the two drawings.

Bring the whole group back together and discuss the activity:

- How accurate were the drawings?
- Was it easy or hard to replicate the original? Why?
- For pairs whose drawings were accurate, what did they do?
- With those that were less accurate, what could they do differently?
- What can we learn from this exercise about successful facilitation?

Try to elicit some of the following learning points:

- The meaning of what we say may be interpreted very differently by our listeners, depending on their understanding of a particular word. This might depend on their culture, history, political allegiance, mood on that particular day, personal experiences associated with the word, etc.
- When giving instructions for activities, facilitators should take care to anticipate or watch out for different constructions that listeners might place on their words, and they should modify or clarify the wording of their instructions accordingly.
- Be as specific as possible; break things down into small steps.

Then present the guidelines for giving instructions or information that are listed in Handout 15.

HANDOUT 14
Line drawing

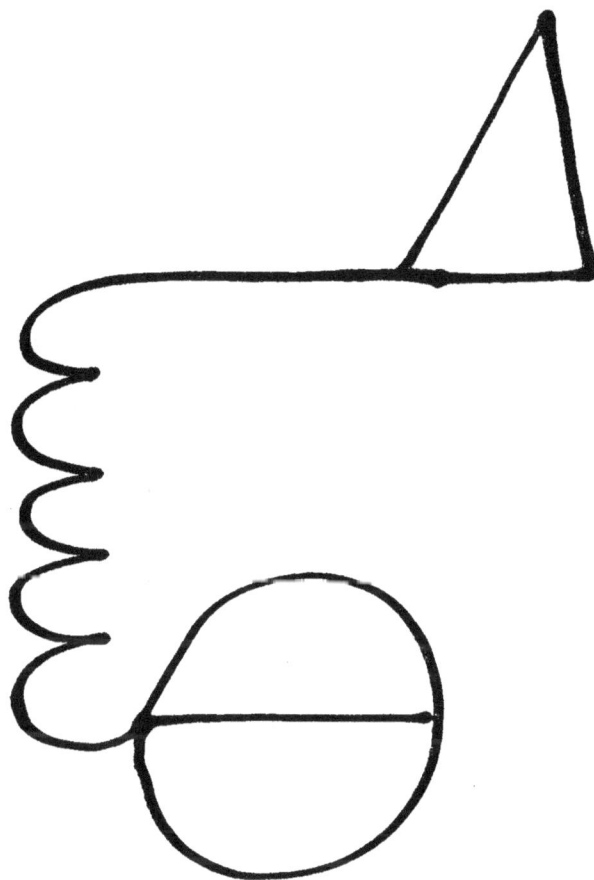

HANDOUT 15
Guidelines for giving instructions or information

1. Facilitators need to be able to explain clearly both what they want participants to do, and why they want them to do it. If participants understand the relevance of an exercise, they will be more interested in it.

2. The structure of the facilitator's input or explanation can help to ensure that it is easily understood:

   - **Introduce**: tell participants the main points of what you are going to tell them (and why).

   - **Explain**: tell them, with details, what you want them to know or to do.

   - **Summarise**: tell them the main points of what you have told them.

   Use the following tools to help you to structure your input, such as:

   - '**road signs**' that tell listeners what to listen out for next, and what stage you have reached in your talk ('another way to think of this is ...', 'to conclude ...');

   - '**flags**' that clearly highlight key points ('the most important thing is ...', 'it is vital to ...');

   - **links** that make a logical bridge between statements, or between one issue and the next. ('As we identified in last week's session, access to education is a big problem in our community. Let's now spend some time considering the options for solving this problem.')

3. Use simple, short sentences, supported by appropriate gestures and facial expressions.

4. Use nouns (such as 'the exercise' or 'non-disabled people'), instead of pronouns (such as 'it' or 'they').

5. Repeat the main points, to emphasise what is important. But do not do this to excess, or participants will become bored and feel patronised.

6. Vary your tone of voice and the speed at which you talk, and pause when necessary.

7. Have a friendly, open approach.

8. Show interest in the subject.

9. Do not fidget; avoid 'non-words', such as 'er', 'you know', 'um', 'kind of'.

Practice in facilitation

To reinforce the principles of facilitation that this section has emphasised, you could set aside half a day or a whole day in which each participant gets an opportunity to facilitate an activity with a small group. Allow time for the others to give feedback on their performance.

The activities suggested below give participants exposure to a range of group-work methods. Photocopy the activity and give each participant a copy. Allow 20 minutes' thinking time before they try out their activities. Each facilitator should decide:

- How to introduce the exercise.
- How to give the instructions.
- Any necessary modifications to make the activity accessible for all participants.
- How to summarise and end the exercise.
- What are the learning points about facilitation from this exercise?

Creating group solidarity: *What I like about you* (7.2.7)

Fostering self-esteem: *What I am proud of myself for* (7.2.8)

Pair work: *I respect you/you respect me* (7.4.3)

Facilitating discussion with a large group: *The right to education* (9.3.13)

Brainstorming: *Discussion of good and bad listening* (8.2.3)

Analysing problems: *Problem-tree exercise* (9.2.2)

Using role play: *Improvised drama about disability rights* (9.3.11); *Puppets exercise* (9.3.14)

Using mime and movement: *Two ways to cross a river* (9.3.15); *The game of life* (9.4.6)

Using visual aids and objects: *Prevention in the home* (8.4.3); *Camouflage game* (9.3.1); *Know your apple* (9.3.6)

Using case studies: *Barriers case study* (9.2.5)

Speaking in front of a group: *Prevention of impairment* (8.4.1)

8.2.12   Facilitation checklists

Time   40 minutes

Objectives   To conclude the focused work on facilitation skills, we included this exercise to give participants an opportunity to reflect on, share, and summarise their experiences during the practice sessions, as well as information taken from the facilitators' input, discussions, etc.

It also gave the facilitators the opportunity for an informal evaluation of participants' learning about facilitation to date.

Preparation   Large sheets of paper and pens

Process   Participants take a few minutes to think back over their own facilitation of the practice sessions: what went well and what they found difficult. They should think also about everything they have learned from the facilitator and other participants about facilitation skills.

In pairs, they should make a checklist for themselves – to remind themselves of important points to keep in mind next time they are facilitating.

One partner can write for both people in the pair. They have 15 minutes to do this, on a large sheet of paper.

Display all the lists around the room. Give people time to move around and read each other's lists.

Ask them to make a (mental) note of anything that is not clear to them. When everyone has read all the lists, bring them back together and give time for questions, clarification, and comments.

If the group includes people who have impaired sight, or are not literate, or experience pain when moving, adapt the methods of making the list and of getting feedback from the whole group to suit their needs.

Further practice in facilitation   In the Oxfam course in Kosovo, further opportunities to practise facilitation were built in. Each week one pair of participants chose and facilitated the introductory (or warm-up) exercise, and another pair chose and facilitated the evaluation exercise. Pairs volunteered for these tasks one week in advance, in order to have time to prepare. In addition, every week for six weeks, a small group was given written instructions for an exercise to be facilitated the following week. The exercise fitted into the rest of the day's content. The group worked out and practised the exercise among themselves in the intervening week.

Participants gained confidence in speaking in front of the group, and practice in giving clear and structured presentations, through frequent five-minute reports/feedback on small-group work to the whole group.

On the final evaluation form, participants reported that enough practice had been provided, and they felt confident about facilitation. However, the three co-facilitators felt that on future courses more time should be allowed for more practice sessions, and that as facilitators they should have given more (and more structured) feedback to participants. We note this here, not as a reflection on participants on the course, but simply to stress that the more one is actually exposed to the experience of being a facilitator, the easier and more effective it becomes.

8.3   Planning workshops

Careful planning is one of the most important elements of a successful
workshop. Facilitators should pay equal attention to the staging of the
workshop, the agenda, and the contents.

8.3.1   The eight sunrays of planning

Time 40 minutes

Preparation Handout 16

Process Explain that the image of eight sunrays of planning is a useful tool to
help us to remember the key elements of planning. (Without the sun's
rays, clouds and rain move in and ruin the event.)

On a large sheet of paper, or a blackboard, draw a round sun, with
eight sunrays coming from it. Starting at the topmost ray on the right,
label each ray in turn:

- **Who?** (as you write, ask 'Who should be involved?'
- **Why?** (ask 'Why should they be involved? What is the aim?
  What will they/you gain?')
- **When?** ('When should it happen?')
- **Where?** ('Where should it happen?')
- **What for?** ('What objectives do you want to achieve?')
- **What?** ('What needs to happen in order to achieve the objectives?')
- **How?** ('How should it happen? What methods should you use?')
- **With what?** ('With what resources, such as people, money,
  materials, etc.?')

Explain that the cyclical rays remind us that planning is an on-going
process, one that should be applied to each stage of whatever event or
activity is being planned, from the general concept to the practical
details. Many of the questions are interrelated.

Applying the eight sunrays to a practical example, ask the group to
imagine that they are facilitators, planning a workshop. Go through
the sunrays one by one, asking them to call out answers to the eight
questions. Take one suggestion given in answer to the first question
and then build the rest of the exercise around it. Here is an example
given by the group in Kosovo:

- **Who?** Parents of disabled children.
- **Why?** To get them more involved in the disabled children's community centre.
- **When?** On a date and at a time that would ensure the biggest attendance.
- **Where?** At the disabled children's community centre. (Go back to 'why?'. To help the parents to get to know the centre and help them to feel comfortable there.)
- **What for?** So that parents will learn about child development and the role of the centre.
- **What?** Skills, knowledge, attitudes, leading to changes in action.
- **How?** Role play, round-table discussion, pairs exercises. (Go back to 'when?'. In what order should you introduce the exercises and activities, which are designed to achieve the 'what for?', which is dependent on the 'what?' and 'how?'?)
- **With what?** Money for materials, transport costs, and driver's wages; donated refreshments. (Go back through the cycle to plan who is going to be responsible for obtaining which resources, and how.)

Allow time for questions or comments. Ask participants to relate this exercise to their own experience of planning some event or activity (not necessarily a workshop).

Link   That was a quick general example. In order to look into this in more depth, we will do an exercise in pairs, to focus our attention on the organising of the workshop itself.

HANDOUT 16
The eight sunrays of planning

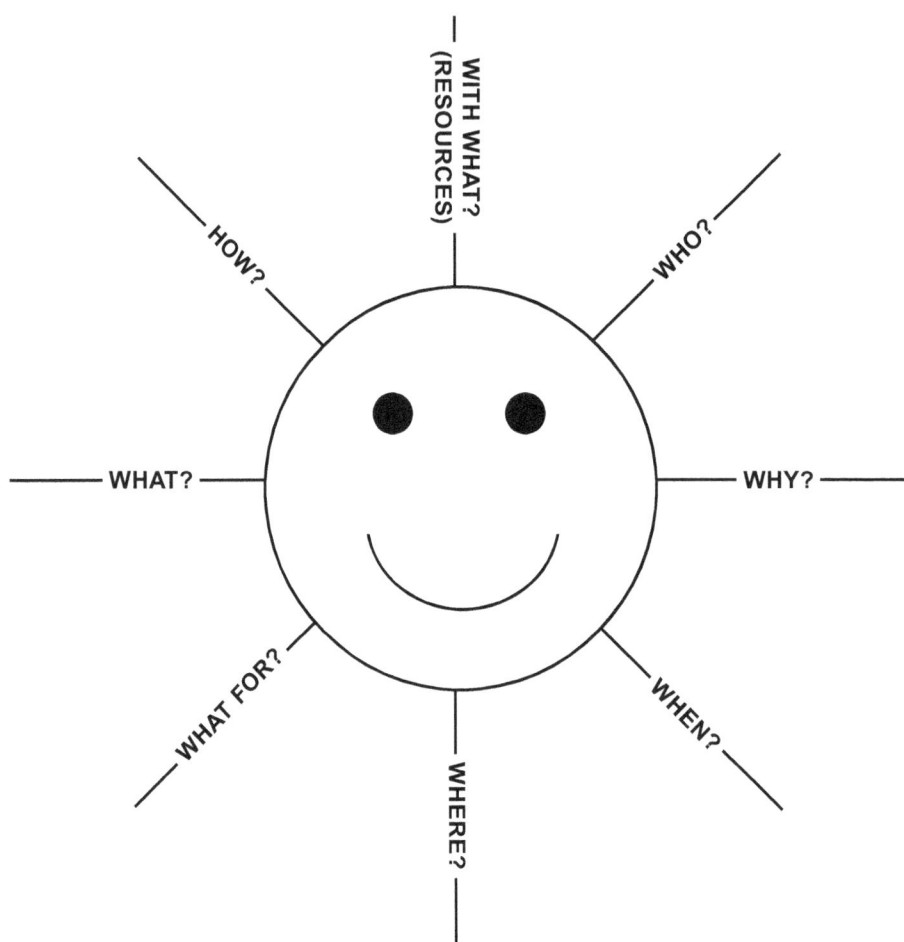

WITH WHAT?
(RESOURCES)

HOW?

WHO?

WHAT?

WHY?

WHAT FOR?

WHEN?

WHERE?

8.3.2 Organising the workshop: a two-part exercise

(Adapted with permission from *Training for Transformation*, Book 2)

Objectives   For participants to apply planning skills to a worked example.

To help participants to appreciate the amount and type of preparation that must be done before a workshop, and the length of time involved.

Preparation   Handout 17

Part 1

Time   45 minutes

Process   Ask participants to work in pairs. They should imagine that they are co-trainers, responsible for planning, administering, and facilitating workshops with their local DPO.

Hand out the list of 17 tasks (lettered A–P) that need to be done in order for the workshop to run.

They have 20 minutes to decide in which order to do the tasks, according to what they think should be done first, second, etc. Which tasks should be done at the same time? Then they should write their list on a sheet of paper.

They may find it helpful to refer back to the eight sunrays of planning during this activity. Leave the drawing up where it can be seen.

For feedback, ask one pair to join up with another pair to compare their answers.

Ask the whole group for their feedback. Did everyone agree on the best sequence for the tasks? If not, why not? Are there any important activities that should have been included and were not? What? At what point might they have been done? Conclusion: there is not necessarily one 'right' order, or one 'right' way. It is important to include all the necessary elements and sequence them in the way that best fits your circumstances.

Possible solution:

1.	E	7.	K
2.	I	8.	D and H
3.	M and Q	9.	O and L
4.	B and G	10.	C
5.	A	11.	F
6.	P	12.	N and J

HANDOUT 17
Planning a workshop: task list

A.   Invite all participants (by letter, telephone, or personal visit) and inform them where and when the workshop will take place, what topics it will cover, etc.

B.   Find an accessible venue, of the appropriate size, and book it for the day required.

C.   Begin the workshop.

D.   Prepare written materials for handouts; make copies for participants.

E.   Meet with your local DPO representatives (staff and ordinary members). Discuss the possible objectives and scope of the workshop, and who should be invited.

F.   Take home any participants who need assistance with transport.

G.   Arrange refreshments for the participants and trainers.

H.   Prepare flipcharts and make puppets.

I.   Meet with your co-trainer to decide on the outline of objectives, content, methods, probable agenda, number and types of participants to invite.

J.   Make payments for refreshments, venue, etc.

K.   Buy paper, pens, etc.

L.   Arrange seating in the workshop room.

M.   Meet with local DPO activists to tell them your proposed objectives, content, method, agenda, number and types of participants; finalise the date of the workshop, in consultation with them.

N.   Evaluate the outcome with local DPO activists: what changes would they have made to any aspect of it?.

O.   Send vehicles to collect participants who need assistance with transport and bring them to the venue.

P.   With your co-trainer, work out in detail the content and methods of the workshop, the approximate timing of activities, and the division of work between you: who will facilitate which activities?

Q.   Make arrangements for transport, if required.

Part 2

Time   50 minutes

Process   Introduce the activity: 'Now we know what has to be done and in what order, we need to think more about the timing of all these tasks. We need to allow enough time in which to do everything. Each pair should work on their ordered task list, and convert it into what is called a time-line. This is what a time-line looks like.'

Put up a piece of flipchart paper horizontally and draw a horizontal line through the middle from one edge to the other. A few inches before the right-hand end of the line, make a mark and write a capital C (to identify the task that says 'Begin the workshop'). Above the letter C, write the date of the imaginary workshop, say 6 May.

Tell participants that they should work backwards from the date of the workshop, and put in the other tasks, in their agreed order, adding approximate dates for the tasks.

Ask people to work in their original pairs, and give them flipchart paper and pens. They have 25 minutes for the activity.

For feedback, ask each pair to display their time-line on the wall. Everybody should spend 10 minutes walking around looking at each other's solutions. Display your own solution too. Note: focus on how much time people have allowed. Did they start their first task a couple of weeks before the workshop, or a couple of months before?

Bring the group back together, ask them for their impressions and comments. What have they learned?

Give participants feedback on key points that you identified from their timelines, including general conclusions and potential problems. Did anyone think of allowing extra time for working out the details of the workshop contents (letter P)? This is something that usually takes more time than expected, so plenty of time should be allowed for it.

Refer to Handout 18: 'The whole training process', which participants may take away and keep for future reference.

Possible timeline solution:

Feb.		1 Mar	6 Apr	30 Apr		6 May		9 May
E	I	M	B G	P K	D	P P P	OCF	N
		Q	A		H		L	J

→

HANDOUT 18
The whole training process

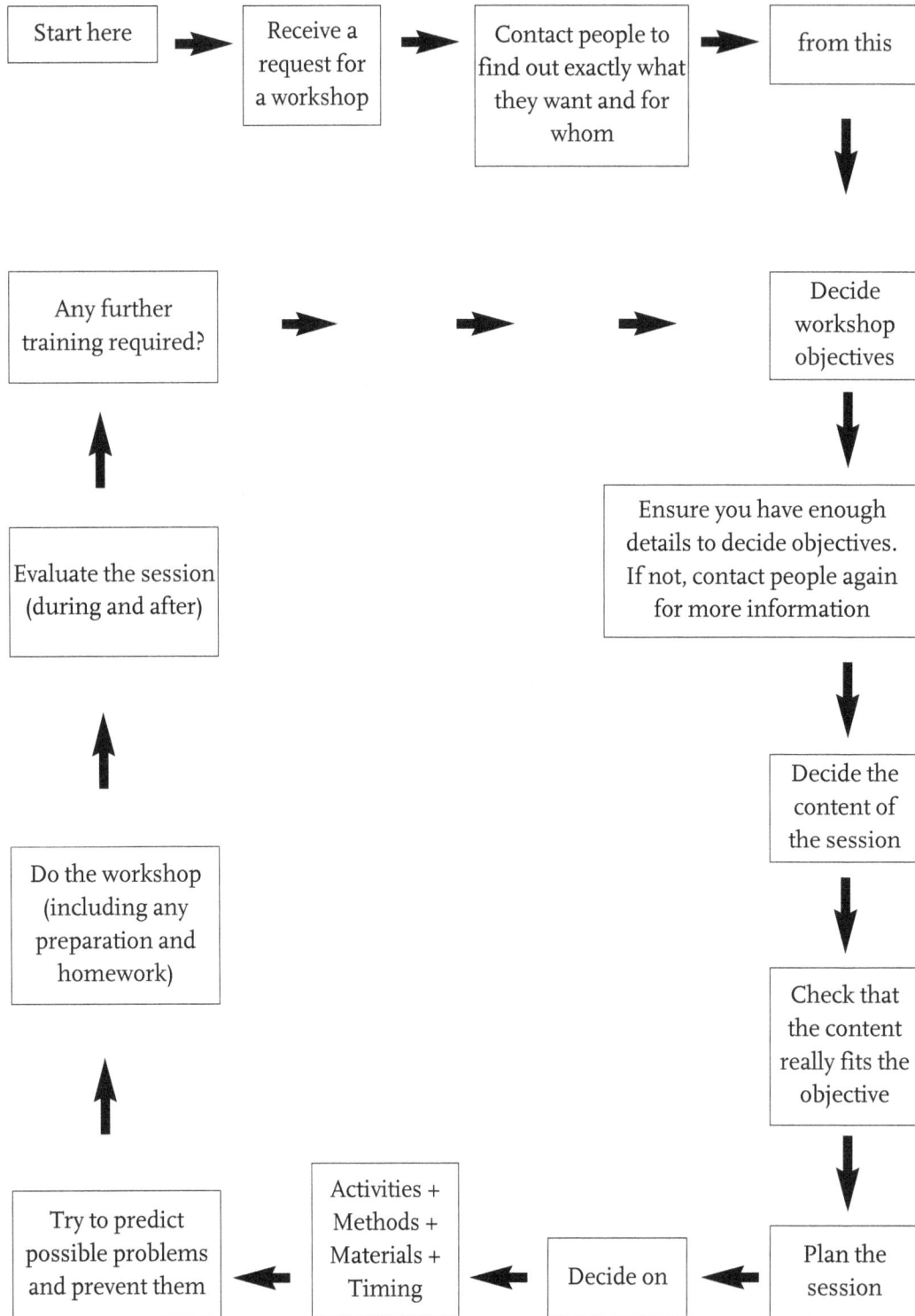

```
┌───────────┐      ┌───────────┐      ┌─────────────────┐      ┌───────────┐
│ Start here│ ──▶  │ Receive a │ ──▶  │ Contact people  │ ──▶  │ from this │
│           │      │ request for│     │ to find out     │      │           │
│           │      │ a workshop│      │ exactly what    │      │           │
│           │      │           │      │ they want and   │      │           │
│           │      │           │      │ for whom        │      │           │
└───────────┘      └───────────┘      └─────────────────┘      └───────────┘
                                                                     │
                                                                     ▼
┌───────────┐                                            ┌─────────────────┐
│ Any further│ ◀── ── ── ── ── ── ── ── ── ── ── ── ──   │ Decide workshop │
│ training   │                                           │ objectives      │
│ required?  │                                           │                 │
└───────────┘                                            └─────────────────┘
     ▲                                                           │
     │                                                           ▼
┌───────────┐                                          ┌───────────────────────┐
│ Evaluate   │                                         │ Ensure you have enough │
│ the session│                                         │ details to decide      │
│ (during and│                                         │ objectives. If not,    │
│ after)     │                                         │ contact people again   │
│           │                                          │ for more information   │
└───────────┘                                          └───────────────────────┘
     ▲                                                           │
     │                                                           ▼
┌───────────┐                                            ┌───────────┐
│ Do the     │                                           │ Decide the│
│ workshop   │                                           │ content of│
│ (including │                                           │ the session│
│ any        │                                           │           │
│ preparation│                                           └───────────┘
│ and        │                                                 │
│ homework)  │                                                 ▼
└───────────┘                                            ┌───────────┐
     ▲                                                   │ Check that│
     │                                                   │ the content│
     │                                                   │ really fits│
     │                                                   │ the       │
     │                                                   │ objective │
     │                                                   └───────────┘
┌───────────┐   ┌───────────┐   ┌───────────┐   ┌───────────┐
│ Try to    │◀──│ Activities+│◀──│ Decide on │◀──│ Plan the  │
│ predict    │   │ Methods +  │   │           │   │ session   │
│ possible   │   │ Materials +│   │           │   │           │
│ problems   │   │ Timing     │   │           │   │           │
│ and prevent│   │           │   │           │   │           │
│ them       │   │           │   │           │   │           │
└───────────┘   └───────────┘   └───────────┘   └───────────┘
```

8.3.3 Planning the agenda and contents of a workshop

Time 1 hour 15 minutes

Objectives To practise planning the content and timing of a workshop.

Preparation Make up one set of 12 activity cards per small group, using topics and activities taken from this manual, or making up your own to suit. See the examples in Handout 19. Leave three cards in each set blank. Include introductory and evaluation activities, energisers, etc.

Process Ask participants to form groups of four people; give each a set of cards.

They have 30 minutes to work together to plan a two-day training schedule, using the activity cards and deciding what to include and what to leave out. There are some blank cards in each set, so they can invent their own if they wish.

They should also decide approximately how much time to allow for each activity, and write this in on the card.

When they have put their chosen cards in order and filled in the timing, they should stick them in sequence on a large sheet of paper.

One person from each small group should present the group's work to everybody. Facilitate the feedback. Allow time for comments, questions, and discussion, using the following questions as prompts:

Questions • Was it easy/difficult to decide on the sequence? Why?
• Was it easy/difficult to decide on the timing? Why?

• How long would they allow themselves in real life for working out the exact content and proposed agenda for a workshop? Emphasise that this is actually a time-consuming process (lasting much longer than 30 minutes!), so facilitators need to invest a lot of thought and time in preparing for a workshop.

• If any groups used all the cards, ask their reasons for this. Point out that there would not be enough time in two days to cover all the topics in depth, so it is important not to do too much, and to cover fewer things more effectively. There is a limit to what workshop participants can absorb in one day!

Options To save time, omit the individual feedback. Ask participants to display their solutions on the wall, and ask everyone to walk around and look at them during a break. Then bring the whole group together for comments and discussion, based on the questions above.

HANDOUT 19
Sample activity cards

Activity:

The three models of disability: presentation and discussion

Time allowed:

Activity:

Rights: Calendar game

Time allowed:

Activity:

Agreeing group guidelines

Time allowed:

8.4 Handling difficult topics

The Oxfam course in Kosovo included a consideration of the psychological impact and prevention of disability/impairments, in order to expose participants (future facilitators) to ways of thinking about these personal, complex issues, as well as giving them practice in facilitating group work on potentially difficult issues. Such sensitive subjects should not be addressed until participants have gained confidence, feel comfortable with each other, and have become familiar with the concept of the social model of disability and the human rights of disabled people.

This section is relevant also for DPO activists, who often have to deal with such topics in the course of their work, and for professionals working in the fields of medicine and public health.

The psychological impact of impairment and disability

We included this topic in the workshop because it is one of the principal issues of concern for KAPP/Handikos and its volunteer members, many of whom are not disabled but spend much of their working time visiting disabled people in their homes. The visits are largely a waste of time if members do not understand the normal psychological processes that disabled people go through in reacting to their impairment, or if the visitor has no strategies to use to reach out to the disabled person. Often this leads to misunderstandings, to negative labelling of the disabled person, and to the offer of inappropriate assistance.

By the psychological impact of **impairment**, we mean the effects of the trauma – both physical and psychological – experienced by people when their faculties or capabilities are first impaired (through illness, war, accident, etc.). By the psychological impact of **disability**, we mean the effects on people's lives and well-being caused by the (discriminatory) reactions of society to their impairment – whether they were born with it or acquired it later.

Given that our participant group contained a mix of disabled and non-disabled people, women and men, we felt that the most appropriate way to approach these issues was to invite a disabled person – in this case Halit Ferizi, the President of KAPP – to share his first-hand knowledge and experience with workshop participants. Below we reproduce a summary of the session that he led.

The physical and psychological isolation experienced by disabled people means that they rarely have an opportunity to discuss personal issues and work through them with their peers. Some of these issues are common to men and women, but some are specific to one sex or the other. Informal peer-support groups can offer space for personal concerns to be raised, experiences to be shared, and solutions to be considered. It is not appropriate to encourage people to deal with them in mixed-sex groups.

Summary of the session led by the President of KAPP

The work of the KAPP starts with each individual, and must respond to each individual's needs. People who were born with an impairment, and grew up disabled, are in a different situation from people who became disabled later in life. They are less likely to have been able to attend school, or they may have received a second-class education in a 'special' school; they are less likely to have been employed, married, etc. These types of discrimination often make people feel less confident about themselves and their abilities.

People who become disabled as children or adults, as well as going through physical trauma, also experience a radical change in their life: they are often in shock, and have to begin their lives again from zero. Suddenly they don't know who they are, and they lose confidence. These problems are compounded by the attitudes of society and the barriers that they start to encounter.

The experience of hospital and rehabilitation can be disempowering if it is concerned only with operations and therapy. What was useful about rehabilitation for me was meeting other disabled people and learning from them, finding out what was possible, and how they had organised themselves into self-help groups. It helped me to move beyond the shock and trauma.

One thing that disabled people share – no matter when or how they became disabled – is the fact that impairments and disability can be a source of strength and motivation. However, very often disabled people internalise other people's negative attitudes. In Kosovo, society alienates disabled people, who as a result may become isolated and depressed, and start withdrawing from contact with others, even refusing food until they become undernourished and vulnerable to illness and death. Some families will tell you that the disabled person is neurotic and aggressive. Is it because of their impairment, or because of the influence of their environment – their family or community? Who would not react with anger if they were treated as perpetual children, or locked alone in a room?

Sometimes families prevent KAPP members from visiting their disabled family member, or they are hostile to visitors. Sometimes the disabled person has become so isolated that he or she does not want to see anyone.

Volunteers need to think about all these things in their work and adapt their approach, interaction, and advice to suit each individual, in order to help them to become motivated, to gain confidence, stop thinking negatively about themselves, and participate or return to participating in life.

Some ways to help isolated disabled people

- Arrange for a disabled activist to visit them.
- Arrange peer support, one-to-one, or in informal groups.
- Build a relationship with the person, gradually over time.
- Don't expect them to be comfortable talking to you straight away, especially about personal matters.
- Help them to recognise their emotions – shock, trauma, denial, anger, lack of self-confidence – as normal reactions to their situation, and to see that they can move forward. They can help themselves, and others with disabilities, by developing a positive approach, refusing to be frustrated or de-valued by other people, turning to other disabled people for support when things are difficult.
- Talk directly with them, not (only) with their family.
- Call them by their name; don't refer to them as 'the patient'.
- Be friendly, not official.
- Find out what they are interested in and talk about that – not just about their impairment.
- Identify the barriers that they experience at home; help them to work out ways to remove them.
- Analyse yourself, your experience and knowledge, and how that can help.
- Use and share information about disability rights, the disability movement, etc.
- Encourage and motivate, using positive examples.
- Focus on what disabled people can do, not what they can't, and build on that.
- Don't fall into the trap of telling someone that his or her impairment 'is not as bad as' someone else's, that 'it could be worse', and they should be 'thankful that it's not'.
- Invite them to meet you somewhere outside the home, or to join you in attending an event in the community or one arranged by the DPO.

Causes and prevention of disability/impairments

Some people might initially question the inclusion of this issue in a Disability Equality course. It is indeed true that in most countries prevention is a difficult subject to tackle, because many people consciously or unconsciously subscribe to the idea 'Better dead than disabled'. The aim of this section of the manual is to give facilitators (and/or DPO members) a means of challenging that very negative notion of prevention, and to suggest an alternative.

The conventional understanding of prevention focuses on 'preventing disabled people from existing' or 'getting rid of disabled people'. It includes such practices as aborting impaired foetuses; euthanasia for disabled children and adults; and the sterilisation of disabled people to prevent them from having children. Such approaches are often promoted by well-meaning members of the medical profession to whom the families of disabled children and adults turn for advice. But often that advice is one-sided, insensitive, and ignorant of the value of disabled people's lives. It is not unknown in so-called 'developed' countries for doctors to advise the parents of children born with Downs Syndrome, for example, to put them in an institution and forget about them, 'because he/she will be dead by the age of eleven anyway'– in ignorance of the fact that most such children live to healthy adulthood and can make their own unique contribution to the lives of those around them. Sophisticated technology is used to detect impairments before birth, based on the virtually automatic assumption that abortion is the only appropriate solution. In Kosovo and elsewhere, it is common for disabled babies in hospital to be 'allowed to die'; it even happens that parents of disabled children who consult a doctor for a condition unrelated to the disability, like influenza, are sometimes offered euthanasia for the child.

The underlying message of this approach is that the most efficient way to prevent 'disability' is to eliminate the person with the impairment. Such a gross abuse of the right to life makes it an appropriate and significant topic for consideration in a longer course based on disability rights. It is especially relevant on a course for trainee facilitators, or for activists who will have to deal with the issue in the course of their work. But discussions need to be handled very carefully, because many disabled people have internalised the negative values of the context in which they live.

An alternative approach to disability prevention consists of two elements. The first is to recognise that disability is a social construct, and to challenge society's hostile, disabling reactions to people with impairments. Disability can be prevented by creating an enabling world (see further the sections on Models and Barriers in Chapter 9).

The second element is to recognise that many physical and mental impairments are caused by the abuse of basic human rights: injuries resulting from landmines are a prime example. To prevent impairments, society should start by taking active steps to protect people's rights: for example by banning landmines, providing health education about proper nutrition for pregnant and nursing women, ensuring immunisation against infectious diseases, and passing and enforcing labour laws that provide protection for workers in hazardous conditions.

Here we present a small selection of activities and discussion-based exercises which cover a range of target participant groups and give scope for consideration of the topic on global or local levels, or both. The exercises may be used separately or in various combinations. We hope they will encourage readers to develop their own ideas for their own workshops.

8.4.1 Prevention of impairment: presentation and discussion

Time   45 minutes

Objective   To provide information about:

- the main causes of impairments (as distinct from disability)
- preventing impairments by addressing the causes
- preventing impairments by protecting people's rights

Preparation   Prepare the presentation (see the suggestion below, and/or refer to Handout 20), and prepare flipcharts to support the presentation.

Process   Introduce the topic. Suggested presentation: start by differentiating between the concepts of preventing disability (changing society's attitudes and construction) and preventing impairments. We need to start by looking at the causes of impairments. They include the following:

- **Poverty:** inadequate medical care and information; poor nutrition and sanitation; overcrowding. Examples: blindness due to vitamin deficiency; diarrhoea, leading to dehydration and brain damage in malnourished babies; paralysis caused by improper use of injections; tuberculosis arising from malnutrition and overcrowded, insanitary living conditions.

- **War:** injuries inflicted on civilians and military personnel. Examples: amputations and blindness caused by landmines.

- **Accidents:** on roads, at home, at work. Examples: paraplegia and brain damage resulting from crashes on badly maintained roads; burns from cooking pots; amputations necessitated by accidents with machinery; loss of hearing in noisy factories; chronic muscular and respiratory problems in work-places where health and safety are disregarded; paralysis and the loss of sight caused by the use of pesticides without safety precautions, etc.

Such causes are responsible for the majority (perhaps two-thirds) of all impairments.

Facilitate a discussion, based on the following questions:

- What rights are being abused in situations like these?
- Who is responsible for these abuses?
- How can these types of impairment be prevented? (By protecting people's rights, eradicating poverty, providing safe and decent working conditions, etc.)

Presentation continues (write key words on a blank sheet of flipchart paper as you speak): in many countries it is common to prevent impairments in a different way: by eliminating the people affected, using the following methods: abortion of impaired foetuses; euthanasia (by denying medical treatment or food so that disabled adults and children die); eugenics (forced sterilisation, or not allowing disabled people to marry or have sexual relationships, in case they produce children with genetic impairments).

Facilitate a discussion, using the following questions:

- What rights are being abused in these cases?
- Why do some people in society think that disabled people have less right to live than non-disabled people?
- What do participants think about the policy of employing abortion, euthanasia, and eugenics in response to the problem of disability?
- Why do governments often prefer such policies to the option of protecting human rights and preventing impairments?

HANDOUT 20
Disability – incidence and causes

Disability and poverty are linked, both at an individual level and at the level of countries and continents. The World Bank estimates that disabled people may account for as many as one in five of the poorest people in the world ('Poverty and Disability: A Background Paper for the World Development Report', World Bank, 1999). Wherever they live, they are accorded low social status and are discriminated against when they try to find paid employment. Eighty per cent of the world's disabled people live in Asia and the Pacific region, but they receive just 2 per cent of the resources allocated to the needs of disabled people worldwide (according to Action on Disability and Development, Five-Year Strategic Plan, 1998–2002). Recent UNESCO studies have suggested that only two per cent of disabled children in developing countries receive an education ('Disability, Poverty, and Development', UK government Department for International Development).

It is difficult to interpret statistics, since official surveys tend to use only medical sources of evidence, and to classify impairments only by clinical criteria. Also, it is not easy to compare statistics gathered in different societies, which might employ different definitions. But the World Health Organisation's estimate is widely accepted: 10 per cent of the world's population is disabled in some respect.

The major causes of impairment are poverty, accidents, and war. As many as 50 per cent of all cases are preventable and directly linked to poverty. Broad classifications of the causes are given below:

Malnutrition	20% of all cases
Accident/trauma/war	15%
Infectious diseases	11%
Non-infectious diseases	20%
Congenital conditions	20%
Other (including ageing)	13%

(Source: *Overcoming Obstacles to the Integration of Disabled People*, UNESCO, 1995)

However, such figures raise many questions, and can confuse rather than clarify matters. For instance, some congenital (pre-birth) conditions can be linked to malnutrition, which is fundamentally related to poverty. Similarly, many infectious and non-infectious

(continued)

diseases are secondary to poverty-related factors, such the drinking of polluted water.

It is also difficult to allow for ageing as a cause of impairment and disability. In the rich industrialised countries, a large proportion of 'disabled' people are over the age of 60, a proportion which increases as life expectancy increases. Ageing is also a factor in poor countries of the South – but less so, because life expectancy is lower there.

Poverty

A large proportion of the populations of poor and conflict-torn countries don't get enough to eat. Added to this is the problem of dietary deficiencies. Approximately 100 million people have impairments caused by malnutrition. In India, 15,000 children go blind every year from lack of vitamin A, because their families have no land on which to grow vegetables and no money with which to buy them. Globally an estimated 200,000 children each year lose their sight through vitamin deficiencies.

'To prevent the disabilities that result from poverty, big changes are needed in our social order. There needs to be a fairer distribution of land, resources, information and power. Such changes will only happen when the poor find the courage to organize, to work together, and to demand their rights. Disabled persons and their families can become leaders in this process.' (David Werner, *Challenging a Disabling World*)

Accidents and war

Some 78 million people (16 per cent of disabled people) have impairments caused by accidents and trauma (including road accidents). Hazardous working conditions are common in developing countries, because people are so desperate for paid work that they will tolerate very dangerous conditions, often working for companies that have deliberately based themselves overseas to escape European/north American health-and-safety legislation, in order to produce goods as cheaply as possible. The mining and chemical industries are notorious for dangerous practices.

Conditions in Angola dramatically illustrate the link between war and disability. It was estimated in mid-2002 (*Jornal de Angola*, 27/06/02) that 80,000 people had been mutilated by unexploded landmines during the civil war. Between 4 and 5 million landmines remain in place. Accidents continue at the rate of 60 per month, and 30 per cent of those injured die of their wounds.

8.4.2 Prevention of impairment: small-group discussion

Time One hour

Objectives For participants to share knowledge or raise questions about the prevention of impairment in their community.

To identify potential sources of information about the prevention of impairment.

Preparation Flipchart paper and pens

Process Divide people into groups of four and ask them to make a list of the five most common types of preventable impairment in their country (region, community, etc.).

Next they should think about the cause of each of the impairments on their list, and write it next to its corresponding impairment. As an example, the typical Kosovan custom of swaddling fevered babies in many layers of blankets can lead to brain damage.

They should consider how each impairment might be prevented. (In the Kosovan example, by health education and access to information.) If they don't know, or are not sure, it doesn't matter: they should just put a question mark.

After 30 minutes, each small group reports back to the whole group for five minutes.

If there are any question marks on the lists, ask other participants for suggestions. Again, it's OK if no one can answer. You can use this as an opportunity to emphasise the importance of having access to information, which most people are denied. Most people try to do the best they can, but often end up harming themselves or their relatives or patients because they cannot get the information that they need.

Where, in this community, can we get information about these things? (Other people who have had similar experiences; doctors and community workers who are trained in preventing impairment and disease; traditional healers who have a positive approach to disabled members of the community; books and newsletters; trade-union officials or other people who know about workplace safety, etc.)

Options Depending on the composition of the group, this exercise can be done without writing, either in small groups with whole-group feedback, or in the whole group from start to finish.

8.4.3   Prevention in the home: picture-based exercise

Time   20 minutes

Objectives   To raise participants' awareness of potential causes of disability in the home.

Preparation   If appropriate, redraw the picture in Handout 21 to fit local culture and circumstances, making sure not to omit any of the five potential accidents.

Make one copy per participant (or draw it on a board or large sheet of paper).

Process   Give out the pictures and read out the story: 'Like many girls, nine-year-old Amina regularly looks after her baby brother. One afternoon her mother is suddenly called away from home. She asks Amina to look after her brother and keep an eye on the evening meal, which is cooking on the paraffin stove. Amina settles at the table to do her homework, while the baby plays in one corner. Then Amina hears a friend calling her name. She hurries to the door. Meanwhile, the baby is curious and crawls to the other side of the room.'

Participants work in pairs. They have five minutes to look at the picture and identify five things that might cause an accident, disability, or death.

Bring the whole group back together, and ask participants to call out their answers. Keep going until they have called out all five causes. Supply the answers if they miss any of them.

Can they think of other causes of accidents in the home that might put a child in danger, possibly resulting in an impairment?

Answers

1. **Unprotected cooking pot:** baby might burn himself on the pot; liquid from the pot might scald skin or damage eyes; an older child might tip the pot over, scalding and burning skin.

2. **Paraffin stove:** unguarded flames can burn skin, hair, and clothing; baby might tip the stove over, causing flames to spread; paraffin might spill, causing fire to spread; fire can spread quickly and baby cannot escape; thick smoke can cause breathlessness, disorientation, and slow reflexes.

3. **Paraffin bottle:** a baby or young child might tip an open bottle over, causing paraffin to spill on skin; or he could be poisoned by drinking paraffin.

4. **Matches:** baby might put matches in his mouth, causing obstruction or choking or poisoning; an older child might strike matches,
    causing burns or creating a fire that gets out of control.

5. **Knife:** young children could cut themselves on sharp edges.

Other dangers for discussion:

Burns: caused by open fires, faulty electrical appliances, or dangerous fluids, such as bleach, petrol, etc.

Cuts: from jagged tins, broken glass, etc.

Poisoning: from eating or drinking harmful things, such as fuel, medicines, etc.

Falls: from unsafe and unsupervised fixtures, stairs, balconies, ladders, etc.

HANDOUT 21
Preventing accidents in the home

(Reproduced with permission from *Child Health Dialogue* 7, 1997,
© Healthlink Worldwide, London)

8.4.4 Fishbowl exercise

This exercise is designed to address the links between disability and human-rights abuses. It can also introduce participants to the use of fishbowl exercises, in which some of the group engage in a role play and others observe the discussion from the outside. By tapping them on the shoulder, you can get the observers to take the place of any of the role-playing participants at any point during the discussion.

The example given here was developed to fit local circumstances and structures in Kosovo, some of which will be familiar and some unfamiliar to readers in other societies. We hope that readers will use it as a starting point, and adapt it to fit their own specific contexts.

Time One hour

Objective For participants to think about and discuss a locally specific example of the abuse of disabled people's rights.

For trainee facilitators to experience the use of 'fishbowl' exercises to explore difficult issues.

Preparation No written materials to prepare. Work out a scenario and roles to suit your situation, or use/adapt the example given.

You can either ask for volunteers to play roles, or, if you think it will make the exercise more effective, you can assign particular roles to particular participants before the session (but remember their right to opt out if they don't feel comfortable about an activity).

Process Announce the roles: four doctors, one representative of the local DPO, and one (or more) observer(s). Give each set of people their instructions separately.

- **The DPO representative:** you have invited doctors from the local health clinic to a meeting, because your organisation is concerned to hear reports from its members that some doctors are routinely telling parents who have a disabled child not to have any more children. The point of the meeting is for the representative to learn about the doctors' opinions and policies; to facilitate a discussion about the advice being given to parents; and to get the doctors to consider the human-rights issues involved. (These include the parents' right to have full information and make an informed choice about whether they want to have more children or not.)

- **The doctors:** your role is to participate in the discussion as you think a doctor would (which may be different from your own personal views, which you should forget about for now). Explain that they are meeting with the local DPO representative to share what advice they would give to parents who have a disabled child and are wondering whether to have more children or not.

- **Observer(s):** your role is to watch and make a note of the dynamics of the discussion: the relationships between the various participants; how people are feeling (interested, bored, angry, insulted, argumentative, co-operative, open-minded, not listening, etc.) and how the DPO representative, as the facilitator of the discussion, responds to those reactions throughout the discussion. You should be prepared to give comments at the end about what you have seen.

- The doctors and the DPO representative should sit in a circle. The observer and the rest of the group should sit around them.

- Allow twenty minutes for discussion in role. Then bring everyone together for feedback.

Questions

Do people agree/disagree with the doctors' views? Why? Why not?

Deciding to abort a foetus solely because it has an impairment is like making a statement that disabled people and their lives are without value. How do participants feel about that statement?

How does that policy fit with the Universal Declaration of Human Rights, which asserts that we are all equal and all have the right to life?

On the facilitation process: how/what did the various participants feel or observe? What happened, and why? If there were perceived difficulties (such as silences or anger), why do people think they happened? How did the DPO representative deal with it? What would others have done in his/her place?

Can difficult moments (such as silences and disagreements) be used constructively in group situations? When? How? What is the responsibility of the facilitator at such times?

9 Disability Equality in practice

This chapter contains activities and exercises designed to introduce the concept that a person's disability is not defined by his or her actual impairment, but by the way in which non-disabled people think and feel about it and represent it. The quality of disabled people's lives is determined more by social attitudes than by actual impairments.

An alternative starting point would be to consider the main causes of impairments (see section 8.4: *Handling difficult topics*, Handout 20 and the small-group discussion), because this helps to confront, explore, and dispel myths; and it creates a space for people to rethink their attitudes to disability.

9.1 Models of disability

9.1.1 Introducing the topic

Here are three different options for prompting people to think about what 'disability' is and getting a variety of ideas flowing. The second and third suggestions involve small-group work and so take more time, but they are good for groups for whom brainstorms are not effective. They also have the bonus, if the group is new to you, of giving you an opportunity to observe the members early on and to form an idea of who the most and least dominant people are, so that you can work towards more equitable involvement of all the group. The second option is also good for use with non-literate groups.

Time 10–60 minutes (depending on which introductory activity is chosen).

Objective To stimulate a consideration of what disability is.

Key learning points DPOs believe that two common approaches to disability, known as the medical and charitable models, do not really solve the problems experienced by disabled people.

An alternative approach, the social model, shows how the real problem of disability is not the fact of having a physical or mental impairment, but the way in which society reacts to that fact, and the ways in which society is constructed to exclude disabled people.

Process   Option 1: **Brainstorm**
Write the word (for) 'disability' in the centre of a large piece of paper, and ask the group to brainstorm for five minutes all the different words or images that come to mind when they hear the word 'disability'. Nobody should comment on the words suggested at this stage. Write up all their suggestions, then move on to the link presented below.

Option 2: **Small-group work – pictures**
Ask people to form groups of four. Give each group two pieces of flip-chart paper and coloured pens. Ask each group to draw two pictures. The first should represent disabled people's lives as they actually are, in their village, or town, or region; the second should represent how they would like disabled people's lives to be, in their village, town, or region. Give them 20 minutes. Before they start work, tell them that each group should appoint someone who will take five minutes to present their pictures to the whole group. Facilitate their feedback, thank them for their ideas, then move on to the linking activity below.

Option 3: **Small-group work – disabled people's needs**
Ask people to form groups of four. Give each group one piece of flipchart paper and pens. Ask them to discuss together what they think disabled people's needs are, and then to list the 10 most important needs on the flipchart. Give them 20 minutes. Before they start work, tell them that each group should appoint someone who will take five minutes to present their list to the whole group. Facilitate their feedback, then move on to the link (below).

Link   Whichever option you used, spend 5–10 minutes giving feedback on the groups' suggestions. Note that their contributions represent differing types of approach to disability and disabled people; give some examples. The way in which people (whether disabled or not) perceive disability is important, because it defines what they do, and the conditions of disabled people's lives.

Disabled people's organisations have identified three common approaches to disability. These different approaches, or models, as they are known (decide in advance if it will be necessary to include a five-minute explanation of the term 'model') are usually called the medical model, the charity model, and the social model. Most of the words and ideas written on the flipcharts fit into one or other of the models.

Remove the written/drawn materials from the main presentation area, but display them somewhere else in the room, so that participants can refer back to them during or after your presentation.

9.1.2 Presentation of the three models

Time 30 minutes

Objective Participants will be able to describe the three basic models of disability.

Preparation Copy the diagrams of the three models in Handout 22 on to large sheets of paper, or a blackboard.

Process Start by explaining that the first two approaches, the medical model and the charity model, are the traditional ways in which disability and disabled people have been seen and treated by others. The third approach, the social model, represents the way in which many disabled people themselves have come to see disability. Now talk through in turn the flipcharts of the medical model, charity model, and lastly the social model (see the facilitator's notes for ideas of what to say).

Facilitator's notes The way in which we see a problem determines what we do to resolve it. Our approach to a problem may be called a 'model'.

The medical model sees disability as a problem, and the problem lies with the disabled individual. To solve the problem, it is necessary to work on the individual – starting with a diagnosis of what is 'wrong' with him or her. The person and his or her life becomes defined solely in terms of the diagnosis. Someone with a diagnosis is a patient: no longer a person, just a case for clinical treatment.

So the main need of disabled people is perceived as medical services (hospitals, specialist doctors, nurses, therapists, etc.). Medical personnel focus on the things that the disabled person cannot do: can't walk, can't see, can't talk, for example. (It is often assumed that not being able to think, decide, and act for oneself are unavoidable consequences of not being able to walk, see, talk, etc.) In response to their diagnosis, medical personnel do their job and try to find a cure. If a cure is possible, all energy and resources are used to achieve it.

If there is no cure, this is seen as tragic, and it is considered that the individual will need to be cared for instead. Care is to be prescribed and provided by a range of specialist professionals, social workers, counsellors, therapists, psychologists, etc., who will work with the individual or his or her family to reduce the 'problems'.

Because the disabled individual is different from what is considered to be the norm, s/he is considered to need a range of different, or special, services. In many countries medical services are the only services deemed necessary; but some countries provide special transport, special buildings, special schools (where the courses are very often less challenging and academic than in mainstream schools, making it harder or impossible for disabled people to enter higher education and employment), special sports and recreational facilities, sheltered employment workshops, etc.

The charity model shares with the medical model the fact that the 'problem' of disability is seen as inherent in the individual who has the impairment. It assumes that a disabled person's main need in life is to be looked after. Again, the focus is placed on what the person cannot do: can't walk without crutches, can't hear without a hearing aid, can't use his or her arms, etc. It is often assumed that disabled people can't think, decide, or act on their own behalf, and that someone else needs to do those things for them.

Typically, the individual is seen in one of three ways: as sad, tragic, and passive; or bitter, twisted, and aggressive; or brave, courageous, and inspirational. Disabled people are perceived as needing help, protection, care, pity, charity, sympathy, special services, special schools, and charitable donations. But what would really make a difference to their lives would be enabling them to earn their own living, in useful and productive ways. Often 'giving to charity' is a way of covering up and ignoring the real problems in our communities.

Many disabled people themselves have adopted and internalised one or both of these two models: like everyone else, disabled people see themselves in the mirror of the people around them. If the people around them think that disabled people are incapable of independent living, sooner or later the disabled person may end up believing it too.

Refusing to be defined by the medical or charity model does not mean that disabled people reject the support of doctors, social workers, rehabilitation workers, and other professionals. Their work is very important. Everyone, disabled and non-disabled, needs medical services and other forms of help sometimes. But this is only part of our lives, and if we see a disabled person only and always as someone who needs help or charity (and not as a whole person), we are actually doing more harm than good.

The social model is the term used by disabled people's organisations who have decided that the other two models severely and unnecessarily restrict the roles that disabled people can play in life. Treating disabled people according to the medical or charity models makes them dependent on certain (non-disabled) people and separates them from the rest of society. For many DPOs, the social model describes the true nature of the problem of disability: the problem is not the individual, nor his or her impairment. The main needs of a person with an impairment are the same as anyone else's: life, love, education, employment, having control and choice in one's life, and access to adequate services (including medical and rehabilitation when necessary) as of right. (It is worth remembering that these are essentially the same needs or demands that other civil-rights movements – such as those fighting for the rights of women, and ethnic minorities – are working for in many parts of the world.)

The problem of disability lies in how society responds to the individual and his or her impairment, and in physical and social environments which are designed (by non-disabled people) to meet the needs of non-disabled people only. As an example: transport is inaccessible to many disabled people, so children with mobility problems cannot go to school. Even if they can get there, school buildings are inaccessible, or the school director may have a negative attitude and won't accept them because (it is claimed) other children's parents will be upset. So they cannot get a decent education. Or perhaps the only school that disabled children are allowed to attend is a 'special school', where they are much less likely to receive a decent education, and where they will be denied exposure to and interaction with their non-disabled peers. Without a decent education they cannot find work, and without work they end up poor and reliant on others (family, the State, charity, etc.).

Medical and social services (where they exist) are designed and provided for disabled people by non-disabled people, many of whom have a negative attitude to disabled people (assuming that there is something 'wrong' or 'abnormal' about them). For this reason, disabled people themselves are not consulted, and the services available to them are often inappropriate or inadequate. The services are often called 'special'– and anything that is special is usually considered extra or not essential. This means that when resources are limited or budgets are being cut, the first things to be lost are the extra or 'special' items.

To conclude, under the social model a person who has an impairment is disabled not because of the impairment, but because of the attitudes of society, and poorly constructed physical and social environments. These are all problems that can be resolved. It is not possible to make all paralysed people walk, or all blind people see (and indeed it is not necessary to walk or see in order to have a worthwhile and enjoyable life); but ramps and lifts can be built, guide dogs can be trained, and non-disabled people can learn to think in a different way about disabled people. The social model can therefore be a helpful tool for disabled people and their allies to make positive changes in their lives, and for non-disabled people to understand more about disability.

HANDOUT 22
The three models of disability

The medical model of disability

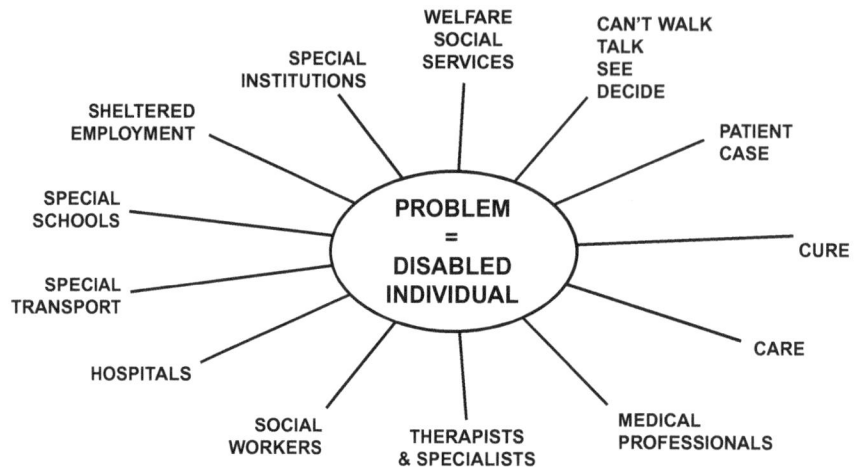

SPECIAL INSTITUTIONS

WELFARE SOCIAL SERVICES

CAN'T WALK TALK SEE DECIDE

SHELTERED EMPLOYMENT

PATIENT CASE

SPECIAL SCHOOLS

PROBLEM = DISABLED INDIVIDUAL

CURE

SPECIAL TRANSPORT

CARE

HOSPITALS

SOCIAL WORKERS

THERAPISTS & SPECIALISTS

MEDICAL PROFESSIONALS

The charitable model of disability

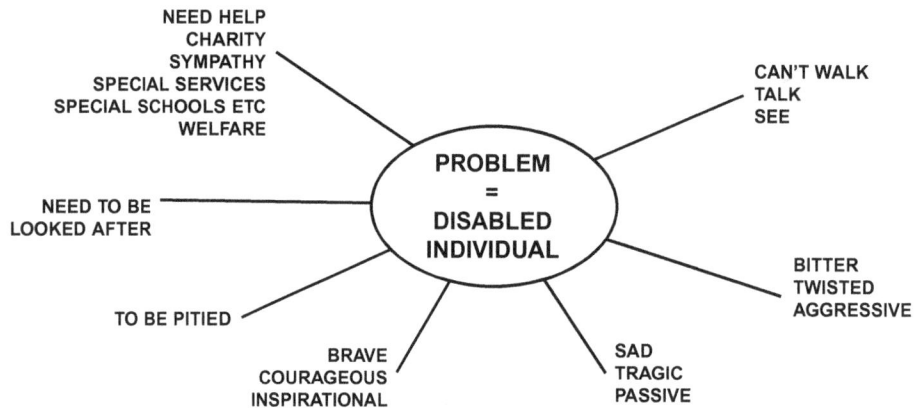

NEED HELP
CHARITY
SYMPATHY
SPECIAL SERVICES
SPECIAL SCHOOLS ETC
WELFARE

CAN'T WALK
TALK
SEE

NEED TO BE LOOKED AFTER

PROBLEM = DISABLED INDIVIDUAL

BITTER TWISTED AGGRESSIVE

TO BE PITIED

BRAVE COURAGEOUS INSPIRATIONAL

SAD TRAGIC PASSIVE

The social model of disability

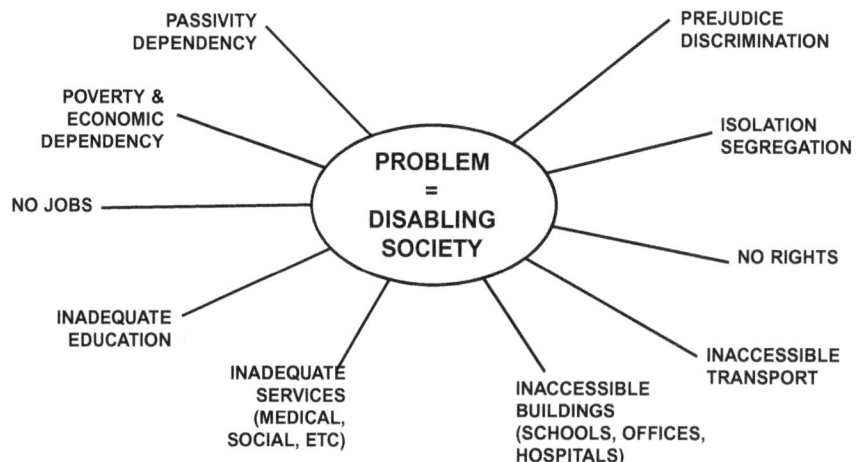

PASSIVITY DEPENDENCY

PREJUDICE DISCRIMINATION

POVERTY & ECONOMIC DEPENDENCY

ISOLATION SEGREGATION

NO JOBS

PROBLEM = DISABLING SOCIETY

NO RIGHTS

INADEQUATE EDUCATION

INACCESSIBLE TRANSPORT

INADEQUATE SERVICES (MEDICAL, SOCIAL, ETC)

INACCESSIBLE BUILDINGS (SCHOOLS, OFFICES, HOSPITALS)

9.1.3   Discussion of the three models of disability

Time   30–40 minutes

Objective   Participants will be able to analyse which model would be most helpful in creating positive change for disabled people in their community/ country/work.

Preparation   No materials to prepare

Process   After the presentation on the models (see 9.1.2), ask for comments and questions. If they are appropriate, you can refer back to the sub-groups'original ideas (9.1.1), to remind them what they have already identified and to revise what was new about the models for them.

This can lead into a whole-group discussion, based on some or all of the following questions. (If working with a mixed group, observe if there is a difference in the responses of disabled and non-disabled participants, and raise this and its relevance with the group – if they do not comment on it themselves.)

- Do participants recognise any of these models in their own society?
- What are the similarities and the differences?
- Which do they think is most unhelpful to disabled people? Why?
- Which do they like most, why?
- Do they think that a completely different model applies to them? If so, can they describe it? Is it helpful or unhelpful to disabled people?
- Do they think that the social model should be introduced or promoted?
- If yes, why? And how would it need to be modified to fit their local circumstances?
- If no, what would they do instead?

Sum up.

9.1.4   Life stories: activity based on the models of disability

This activity could be done in place of the discussion in 9.1.3.

Time   One hour

Objectives   For participants to use the models as a tool to analyse their impact on disabled people's lives.

Preparation   No materials to prepare

Process   Divide the group into sub-groups of four. Each sub-group will work together to create either a written story or a short play.

The story or play should be in two parts. The first should tell the life story of a disabled person from childhood, in terms of either the medical or charity model of disability.

The second part should re-tell the person's life story from the perspective of the social model of disability.

Participants should create an imaginary disabled person, but may use their own experiences for ideas.

Allow 30–40 minutes, then bring everyone back together. Each sub-group shares its story or play with the whole group.

Allow time for questions, comments, and discussion. You could use some of the questions from exercise 9.1.3 to focus the discussion.

9.1.5 How can I help?

Time 50 minutes

Objective For participants to consider the traditional roles of disability professionals and traditional disability programmes.

Preparation Make copies of Handout 23.

Process Remind participants about the three models of disability (activity 9.1.2).

Divide participants into four numbered groups and give out Handout 23.

Allocate Quotation 1 to Group 1, Quotation 2 to Group 2, etc.

Each small group should discuss their quotation. What do they think about it? How does it relate to their own work? Or to their own experience of disability and impairments?

Ask them, still in their small groups, to exchange experiences and ideas of how to work appropriately with disabled people, and to make three suggestions to present to the whole group.

Bring the whole group back together. One person from each small group should read out their quotation and present their three suggestions. You can write these up on a flipchart (key words only) as they talk.

Sum up.

Facilitator's notes This exercise may be used with DPOs or agency staff (planners, funders, medical staff, social workers, etc.). It needs careful handling, because some people may feel threatened by challenges to their professional authority. You may need to emphasise that working in partnership with disabled people to identify and meet their basic needs (not merely their medical needs, or needs related to rehabilitation) is better for everyone, disabled people and professionals alike.

HANDOUT 23
How can I help?

1. 'The [disability] movement does not reject the role of professionals. What we reject is the inappropriateness of so much of the work that is being done, and the inappropriateness of their attitudes, and the complete inappropriateness of their seeking to represent us. We do need professionals, we need services, we need rehabilitation. But I would hasten to add that rehabilitation is something that happens to us for a very short period in our lives. It is by no means the most important thing in the life of a disabled person.'(Mike du Toit, South Africa)

2. 'I think that professionals ... should be managed by organisations of disabled people. Their job is to deal with the impairment only. But to get them into an activist role is a very dangerous thing, because they have so much power from their expertise ...We should not make them more powerful than they already are.'(B. Venkatesh, India)

3   'Implicit in any model of who we think we are is a message to everyone about who they are ... The more you think of yourself as a "therapist", the more pressure there is on someone else to be a "patient". The more you identify as a "philanthropist", the more compelled someone feels to be a "supplicant". The more you see yourself as a "helper", the more need for people to play the passive "helped". You are buying into, even juicing up, precisely what people who are suffering want to be rid of: limitation, dependency, helplessness, separateness. And that's happening largely as a result of self-image.'(From *How Can I Help?* by Ram Dass and Paul Gorman, London: Rider, 1985)

4   'In a recent survey, disabled people in Uganda were asked to list their needs in order of priority. At the top of their list came income, then housing, then transport, then sex. Rehabilitation came a bad fifth.'

(Quotations 1, 2, and 4 taken from *Disability, Liberation, and Development* by Peter Coleridge (Oxford: Oxfam, 1993))

9.2 Barriers to equal participation

We have seen that the real problem of disability is not physical or mental impairments, but the ways in which society is constructed – in physical, institutional, and attitudinal terms – to exclude disabled people, and to focus solely or mainly on meeting the needs and rights of non-disabled people. In this section we will consider in detail the barriers that prevent disabled people from claiming their rights and impede their participation in society on equal terms with non-disabled people.

9.2.1 Identifying barriers: the wall exercise

Time One hour

Objectives Participants will be able to describe the three principal types of barrier that prevent disabled people from participating in the rest of society.

They will be able to identify and describe the commonest barriers in their own community.

Preparation Prepare three flipchart sheets, one for each of the three principal categories of barrier (**environmental, institutional,** and **attitudinal** – explained in Handout 25). Using Handout 24 as a model, draw a brick or stone wall on each flipchart, with aspects of each type of barrier written on individual bricks. Leave some bricks empty.

Provide post-it notes or small pieces of paper.

Make copies of Handouts 24 and 25.

Process Ask participants to form groups of four. Give each group a pile of post-it notes and some pens.

Ask them to work together to identify the obstacles in their community that prevent or limit disabled people's participation in everyday life. They should think about all types of barriers, not just the physical ones.

They should write a note about each barrier on a separate post-it note.

After 15 minutes, bring the whole group back together, and display the three pre-prepared flipchart sheets next to each other, to form a continuous wall.

Explain that the bricks of the walls represent barriers identified by disabled people in other countries. They have been categorised into three types: **environmental, attitudinal,** and **institutional**. Give people a few minutes to look at them.

Ask one person from each group to come up, one at a time, and stick their post-it notes on to corresponding bricks in the wall. They should announce each barrier as they display it.

If some of their barriers are not included on the wall, they should stick them on to an empty brick under the relevant category.

When this process is finished, review what people have identified. You could use the following questions to draw out they key points.

Questions

Do the barriers shown on the pre-prepared wall resemble disabled people's experience in this particular community?

What are the differences, if any?

Are there any barriers shown on the wall that the group does not understand? Take time to explain them and answer questions.

Was one barrier mentioned several times, indicating perhaps that it is particularly significant?

Are there any barriers on the pre-prepared wall that participants did not identify? Are they applicable to their own experience or not? Use this opportunity to encourage consideration of barriers that participants had not previously thought of as barriers (see facilitator's notes).

Facilitator's notes

Often people fail to identify the family, or political and legal systems, or religion as barriers; but these often play a crucial role in determining the status of disabled people.

Families might be considered a barrier for three main reasons: the commonest is that they tend to overprotect their disabled member and so prevent him or her from developing independence; or they want to help but they lack information, or have the wrong information; or they try to hide or get rid of their disabled relative. Families need to be supported to find appropriate ways to help their disabled members. Some **religions** teach that disability is a punishment for sin, and therefore a source of shame, which leads to the exclusion of the disabled person, and sometimes his or her family, from community life. Disabled people's **lack of access to the political life of their community** or nation means that they are excluded from the policy-making process. So important decisions are made without taking into account their existence, rights, wishes, and needs.

Often participants identify 'other people's attitudes' as a barrier, but only in general terms. The 'wall' device may help them to think more specifically about the particular forms that prejudice can take, including some which might seem benevolent but are in fact oppressive. For example, disabled people are expected to be passive, compliant, and grateful for whatever help other people see fit to give them. If they accept the help, they earn condescending approval – but are still perceived as inferior to the rest of society. If disabled people react against patronising or abusive behaviour, they risk being labelled 'bitter' or 'aggressive'. But who would not react with anger to being locked up in a room at home, or being subjected to years of hospital-isation and pointless, painful operations, or being given 'special' treatment, based on pity? Anger would seem to be the most normal human reaction to such experiences.

The point of this exercise is not to make non-disabled participants feel guilty! Seeing negative attitudes named on the wall allows them to be raised and discussed in a neutral manner, without participants feeling threatened or having to confess. It also allows for the discussion of issues that might otherwise be taboo, for example the negative influence of some religious teaching about disability.

This exercise may also be useful for raising disabled participants' awareness of barriers faced by people with disabilities different from their own: for example, a wheelchair-user may think of access to buildings in terms of ramps and handrails, but may not be aware that changes to lighting and wall textures could make the buildings more accessible for blind people. Likewise, people with physical or sensory disabilities are not necessarily conscious of the particular attitudinal barriers faced by people with learning difficulties.

Link   The wall looks very big, and it seems that it would be hard to dismantle the barriers that disabled people face. Even each individual brick represents a big problem in itself. It may be hard to know what to do, where to start, to solve such problems. The following exercise will give us a method of assessing the whole problem and breaking it down into smaller, more manageable parts. It will help us to decide where we can start taking action, and what needs to be done.

HANDOUT 24
Wall of barriers

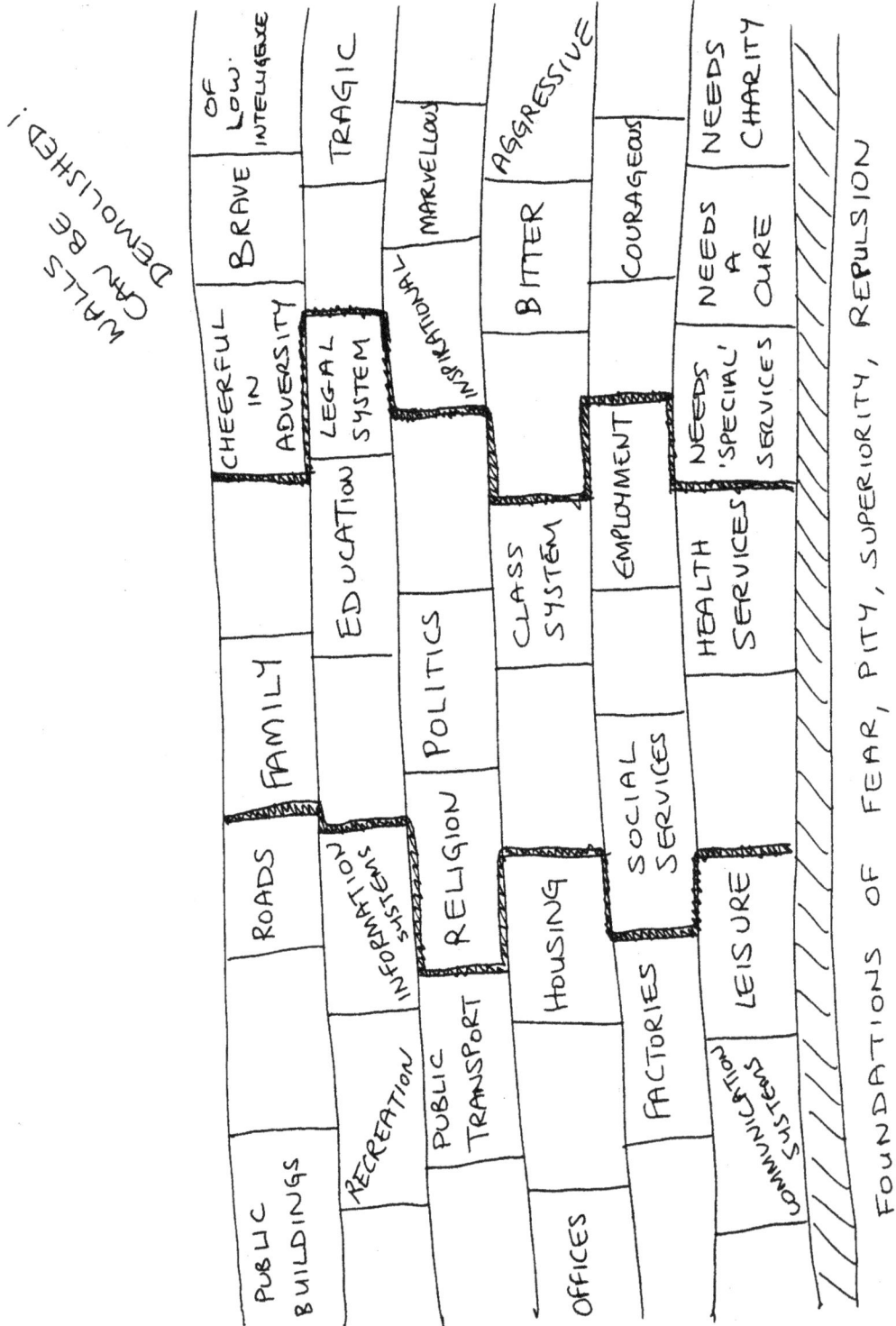

WALLS CAN BE DEMOLISHED!

PUBLIC BUILDINGS — ROADS — FAMILY — EDUCATION — CHEERFUL IN ADVERSITY — BRAVE — OF LOW INTELLIGENCE — TRAGIC

RECREATION — INFORMATION SYSTEMS — RELIGION — POLITICS — LEGAL SYSTEM — INSPIRATIONAL — MARVELLOUS

PUBLIC TRANSPORT — HOUSING — CLASS SYSTEM — BITTER — AGGRESSIVE

OFFICES — FACTORIES — SOCIAL SERVICES — EMPLOYMENT — COURAGEOUS

COMMUNICATION SYSTEMS — LEISURE — HEALTH SERVICES — NEEDS 'SPECIAL' SERVICES — NEEDS A CURE — NEEDS CHARITY

FOUNDATIONS OF FEAR, PITY, SUPERIORITY, REPULSION

HANDOUT 25
Explanation of barriers

Disabled people encounter **environmental barriers** in the following areas:

public transport	housing
public buildings	roads
pedestrianised streets	leisure and recreation facilities
offices and factories	places of worship
communications systems	access to information

It is relatively easy, once alerted, to see the environmental barriers that disabled people face: inaccessible offices, shops, cinemas, toilets; inaccessible public transport; and poor signposting throughout. But it is probably less easy to see how barriers in communications systems are disabling for a range of people, particularly those who are deaf, or hard of hearing, or who have impaired sight.

Take, for instance, bus or railway stations, where travel information is given visually and not always supplemented by information on a loudspeaker system for the benefit of people who are blind or partially sighted. Signs for services on the station may also be difficult to read or badly placed. Deaf people are disadvantaged when last-minute changes to timetables and platforms are announced on the loudspeaker but not altered on indicator boards.

Attitudinal barriers are less obvious than environmental barriers, but they can create major problems for disabled people in their efforts to lead ordinary lives. Disabled people are commonly and automatically assumed to fit into one or more of the following categories:

incapable/inadequate	marvellous/exceptional
brave and courageous	embittered, resentful
tragic	in need of cure
aggressive	inspirational
in need of charity	of low intelligence
smiling and cheerful in adversity	needing 'special' services

These assumptions are damaging and offensive, because they represent unthinking value-judgements which are based on negative generalisations. The person making such a judgement has failed to respond to the individual person who is disabled: his or her personality, strengths, weaknesses, etc.

(continued)

At a deeper level, non-disabled people may respond with feelings that include fear, pity, repulsion, or a sense of superiority. Too often, such assumptions and emotions are reinforced by literature, films, newspapers, and television. The use of negative language reflects and perpetuates prejudices, but disabled people are now setting the pace in rejecting terminology that they feel is offensive. The influence of the Bible is strong in Western culture, and its treatment of disability, particularly in the Old Testament, is generally negative. (However, the New Testament could be interpreted as presenting a less negative view of disability.)

Institutional barriers also exclude or segregate disabled people from many areas of society. Key institutions (or systems) include:

the family	religion
education	health services
social services	the legal system
the class system	employment
the political system	humanitarian and development agencies

Many of these institutional barriers link directly to environmental and attitudinal barriers. But it is only by looking at institutions as a whole that we can identify the way in which these barriers interlock, and see the ways in which disabled people are segregated and disempowered.

In many countries, the marginalisation and exclusion of disabled people (for instance in terms of employment or political representation) is similar to – and compounded by – the negative treatment of women and members of ethnic-minority groups. In the UK, for example, black men and women with impairments experience double disability at all levels.

For disabled people generally, the effects of exclusion from institutions such as education and training are cumulative. Segregated education makes fewer academic demands on pupils, and much smaller schools and classes expose them to a more limited range of cultural stimuli and experiences. The virtual exclusion of disabled people from teacher-training colleges also limits the numbers of qualified disabled teachers who are available as role models for disabled and non-disabled pupils in mainstream schools.

(adapted with permission from *Challenging a Disabling World,* by David Werner, published by Milton Keynes World Development Education Centre, now known as Global Education Milton Keynes)

9.2.2 Problem-tree exercise

Time One hour (or longer)

Objectives Participants will know how to use problem-trees as a method of solving problems.

They will understand the causes of specific barriers that confront disabled people.

They will be able to explain the relationship between the causes and consequences of the problems that they identify.

Preparation Prepare a sample problem-tree for yourself in note form. (You could use the example given below, or compose one that is not necessarily related to disability.)

Process • Draw a picture of a tree, with leaves, trunk, and roots, in the top left-hand corner of a large sheet of flipchart paper.

• Explain that the tree represents an entire problem. The roots symbolise the causes of the problem; the trunk is the statement of the problem itself; and the leaves are the consequences of the problem.

• Label the roots: **causes**; the trunk: **statement of problem**; the leaves: **consequences**.

• Work through your example, to help participants to understand what to do. Start with the problem statement: '*lack of employment for disabled people*', and write this across the middle of the paper. Now work back to find the root(s) of this problem, by asking the question '*Why [is there lack of employment for disabled people]?*'. If there is more than one answer, each of these makes a separate root:
  – because employers don't want to hire disabled people
  – because of the poor quality of education available for disabled people
  – because the State encourages disabled people to take a pension instead of working.

• Work on one answer-root at a time, and keep asking *why?* until you feel you have got to the bottom of the problem. Then work through all the rest of the roots. If there is more than one answer to a 'why?' question at any level of the root, the root could be subdivided. As an illustration, work through the first root:
  – Why [do employers not hire disabled people]?
  – Because they assume or are afraid that they won't be able to do the job. *Why?*

- Because they think that a person's impairment means that he or she can't do anything at all, even tasks that are completely unrelated to the impairment. *Why?*
- Because they don't see anything about the person, apart from his or her impairment. *Why?*
- Because they have never thought about disability in an unprejudiced way. *Why?*
- Because they do not know enough about disability. *Why?*
- Because they have never met a disabled person. *Why?*
- Because disabled people are kept separate from mainstream society. *Why?*

etc., etc.

- Next consider what the consequences of the problem can be. Unemployment can lead to dependence on others (the State, the family), and thus to
  - poverty
  - low status in society
  - lack of friendship and communication
  - isolation
  - low self-esteem
  - depression
  - loss of interest and involvement in life
  - inactivity
  - prejudices about disabled people
  - so the cycle continues.

- Divide people into groups of four, and give out pens and flipchart paper.
- Each group should choose one problem or one barrier from the wall to work on. Ask them to break down in detail all the different elements of the problem that they have chosen. They should start by drawing their tree and then work from the statement to the roots, and then to the consequences. They have 30 minutes for this.
- One person from each small group then presents their tree to the whole group (for no more than five minutes each).
- After the presentations, ask participants what they have learned from their problem-trees. You might focus the discussion on the following questions.

Questions   If at the start of the exercise the problem seemed too big to tackle, how do they feel now?

Use the discussion to draw out learning points such as the following.

- The cyclical link between the causes and consequences of most problems.

- The interlocking barriers that confront disabled people.
- The fact that negative attitudes on the part of non-disabled people are at the root of many problems faced by disabled people.
- The exclusion of disabled people from the process of making policies and decisions.
- The unequal allocation of resources: there is money for the needs of non-disabled people need but not for what disabled people need. Can participants think of some examples of such unequal resource distribution?

Now that they have broken down some barriers into their component layers, can they identify where they might start taking action, and what they might do? (See 9.2.3 and 9.2.4.)

Options   With aid-agency staff or medical professionals, you can ask each group to work on a barrier that is relevant to their line of work. For example: small groups of health-care or rehabilitation workers could examine the assumptions of their profession about the needs of disabled people; the institutional barriers posed by the management of health services; and the environmental barriers posed by the physical design of clinics.

Facilitator's notes   Some groups end their examination of the roots when they get to the point 'because there is no (or not enough) money'. Watch out for this as you go around the small groups. Help them to refocus by encouraging them to keep asking *why*? (*Why is there not enough/no money?*, etc.) This will help them to discover further layers that they had previously not considered, and to challenge the *status quo* in which resources are distributed unfairly.

Here are some examples of unfair distribution which arise from the failure to consult disabled people:

- Non-disabled people use steps to move from one level of a building to another. The space and money needed to construct the steps is never questioned. If the building has more than a certain number of storeys, an elevator will be installed, so that non-disabled people don't have to walk up lots of stairs. Some disabled people need ramps or elevators – but often they are not provided, because they are considered unnecessary or 'not cost-effective' by the non-disabled architects and engineers.

- In many aid agencies, foreign employees are provided with interpreters to enable them to communicate and do their job. This is accepted as a necessary cost, and some people even think it quite prestigious to have an interpreter. In the same agency a deaf person who needs a sign-language interpreter will probably not be employed, because 'there is no money available': the cost of the interpreter is seen as extra and unnecessary. The truth is that the agency can budget for the cost of a sign-language interpreter just as well as for the cost of a foreign-language interpreter. It is a question of what decision makers want to do, not what is possible or impossible.

Options   Some groups get very involved in this exercise, so in order to investigate each root thoroughly you will need to spend further sessions working through them.

Others may not be comfortable with the analytical process required by problem-trees. Instead they might prefer to work on problem-triangles, which also illustrate cause and effect. An example (developed by Halit Ferizi) follows.

- Draw a large triangle on a piece of flipchart paper, as in Handout 26. Label one corner '**Hospital**', one '**Ministry of Health and Welfare**', and one '**Person with disability**'. Across the bottom write '**Pressure sores**' (for people with limited mobility a common and potentially life-threatening condition, which can be prevented by the use of anti-decubitus cushions and other devices).

- Tell the story: a disabled person goes before a medical commission (exclusively composed of non-disabled people) at the hospital to request as a medical essential an anti-decubitus cushion (cost to Welfare branch of the Ministry: $10). The commission rejects her request, saying that unfortunately the Ministry of Health and Welfare (entirely composed of non-disabled people) does not pay for these items. The woman goes home and after several months she develops serious pressure sores. The infection spreads and she becomes seriously ill, requiring hospitalisation and medicines (cost to Health branch of the Ministry: $70). But the infection has spread too far, and she dies (cost: her life).

- The Ministry did not wilfully create conditions for the woman to die. But this type of problem confronts disabled people every day, for multiple reasons: the lack of disabled people in decision-making positions and positions of authority; lack of control by disabled people over resources and budgets; lack of information; lack of communication (in this case between government departments), etc. etc.

- Ask participants to work in pairs for 30 minutes to define their own problem-triangle, based on a situation that they themselves have experienced.

- Bring everyone back for feedback, discussion, and conclusions.

HANDOUT 26
Problem-triangle

MINISTRY OF
HEALTH & WELFARE

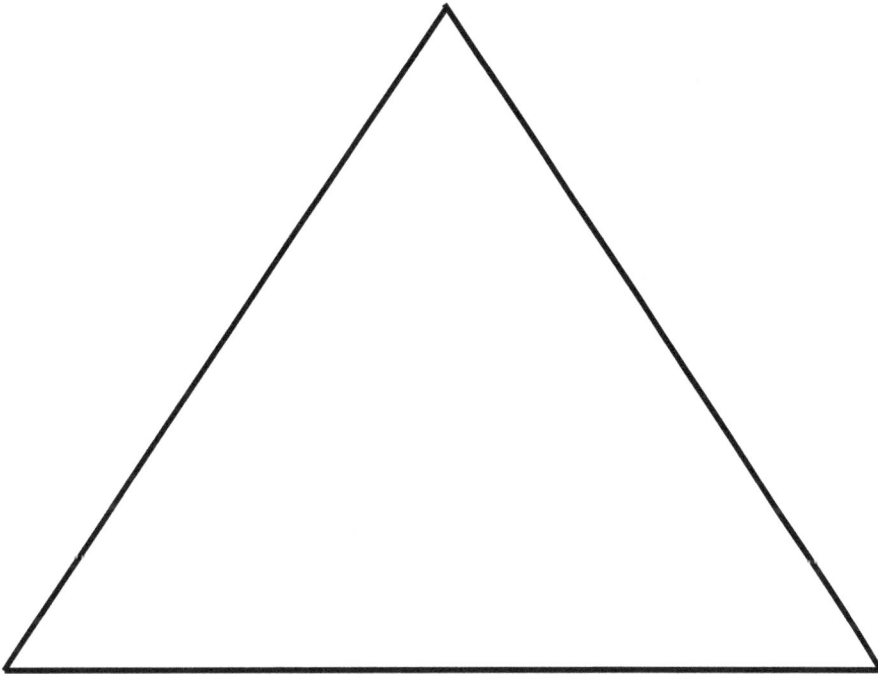

HOSPITAL   DISABLED PERSON

9.2.3   Action-planning to overcome barriers: for DPOs and local community members

If the aim of the workshop includes identifying specific actions that participants will carry out to start breaking down barriers (or solving other types of problems), you can use the problem-tree as a starting point, and then do small-group work to decide what to do, when, with whom, etc. The whole of the next chapter is devoted to action-planning. You will find more ideas for activities there.

In any action-planning exercise, encourage participants not to complicate matters unnecessarily. This is not to discourage vision and ambition, but to encourage people to start with what is possible, develop a strong base, and then go forward from there. Changing attitudes is the first and most important step, which will then lead on to other things. Often this does not require a lot of preparation and resources. For example:

- A group of disabled people could support each other to become visible in their community, on the streets, in the places where everyone else goes – whether or not they are easily accessible. This is not necessarily an easy process: it is hard to cope with being stared or laughed at, and there are of course physical barriers to contend with. But with time, insistence, contact, and familiarity, the attitudes of the non-disabled community will start to change. From that, further actions can be developed.

- Schools and workplaces could invite disabled people to come and talk about their lives, what they do, their dreams, their disability, and the barriers that confront them.

- Non-disabled family members could make a commitment not to talk in place of, and make decisions for, their disabled relative.

9.2.4   Action planning to overcome barriers: for aid-agency staff

You could use the same action-planning exercises as for DPO and community members, or you could design activities which focus specifically on the participants' area of special interest or expertise.

Example 1   With emergency-relief or development engineers, ask them to bring with them to the workshop a plan or drawing of a structure that they are currently working on which does not make allowance for disabled people's access. Invite representatives of DPOs (for example, someone with impaired mobility, and someone with impaired sight) to come and describe the commonest access problems that they experience in typical buildings in the community. (If speakers are not available, find out beforehand from local disabled people what problems of access are posed by typical buildings in their community, and write notes of what they tell you.)

Use the access checklist given at the beginning of Chapter 7, and/or obtain the ISO Building Guidelines (see Resources section for details). Copy and distribute one or both of these texts to participants, who should work in pairs, referring to the checklist/ISO guidelines and devising ways to make their structure accessible. Stress that the ISO Guidelines are guidelines: they will probably need to be adapted and modified to take into account local building practices, available materials, etc. They are, however, very helpful, because they give precise measurements, as well as suggestions for modifications which might not immediately occur to an engineer. The pairs should report back to the whole group, and the DPO representatives should give advice and comments.

Example 2   To consider the issue of employment opportunities for disabled people in aid agencies, enlist the help of DPO representatives. They might accompany participants to their offices, identify the physical barriers there, and work out how they could be removed (although in some cases, the only remedy will be for the office to move to a new location, which it should!). The access checklist in Chapter 7 may also be used for guidance. While at their offices, participants should pick up a copy of the latest 'jobs vacant' announcement issued by the office.

When the group re-assembles, ask for feedback on the physical barriers that they found, and ways in which they might be removed.

Next, ask about the vacancy announcements: did any disabled people apply? If yes, with what result? If not, can they think why not?

What could the office staff do to encourage disabled applicants to apply? What are the views and advice of the DPO representatives?

Often disabled people do not apply for jobs because the discrimination that they face is so widespread that they assume there is no chance at all that they will be hired. One response to this would be to add a sentence such as 'Disabled people are encouraged to apply' or 'All disabled applicants will be interviewed' at the bottom of the advertisement. Often disabled people have no way of knowing when vacancies occur. Information should be made accessible, perhaps by circulating announcements of vacancies to DPOs.

Another major obstacle that disabled people may face is lack of work experience. Many have been so discriminated against that a job has never seemed like a possibility to them. But the prospective employer should consider whether an applicant has other life skills which may be transferable: could training be offered, if the applicant has the required aptitude for the job? This is already commonly done when non-disabled staff are recruited.

9.2.5 Barriers: a case study

Another way to help participants to think about what they might do to break down the barriers faced by disabled people is to work through case studies in small groups. To be most effective, the studies should arise from real-life examples; they should address issues that participants themselves are likely to encounter; and they should be set in a context that is relevant, or familiar, to participants. This means that wherever possible it is best to find, or design, situation studies that specifically suit your workshop. In the following example, we chose to start with a case study from a different country and then apply the learning to the local context, because this may be a less threatening way for people to start to deepen their understanding of barriers (and perhaps to recognise their own contribution to their construction).

Objectives   Participants will apply a barriers analysis to the real-life situation of Mahfuja Akhter Shapla, a young disabled woman in Bangladesh.

Participants will compare Shapla's situation with their own, or with that of disabled people in their own country, and identify similarities and differences.

Preparation   For each participant, make one copy of Shapla's story in Chapter 12.

Process   Give a copy of the case study to each participant and give them five minutes to read it. (If anyone cannot see or read, read the case study aloud to the whole group.)

Ask for a volunteer to read the study aloud to the whole group.

Ask participants to form small groups of four.

Explain that the group should now work together, for 15 minutes, and between them answer the following questions.

- What barriers has Shapla experienced, and how has she overcome them?
- What are the similarities between her experiences and those of disabled people in your country?
- What are the differences?

Bring the group back together, and ask them to present their answers.

In the whole group, ask participants if they have any advice or suggestions for Shapla. And what, if anything, have they learned from her experiences?

9.3   Disabled people's rights: human rights

This section is in two parts. The first introduces the idea and principles of human rights in general, with reference to disability rights as part of the whole. The second part focuses specifically on the human rights of disabled people.

It is not suggested that all of the activities in both parts would be done in one workshop, although they are presented with a certain sequential logic. Deciding which activities to combine will depend largely on the participants' prior experience and knowledge; but even with participants who are familiar with the general principles of human rights, it is recommended to use one or two of the activities from the first part, in order to emphasise the point that disabled people's rights are not something separate or special, but part of the broad range of human rights. So, when claiming their rights, disabled people are not asking for anything special or extra (which is a common misconception).

In many countries, people's initial understanding of the concept of human rights may be limited to a fairly narrow, political interpretation, based on the abuse of individuals by (usually) the State, expressed for example in the form of torture, politically motivated killing, or imprisonment of dissenters. Especially at times of economic or political crisis, or where the rights of the entire population are not respected, some participants may argue, 'It is pointless to think about disabled people's rights when everyone's rights are being abused', or 'We need to sort out this economic (political) crisis first, before we can think about disabled people's rights.'

The point to keep in mind is that the rights of disabled people are usually denied on an everyday basis that is additional to the abuse or denial experienced by the whole population, whether or not there is a national crisis. It is important therefore to keep participants focused on disabled people's specific, everyday experience of human-rights violations, about which usually something can be done immediately.

Here are two examples that might help you (and participants) to think through the issue:

Freedom of movement: where freedom of movement is restricted for all people (disabled and non-disabled) in a context of social unrest and police controls, the freedom of movement of many disabled people may be even more restricted by their own family, who do not want them to go outside the house and be seen by neighbours, or who don't regard a prosthesis as a priority and use their savings to buy a TV set instead.

Employment: in the UK and USA (whose economies and political situations are generally considered to be stable), about 67 per cent of disabled people of working age are unemployed. In the UK, the government often claims lack of money as a reason why it cannot ensure that disabled people have the same rights as the rest of the population – but every year it spends billions of pounds on sophisticated weapons and the armed forces. Economic and political stability are largely irrelevant: what matters is how resources are distributed (however large or small those resources are), and who decides how they are distributed (usually non-disabled people).

If participants are having difficulty with these concepts, activity 9.3.5 may help.

9.3.1 Fairness and rights: camouflage energiser

Time 30 minutes

Objectives Participants will be able to identify and question unfairness.

They will be able to explain the link between rights and fairness.

Preparation Take three balls of wool of different colours. One ball should be a distinctive colour, such as red or bright purple; the others should be colours which blend with the indoor or outdoor surroundings.

Cut out 30 pieces of the distinctively coloured wool, and 20 pieces each of the other coloured wools.

Hide them outside, or in a room other than the workshop room.

Process Divide participants into three teams. Each team should be assigned a colour of wool to look for.

Give them a time limit (10 minutes) and agree on a time-up signal.

Count how many pieces of wool of their colour each team was able to find. The winner is the team with the largest number of pieces.

The team which is looking for the distinctively coloured wool will probably win, because it is easier to find, and there are more pieces of that colour.

Ask the questions below.

Questions What did it feel like to be on the winning team?

What did it feel like to be on the other team?

Which team found most pieces? Why?

If we played again, which team would you like to be on? Why?

Is the game fair?

Can it be made fair? (By making the rules and chances equal for all players)

Think about your community: is everything fair? Who are the people for whom it is not fair? Why? What can we do to make it fair(er)?

Facilitator's notes Use this discussion to draw out from participants the idea that giving equal rights to everyone – the same starting point, the same opportunities – is a way to make things fair. You can also use it to identify which groups of people – including disabled people – do not have fair and equal opportunities, a fact which is developed in more detail later.

Options   If participants include people with impaired sight, instead of differently coloured wool you could use objects that are clearly identifiable because of their different textures, in a room that is known to participants. If participants include those for whom movement causes pain, use a word game or guessing game instead, adapting it to make it unfair to one of the teams.

Link   We have seen why rights are defined and asserted (to try to make things fair for everyone). Now we shall spend time looking at what rights we have.

(adapted with permission from *First Steps*, published by Amnesty International)

9.3.2 **What rights do we have? The calendar game**

Time   One hour

Objectives   Participants will be able to list a range of human rights.

They will be able to explain that rights are universal and indivisible.

Preparation   Gather about 12 photographs or other good-quality pictures of people from around the world, in as many different situations as possible. Include at least a couple that include disabled people. Calendars, newspapers, and magazines are good sources for pictures. If these are not available, you can draw sketches.

Prepare copies of the Simplified Version of the Universal Declaration of Human Rights (Handout 27).

Process   Spread the pictures on the floor or on a table where everyone (who can see) can see them.

Ask participants to work in pairs, and to choose one picture per pair. (If the group is small, each pair may take two pictures.)

Participants have five minutes to discuss their picture and imagine:
- who is in the picture?
- where are they?
- what are they doing?
- how are they feeling?
- what rights are illustrated in the picture?

Each pair then shows their picture to the whole group, and reports back on the rights that they have identified (allow five minutes for each pair).

As participants report back, write up the rights that they identify on a large sheet of paper, or on a blackboard.

Ask participants what the pictures tell them about rights (that they are universal: they apply to everyone, everywhere, including disabled people).

Explain that the rights that they have identified (and others) have been written up in an internationally accepted document, called the Universal Declaration of Human Rights, which nearly every country in the world has signed.

Hand out the Simplified Version of the UDHR, and give participants a few minutes to read through it. (For groups with sight-impaired or non-literate members, read it aloud, or ask the other group members to read it aloud in turn, one right each.)

Use this opportunity to highlight any significant rights which were not identified during the picture exercise, and/or to answer any questions that might arise.

Now ask participants to divide the pictures into piles, each pile corresponding to one of the points in the Simplified Version of the UDHR. Participants will soon realise that this task is impossible, as all rights are linked, so one picture will represent several rights at once. Use this opportunity to explain that rights are 'indivisible'(you cannot enjoy some rights while denying others).

Options   If you want to focus on children's rights (including those of disabled children), or on women's rights (including disabled women), all the pictures that you choose should depict children or women. Use them with the Convention on the Rights of the Child or Convention on the Elimination of All Forms of Discrimination Against Women (both available from your nearest UN office or on the Internet at www.unhchr.ch/html/intlinst.htm).

For groups who include people with impaired sight, working in pairs, one partner (a sighted person) should make a story about their picture, and tell it to his or her partner (a sight-impaired person), who should decide what rights are conveyed by the picture.

(adapted with permission from *First Steps*, published by Amnesty International)

HANDOUT 27
Simplified version of the Universal Declaration of Human Rights

Summary of Preamble

The General Assembly recognises that the inherent dignity and the equal and inalienable rights of all members of the human family is the foundation of freedom, justice and peace in the world. Human rights should be protected by the rule of law. Friendly relations between nations must be fostered. The peoples of the UN have affirmed their faith in human rights, the dignity and the worth of the human person, and the equal rights of men and women and are determined to promote social progress, better standards of life and larger freedom, and have promised to promote human rights and a common understanding of these rights.

A summary of the Universal Declaration of Human Rights

1.   Everyone is free, and we should all be treated in the same way.

2.   Everyone is equal, despite differences in skin colour, sex, religion, language, for example.

3.   Everyone has the right to life and to live in freedom and safety.

4.   No one has the right to treat anyone as a slave or make anyone a slave.

5.   No one has the right to hurt or torture another human being.

6.   Everyone has the right to be treated equally by the law.

7.   The law is the same for everyone; it should be applied in the same way to all.

8.   Everyone has the right to ask for legal help when their rights are not respected.

9.   No one has the right to imprison another human being unjustly or to expel another human being from his or her own country.

10.   Everyone has the right to a fair and public trial.

11.   Everyone should be considered innocent until guilt is proven.

12.   No one has the right to enter another's home or open another's letters without a good reason.

13.   Everyone has the right to travel as they wish.

14.   Everyone has the right to go to another country and ask for protection if they are being persecuted or are in danger of being persecuted.

15. Everyone has the right to belong to a country. No one has the right to prevent anyone from belonging to another country if they wish to.

16. Everyone has the right to marry and have a family.

17. Everyone has the right to own property and possessions.

18. Everyone has the right to practise and observe all aspects of their own religion and change their religion if they want to.

19. Everyone has the right to say what they think and to give and receive information.

20. Everyone has the right to take part in meetings and to join associations in a peaceful way.

21. Everyone has the right to help to choose and take part in the government of their own country.

22. Everyone has the right to social security and to opportunities to develop their skills.

23. Everyone has the right to work for a fair wage in a safe environment and to join a trade union.

24. Everyone has the right to rest and leisure.

25. Everyone has the right to an adequate standard of living and medical help if they are ill.

26. Everyone has the right to go to school.

27. Everyone has the right to share in their community's cultural life.

28. Everyone must respect the 'social order' that is necessary for all these rights to be available.

29. Everyone must respect the rights of others, the community, and public property.

30. No one has the right to take away any of the rights in this declaration.

(Reproduced with permission from *First Steps*, published by Amnesty International)

9.3.3   **The imaginary country**

This exercise may be done as an alternative to the Calendar Game.

Objectives   Participants will be able to

- explain how human rights are based on our own inherent needs;
- recognise that we value some rights more highly than others, depending on our own situation, but that every right is important to someone;
- list human rights contained in the UDHR.

Preparation   Prepare copies of the simplified version of the Universal Declaration of Human Rights (Handout 27).

Process   Divide people into groups of five or six people.

Read out the following scenario: 'Imagine that you have discovered a new country, where no one has lived before, and where there are no laws and no rules. You and the other members of your group will be the settlers in this new land. You do not know what social position you will have in the new country.'

Each participant should individually list three rights which they think should be guaranteed for everyone in this new country.

Now ask them to share and discuss their lists within their small group. Together they should select 10 rights which their whole group thinks are important.

Now ask each group to give their country a name and write their 10 chosen rights on flipchart paper.

Each small group presents its list to the whole group. As they do this, you should make a main list, which should include all of the different rights contained in the small-group lists. Some rights will be mentioned several times; write them on the main list once, and tick them each time they are repeated.

When all the groups have presented their lists, identify the rights on the main list that overlap or contradict each other. Can the list be rationalised? Can some similar rights be grouped together?

When the main list is completed, compare it with the Simplified Version of the UDHRs. What are the similarities and differences between your list and the UDHR?

Use the following questions to draw out the learning points.

Questions   Did your ideas about the importance of certain rights change during this activity?

Are some of these rights denied here [in the region, country etc. where the participants come from]? If yes, how does that feel? If no, how would life be if they were denied?

Do you now want to add any rights to the final list?

Did anyone list a right which was not included in any of the lists?

Is it useful for us to make such a list? Why?

(adapted with permission from *First Steps*, published by Amnesty International)

Link   If we all have rights, we all have a responsibility to respect other people's rights. In the next exercise we shall consider what this means in practice in our lives.

9.3.4   Rights and responsibilities

Time   30 minutes

Objectives   Participants will be able to understand and explain the link between rights and responsibilities.

Preparation   No materials to prepare.

Process   Ask participants to form pairs. Each participant should write down three rights which he or she thinks are important in the context of the training workshop, and three which they consider they should have at home – for example, the right to contribute their thoughts and ideas to family discussions.

Ask each person to swap lists with his or her partner. Each person should think of the responsibilities which correspond with each right that the partner listed – for example, the responsibility to respect the contributions that other family members make to discussions.

From their lists, every pair reports to the whole group two rights and their corresponding responsibilities. The facilitator writes the responsibilities and rights on a flipchart or blackboard.

Start a discussion, using the following questions.

Questions   Was it easy or hard to think of the responsibility corresponding to each right?

Can someone think of an example where a right and a responsibility conflict?

How could that conflict be resolved? Is there always a solution?

(adapted with permission from *First Steps*, published by Amnesty International)

9.3.5 'Choosing' rights

This is a good exercise to do if you have already spent time working on the UDHR, and the group has considered what rights are, and how declarations of rights reflect our own needs (in 9.3.2 *The calendar game* and 9.3.3 *The imaginary country game*, for example), and you want to focus on the concept that we value some rights more highly than others, depending on our own situation, and how this affects the lives of disabled people.

Time One hour

Objectives Participants will be able to explain how we value some rights more highly than others, depending on our own situation, but they will understand that every right is important to someone.

They will have considered how the economic/political situation in their country does or does not have an impact on the rights of disabled people.

Preparation No materials to prepare

Process Either: If you have a list of rights on flipchart paper produced during a previous exercise, such as a brainstorm or the Calendar Game, display it where everyone can see it. For groups which include non-literate or sight-impaired people, read the list aloud.

Or: If you do not have a list, go through steps 1 to 6 of *The imaginary country* (activity 9.3.3).

Divide participants into groups of four or five. Give them flipchart paper and pens, and ask them to discuss as a group what three rights they personally think are most important, and three which they think they could live without. They should draw a line down the middle of the page, and on one side of the line write (or draw symbols to represent) the three that they decide are most important, and on the other side the three that they could live without. (20 minutes)

Bring the whole group back together and ask each small group to present their findings. Explain before they start that this is not a test: there are no right or wrong answers. Ask if anyone has comments or questions.

Facilitate a discussion, using the questions below, if helpful, to bring out the learning points.

Questions Did your ideas about which rights were most/least important change during this activity?

Did it happen that one group identified a very important right which another group thought they could live without? How did that make you feel? (Ask the people who thought it less important first, then the group who thought it very important.)

Did your personal circumstances affect your choice of rights? Why? Why not?

Has the situation in your country affected your choice of rights? Why? Why not?

Facilitator's notes

The exercise from which this was adapted has been used in many countries by Amnesty International. They found that in countries where war is a problem, students value the right to life most highly, while in countries with economic problems the right to work comes first.

This exercise can be combined with activities in the next section which focus on the rights of disabled people to explore the idea that there never is a 'right time' to start working on disabled people's rights: experience from countries all over the world, including the so-called 'developed' ones, shows that there seems always to be 'just one more problem' to solve, one other thing which is more important than the situation of disabled people. Waiting for the 'right time' condemns disabled people to suffer continued violations of their rights.

In places where crisis is given as the reason for not respecting disabled people's rights, you might want to explore, non-confrontationally, whether disabled people's rights were respected before the crisis began. (Make sure that people do not confuse State benefits with rights and equal participation.) You should ask about the impact of the crisis on disabled people (it probably makes life even harder for them, as they are accorded even less priority than usual by the rest of society); and if/how/why participants think that the end of the current crisis is going to achieve the realisation of disabled people's rights, given that this was not the situation before the crisis began.

The learning point to draw out is that the right time to start working for disabled people's rights is NOW. This exercise can also reinforce previous learning about the fact that we all have rights all of the time, even if they are being denied or abused, and about the need to challenge abuse and claim rights at the everyday level: in the family, within DPOs, within the community.

9.3.6 Stereotyping and discrimination: Know your apple

Time 40 minutes

Objectives For participants to understand the concept of stereotyping, and the role that stereotypes can play in discrimination and the abuse of human rights.

(Optionally) to give participants practice in facilitation.

Preparation Bring in apples, or other local fruit, all of the same type, enough for one per participant; and one bag or box to put them in.

Process Ask participants to sit in a circle. Ask them: what are the characteristics of apples? Are all apples the same? Give one apple to each person.

Each person observes his/her own apple for three minutes. Tell them to notice its colour, bumps, marks, or other things that make it different from other apples.

Collect the apples into the bag or box, and mix them up.

Give out the apples, one by one, passing them around the circle. Each person examines each apple in turn. If a participant recognises his/her apple, s/he keeps it.

When all the participants have claimed their apples, they may eat them.

Discuss with participants what they think the point of the exercise is. You can ask some or all of the following questions to help the discussion and to help people learn.

Questions Was it easy (or difficult) to recognise their own apple?

If at the beginning of the exercise some participants thought that all apples looked the same, what do they think now?

The assumption that people are all the same if they share one characteristic (for example, disabled people, African people, doctors) is called 'stereotyping'. Can participants think of examples when they have been stereotyped, or examples of when they have stereotyped other people?

Are stereotypes helpful? Why? Why not?

What are common stereotypes about disabled people? What is the effect of these stereotypes for disabled people? What is the effect for the rest of society?

Facilitator's notes   These are some of the learning points to bring out through the discussion:

- Stereotypes usually express negative prejudices about a group of people, and are usually untrue.

- One of the unhelpful things about stereotypes is that they do not recognise that we are all different but equal, that we are all different but have the same rights.

- Stereotypes usually ignore the value and potential of individuals – which results in some people thinking that they are superior to some other individual or group of people. This leads to discrimination and the abuse of rights.

- Common stereotypes about disabled people are that they are sick, abnormal, and limited in ability. These stereotypes have a negative impact on disabled people's lives, leading to the abuse of their rights and their exclusion from mainstream life. Society suffers, because it needs everyone's contributions. (You could give an example of a local disabled person, or internationally known disabled person and his or her contribution to science, art, politics, the community, etc.)

Handout 28 could be distributed at the end of a workshop as a useful reminder of the principal learning points about human rights.

(adapted with permission from *First Steps*, published by Amnesty International)

HANDOUT 28
Human rights – a summary of learning points

- Rights are universal (everyone has them).

- Rights are indivisible (you cannot enjoy some rights if others are denied).

- Our perception of the importance of rights is based on our own needs: we value some rights more highly than others, depending on our own situation, but every right is important to someone.

- Every right has a corresponding responsibility.

- Rights are inalienable: you can't buy or inherit them; we all have them because we are human.

- We have rights even when it seems we do not: even when they are being denied or abused.

- We need to know what our rights (and responsibilities) are, in order to claim them for ourselves and to respect those of other people.

9.3.7   Global and local discrimination

Time   30 minutes

Objective   Participants will understand some types of discrimination experienced by disabled people around the world, and compare them with their own local situation.

Preparation   Choose five or six of the statistics given in Handout 29 and write them on flipchart paper.

Process   Display the list and talk briefly about the statistics that you have chosen.

For each statistic, ask participants to comment on the comparable situation of disabled people in their country/region/village, etc. Is it similar? different? in what way?

Do disabled people in their community encounter any other types of discrimination, not on this list? What are they?

Optional activity   To take this exercise further, you can ask participants to work in pairs on some research in their community. Each pair should choose one of the statistics from Handout 29, and investigate the corresponding conditions in their community. (They should try to form a general impression, rather than trying to assemble precise statistics, which will probably not be possible.) They can do this by talking to (other) disabled people, visiting schools, workplaces, talking to local officials, etc. This should be done as homework, and participants should be asked to report back at a future session.

Facilitator's notes   The statistics in Handout 29 illustrate the negative discrimination faced by disabled people throughout the world. It includes some information from 'stable'countries in Europe and the USA, which can help you to dispel the common myth that everything is fine for disabled people there.

Link   Because disabled people are one of the groups of people whose needs are most commonly not met, and whose rights are denied, the United Nations has produced international instruments (documents) which, in addition to the Universal Declaration of Human Rights, reaffirm disabled people's rights. Knowing about the rights that are stated in these documents can be the starting point of a campaign to challenge the *status quo* in our own communities.

HANDOUT 29
Disability – some global statistics

There are estimated to be more than 500 million disabled people in the world.

There are 42 million disabled people in the European Union (EU), of whom 51 per cent are women.

On average, between 4 and 10 per cent of any country's population may be described as disabled. However, in South Africa the figure is nearer to 13 per cent, and in the USA the figure is 20 per cent.

The UN estimates that disabled people are two to three times more likely than non-disabled people to live in poverty.

20 million people worldwide who need wheelchairs do not have them.

In some countries, 90 per cent of disabled children will not live beyond the age of 20.

In some countries, 90 per cent of children with learning difficulties do not live beyond their fifth birthday.

Throughout the world, most so-called 'public' transport is inaccessible to disabled members of the public.

In Sweden, which has some of the most enlightened housing policies in Europe, of those disabled people who do not live in institutions, approximately 85 per cent live in housing with difficult access.

Worldwide, access to communications and information, especially for those with impaired sight or hearing, or learning difficulties, is limited (and often non-existent).

In some hospitals in Europe, the medical records of disabled people who are not dying contain the phrase 'Do not resuscitate in the event of heart failure'.

98 per cent of disabled people living in developing countries have no access to rehabilitation services.

(continued)

In Hong Kong, 52 per cent of disabled children do not receive any education.

In India, 98 per cent of disabled boys do not receive any education.

Only 0.3 per cent of disabled children in the UK succeed in entering higher education.

In Tunisia, 85 per cent of disabled adults are unemployed.

In the USA, 67 per cent of disabled adults are unemployed.

Between 50 and 70 per cent of disabled people are unemployed in the European Union. Those with jobs are usually underemployed – not reaching their full potential – and underpaid.

In Europe 400,000 disabled people working in sheltered, supported, or open employment have no proper labour contracts and are outside the protection of labour law.

In some countries, disabled people are denied their right to seek asylum.

The use of sign language is suppressed in some countries.

In many countries disabled people are denied their right to vote or participate in politics.

(*Sources*: Disability Awareness in Action; Disabled Peoples' International; United Nations)

9.3.8   The evolution of documented rights for disabled people

Time   30 minutes

Objective   To give an overview of the development of the codified rights of disabled people.

Preparation   Copy Handout 30 on to a large sheet of flipchart paper.

Make individual copies of Handout 30.

Process   Put up the flipchart display, and give a commentary on it – for example:

- The most relevant of the documents (apart from the UDHR) were developed from the 1980s onwards. 1981 was the 'International Year of Disabled People'. Its motto was *Complete Participation and Equality.*' It resulted in the 1982 UN Declaration of the Rights of Disabled People.

- However, one year was not enough to make much positive change, so the UN held an International Decade of Disabled People from 1983 to 1992, leading to a worldwide programme of action. This was influenced by the growing Disability Movement (disabled people organising, speaking, and acting for themselves).

- One of the results of this was the production, in October 1993, of the UN Standard Rules on the Equalisation of Opportunities for Persons with Disabilities ('the Standard Rules'). Implementation of the rules began on 1 January 1995. The UN appointed a 'special rapporteur', whose duty is to report to the UN General Assembly on how the implementation of the rules is going. The first round of reporting took place in 1997.

- The Standard Rules are important, because they are the most comprehensive documentation of disabled people's rights and the conditions that society needs to create in order to fulfil those rights. They refer to the obligations of signatory States, but also set standards for the rest of us to aim for.

- The Rules are important also because they are written according to principles defined by disabled people's organisations themselves. These include the principle of equal participation in mainstream society. This is very different from previous ideas about disabled people's needs and rights, which generally led to the creation of separate and segregated facilities and services for disabled people, which was generally harmful. The new approach is a great advance.

HANDOUT 30
The development of codified rights for disabled people

1948   Universal Declaration of Human Rights

1981   International Year of Disabled People (motto: *Complete Participation and Equality*)

1982   Declaration of the Rights of Disabled People

1983–1992   International Decade of Disabled People

1993   Standard Rules on the Equalisation of Opportunities for Persons with Disabilities

1995   Start of Implementation of Standard Rules

1997   First report of UN Special Rapporteur

9.3.9 **Applying the UN Standard Rules to real life**

Time   30 minutes

Objective   For participants to become familiar with the UN Standard Rules on the Equalisation of Opportunities for Persons with Disabilities, and to begin to apply them to their own local context

Preparation   Distribute Handout 31 the day before the session, and ask participants to read it in advance. (This activity is suitable only for fully literate and sighted participants.)

Process   Introduce the topic of the UN Standard Rules. The following notes are based on an Information Kit written by Agnes Fletcher and published by Disability Awareness in Action (1995).

- The Standard Rules cover all aspects of disabled people's lives. They offer detailed guidance to show how governments can make social, political, and legal changes to ensure that disabled people become full and equal citizens of their societies.

- They require a strong political and practical commitment by States to take action to equalise opportunities for disabled people.

- Very importantly, they provide an international monitoring system to help to ensure that the Rules are effective. They also provide the basis for technical and economic co-operation among States, the United Nations, and other international organisations.

- Although States cannot legally be forced to implement them, the Rules should become an accepted standard internationally when they are used by a large number of States.

- The adoption of the Standard Rules marks the fact that the international community is starting to understand that disability is a human-rights issue, and that disabled people's rights are abused in every country in the world.

Divide participants into groups of four or five.

Each group should take a different Rule (or set of Rules) from the UN Standard Rules and discuss its relevance to their work or life, and consider how they can ensure that it is applied in their work or life. It is probably simpler if you allocate Rules to groups, rather than allowing them a free choice. Emphasise any Rules that are particularly relevant to the participant group (for example, for medical staff of international NGOs and agencies, Rules 2, 3, 4, 19, 21).

HANDOUT 31
The UN Standard Rules on the Equalisation of Opportunities for Persons with Disabilities

1.   PRECONDITIONS FOR EQUAL PARTICIPATION

Rule 1: Awareness-raising
'States should take action to raise awareness in society about persons with disabilities, their rights, their needs, their potential and their contribution.'

There are nine recommendations under this Rule. They include providing information in accessible forms; supporting public information campaigns about disability; encouraging positive portrayals of disabled people in the media; and educating disabled people about their rights and potential.

Rule 2: Medical care
'States should ensure the provision of effective medical care to persons with disabilities.'

There are six recommendations under this Rule. They include the importance of ensuring that disabled people have the same level of medical care within the same system as other members of society; and ensuring that medical and paramedical personnel are trained in relevant treatment methods and technology.

Rule 3: Rehabilitation
'States should ensure the provision of rehabilitation services to persons with disabilities in order for them to reach and sustain their optimum level of independence and functioning.'

There are seven recommendations under this Rule. These include developing national rehabilitation programmes for all disabled people, based on individual needs and principles of full participation and equality; programmes should include a wide range of activities, for the development of self-reliance, assessment, and guidance; disabled people and their families should be empowered; rehabilitation should be available in the local community; disabled people and their families should be involved in rehabilitation, for example as trained teachers, instructors, or counsellors; the expertise of organisations of disabled people should be used when setting up or evaluating rehabilitation programmes.

Rule 4: Support services
'States should ensure the development and supply of support services, including assistive devices for persons with disabilities, to assist them to increase their level of independence in their daily living and to exercise their rights.'

There are seven recommendations under this Rule, all of which support rights-based services – including, among other things, support for cheap and simple technical aids, available free or at low cost; and the involvement of disabled people in the design and support of personal assistance programmes and interpreter services to support integrated living.

2   TARGET AREAS FOR EQUAL PARTICIPATION
This part of the Standard Rules sets out goals in various areas of life. Meeting these goals will help to ensure equal participation and equal rights for disabled people.

Rule 5: Accessibility
'States should recognise the overall importance of accessibility in the process of equalisation of opportunities in all spheres of society. For persons with disabilities of any kind, States should (a) introduce programmes of action to make the physical environment accessible; and (b) undertake measures to provide access to information and communication.'

There are eleven recommendations under this Rule. They include programmes of action, laws, consultation with organisations of disabled people, and the provision of accessible information and sign-language interpretation services.

Rule 6: Education
'States should recognise the principle of equal primary, secondary and tertiary educational opportunities for children, youth and adults with disabilities, in integrated settings. They should ensure that the education of persons with disabilities is an integral part of the education system.'

There are nine recommendations under this Rule, including the support of integrated education through provision of interpreters and other support services; the involvement of parents and organisations of disabled people; and ensuring that services are available to very young disabled children and to disabled adults, particularly women.

(continued)

Rule 7: Employment

'States should recognise the principle that persons with disabilities must be empowered to exercise their human rights, particularly in the field of employment. In both rural and urban areas they must have equal opportunities for productive and gainful employment in the labour market.'

There are nine recommendations under this Rule. They include making sure that employment laws and regulations do not discriminate against disabled people, and taking action to support disabled people in open employment.

Rule 8: Income maintenance and social security

'States are responsible for the provision of social security and income maintenance for persons with disabilities.'

There are seven recommendations under this Rule, aimed at ensuring that disabled people and their supporters get an adequate income which meets the extra costs of disability, and outlining action to be taken.

Rule 9: Family life and personal integrity

'States should promote the full participation of persons with disabilities in family life. They should promote their right to personal integrity and ensure that laws do not discriminate against persons with disabilities with respect to sexual relationships, marriage and parenthood.'

There are four recommendations under this Rule, all focused on making sure that disabled people can be full and active members of a family and have equal opportunities to enjoy a personal life. There are also recommendations to prevent abuse and to improve negative attitudes.

Rule 10: Culture

'States will ensure that persons with disabilities are integrated into and can participate in cultural activities on an equal basis.'

This Rule has three recommendations, including full access to places of cultural activity, and the support of disabled people to use their creative, artistic, and intellectual potential in the whole community.

Rule 11: Recreation and sports

'States will take measures to ensure that persons with disabilities have equal opportunities for recreation and sports.'

This Rule has five recommendations, covering full access to recreational and sporting venues and the encouragement of all tourist authorities to provide services to everyone, including disabled people.

Rule 12: Religion

'States will encourage measures for equal participation by persons with disabilities in the religious life of their communities.'

This Rule has four recommendations, which emphasise the right of disabled people to take part in religious activities of their choice and which indicate ways of achieving this.

3   IMPLEMENTATION MEASURES

This section outlines ways in which the Standard Rules can be carried out effectively.

Rule 13: Information and research

'States assume the ultimate responsibility for the collection and dissemination of information on the living conditions of persons with disabilities and promote comprehensive research on all aspects, including obstacles that affect the lives of persons with disabilities.'

This Rule, with its seven recommendations, says that research should not merely establish the incidence of disability but investigate the status of disabled people within their communities.

Rule 14: Policy-making and planning

'States will ensure that disability aspects are included in all relevant policy-making and national planning.'

This Rule has five recommendations, designed to ensure that disabled people are involved in general policy-making, as well as having separate policies to meet their own needs.

Rule 15: Legislation

'States have a responsibility to create the legal bases for measures to achieve the objectives of full participation and equality for persons with disabilities.'

This Rule includes four recommendations, emphasising the need for legislation to support the rights of disabled people and the need to include organisations of disabled people in drafting and evaluating legislation.

Rule 16: Economic policies

'States have the financial responsibility for national programmes and measures to create equal opportunities for persons with disabilities.'

This Rule has four recommendations to ensure that policies on disability inform the regular budgets of national, regional, and local authorities, and that economic measures are considered to encourage and support equal opportunities for disabled people, particularly at the grassroots.

(continued)

Rule 17: Co-ordination of the work

'States are responsible for the establishment and strengthening of national co-ordinating committees, or similar bodies, to serve as a national focal point on disability matters.'

This Rule has four recommendations and gives independent, permanent, and legal status to national disability co-ordinating committees, with enough funds to fulfil their responsibilities, and allowing a major role for organisations of disabled people.

Rule 18: Organisations of disabled people

'States should recognise the right of organisations of persons with disabilities to represent persons with disabilities at national, regional and local levels.'

This Rule has eight recommendations which emphasise the importance of the direct representation of disabled people in disability-policy making and development, including at the local community level.

Rule 19: Personnel training

'States are responsible for ensuring the adequate training of personnel, at all levels, involved in the planning and provision of programmes and services concerning disabled people.'

This Rule has four recommendations, covering the training of personnel working with disabled people. The Rule emphasises that training must be based on the principles of full participation and equality, and should involve disabled people, their families, and other community members.

Rule 20: National monitoring and evaluation of disability programmes in the implementation of the Standard Rules

'States are responsible for the continuous monitoring and evaluation of the implementation of national programmes and services concerning the equalisation of opportunities for persons with disabilities.'

This Rule has five recommendations, suggesting how Member States can monitor and evaluate their work on equal opportunities for disabled people, in close co-operation with organisations of disabled people.

Rule 21: Technical and economic co-operation

'States, both industrialised and developing, have the responsibility to co-operate in and take measures for the improvement of the living conditions of persons with disabilities in developing countries.'

This Rule has six recommendations, concerning issues of development and technical and economic co-operation, to ensure that, as a priority, disabled people are involved as full and equal participants and recipients in the process.

Rule 22: International co-operation

'States will participate actively in international co-operation concerning policies for the equalisation of opportunities for persons with disabilities.'

This Rule has four recommendations, outlining how Member States can co-operate internationally through the development of policy, inclusion of disability in general standards, policies and activities, and the dissemination of information.

9.3.10 Interviews in pairs

Time One hour

Objectives To share experiences of discrimination and overcoming discrimination

Preparation Write up the interview questions (below) on a flipchart or blackboard.

Process Ask people to work in pairs; they should choose a partner with whom they feel comfortable.

Each participant should take a few minutes to think about an incident when they experienced negative discrimination on account of their disability (or for another reason, if they are not disabled).

Then in pairs they take 15 minutes to interview each other in turn, to find out about their partner's experience. They can use the following questions to help them, or ask their own questions:

- What happened?
- How did you feel?
- How did you react?
- What were your sources of strength that helped you to deal with the situation?
- Were you able to challenge the treatment that you received?
- If yes – how? what did you do? did you challenge it alone? with the support of others? who?
- If no – what prevented you?

Before they start, tell them that no one will be asked to give detailed feedback about their personal experience of discrimination (unless they really want to), so the pairs should be able to discuss their feelings freely.

Bring the whole group back together for general feedback, which you can structure around the following questions.

Questions How did they feel about the exercise? Any comments? questions?

Ask people to share what their sources of strength were, and write these up on a sheet of flipchart paper headed '**Sources of strength**' as they are called out.

Does anyone want to explain what they did, either alone or with others, to challenge the discrimination? Write up contributions (summarised) on a flipchart sheet headed '**Actions**'.

Sometimes problems can be solved by one person, but sometimes they can't. In instances where you couldn't act alone, who were the people who supported you? Write up contributions, as they are called out, on to a flipchart sheet headed '**Allies**'.

For participants who were prevented from challenging their discrimination, what prevented them? Write up their answers on a flipchart sheet headed '**Obstacles**'. Can they think of anything that they might do now to overcome the obstacles? Do other participants have any suggestions? (Add to the **Actions** and **Allies** charts as appropriate.)

Can anyone think of any other ways of challenging discrimination, or of other potential allies? Add to the lists.

Finally, sum up, highlighting possible actions that could be taken by disabled people, their organisations, and their allies to combat negative discrimination.

Option   If there are a lot more non-disabled people in the group than disabled people, ask the non-disabled people to think about incidents where they witnessed discrimination against a disabled person (otherwise the focus of the exercise will be lost).

9.3.11   Improvised drama about disabled people's rights

In addition to (or as an alternative to) the above interviews-based exercise, you could use improvised drama, as a more light-hearted way of tackling the same issues.

Objectives

For participants to reflect on and share their own experiences of human rights.

To draw out lessons about what people can do to ensure that their rights are respected.

Preparation

Work out a short scenario and appropriate roles, based on a common real-life experience of disabled people in the community (see sample below). The drama should be in two halves: the first shows a situation in which a disabled person's rights are ignored or abused; the second takes the same scene but turns it around so that the disabled person achieves what is her or her right.

Find volunteers to participate (with you) in the drama and improvise it with them beforehand or during a break.

Process

Show the two-part drama to the whole group.

Ask for their reactions. What did they see? What happened in the first part, and why? In the second part, and why? What rights-related issues were involved? Has a similar experience ever happened to members of the group?

Divide people into four small groups. If participants are mostly non-disabled people, make sure that at least one disabled person is in each small group. Stress that the non-disabled people must take their lead from the disabled member(s), who will use personal experience to determine the topic for the next activity.

Ask the groups to work out their own drama, based on their own real-life experiences of occasions when their rights as disabled people were not respected, and the consequences of that; the second part should show what they have done, or might do, to change the situation and achieve their rights.

Each small group performs its drama to the whole group.

Facilitate feedback on each drama, using the same questions that you used in your own example, to draw out the concepts and strategies involved.

Sample drama

Three characters: a doctor; a person with a physical disability (who has stomach pains); a neighbour.

Part 1: Disabled person and neighbour enter doctor's office. From the very start, and throughout, the doctor and neighbour do all the talking, as if the disabled person wasn't there, the doctor asking the neighbour what is wrong with the disabled person, and the neighbour describing the fever symptoms that s/he thinks the disabled person has (which are completely different from the person's actual symptoms). The doctor writes out a prescription for medicines for the disabled person's 'fever'. They leave.

Part 2: Disabled person and neighbour return to the doctor's office three days later, because there has been no improvement. This time, when the doctor and neighbour greet each other and start talking, the disabled person interrupts and insists on speaking for him/herself, explaining that the neighbour doesn't know what the symptoms are: the disabled person's father asked the neighbour to give him/her a lift to the clinic and told the neighbour only that his son/daughter wasn't feeling well. The disabled person explains his/her symptoms, being assertive whenever the doctor forgets and starts talking to the neighbour again. Finally the doctor identifies the real problem and makes out a prescription for medicine to cure the person's stomach ache.

Ask people what they thought the learning point of the drama was. Try to elicit statements such as the following: like everyone else, disabled people have (and need to exercise) a right to speak for themselves, otherwise someone else will do it for them, possibly with disastrous results. Disabled people can speak for themselves as individuals, and as an organised group, with one voice, to make changes.

9.3.12   Identifying allies

Change and action come from disabled people and their organisations, but they also need to reach out to the broader community, to gain support and also to become an accepted part of the broader community. This means finding (or, where necessary, making) allies.

Exercise 9.3.10 will usually elicit broad categories of potential allies (friends, family, disabled and non-disabled people, DPOs, community leaders, officials, etc.). You may want to spend more time identifying specific allies, or people who might become allies if lobbied hard enough! This next exercise can help with this.

Time   One hour

Objective   For people to identify (by name or position) and share knowledge of potential allies for change in their community.

Preparation   Review who the participants are and which communities they come from (by village, town, religion, etc., as appropriate). If they are all from the same community, they can do this exercise in self-selected groups of four. If they are from various communities, work out groups of four which contain people who share similar backgrounds.

Provide pens and flipchart sheets.

Process   Ask participants to consider in greater depth the people who can (or might be persuaded to) help to resolve the problems of discrimination that are experienced by disabled people in their community.

Put them in their small groups, with pens and flipchart paper. They have 20 minutes for this small-group work.

Ask each group to choose one specific example of discrimination against disabled people in their community that they would like to stop. They should label their flipchart sheet with a brief description of the discrimination (for example: 'The Elementary School in Village X won't admit blind children', or 'Families in Village Y won't let their disabled female relatives attend the local women's meetings').

As a group they should either brainstorm a list, or draw a community map, of all the people who they think could or might be helpful in solving the problem. (All suggestions should be encouraged.) If they don't know the name of a particular individual, they can identify him or her by their role or position or some other identifier.

Then they should go through their list or map and mark with one colour the people on it who they know would help now. They should use a different colour to identify those who would need to be lobbied before they would get involved.

One person from each small group should be prepared to present their ideas to the rest of the group (five minutes each).

Bring the groups back together and facilitate the feedback. Even where all participants are from the same community, this sharing of ideas can be very helpful, as they will all have their own ideas or contacts.

Take a few minutes to look at all the lists together and ask participants if they want to comment or draw any conclusions. If helpful, use the following questions to facilitate this discussion.

Questions   Are there any surprises?

Are there some people (or groups of people) who appear on all the lists, and others who are issue-specific?

Who are the people whom they can count on now?

Who are the ones who need to be lobbied and persuaded to give their support?

Options   This exercise can be developed further as part of an action-planning session, where participants take as their examples the problems that they intend to work on in real life.

9.3.13   The right to education: whole-group discussion

Facilitator's note   Lack of access to education is one form of human-rights abuse which has a major and life-long disabling impact on people with impairments. Even people who agree with this observation in principle find it hard to imagine how in practice disabled people might get the education that they want. Usually this is because they have never seen such a state of affairs, and they believe that it could happen only in a 'rich' country. Lack of positive models can limit people's understanding of what is possible when it comes to giving disabled children equal opportunity in education. The article in Handout 32 may be used as a stimulus for discussion and to help to dispel myths about disability and education, to show how integrated education is possible. Although the text is long, the article is reproduced in its entirety here, (a) to provide facilitators with a comprehensive overview of the issues and (b) as a resource that facilitators may wish to adapt for workshop activities.

Time   30–60 minutes

Objectives   For participants to consider and discuss issues related to the education of people with impairments.

To provide a forum where conventional assumptions can be challenged.

Preparation   Make copies of Handout 32.

Option   Use a summary of the article as the basis for the discussion. Or conduct the discussion in two parts, first considering the first section, concerned with disability and literacy, and at a later date considering the second section concerned with 'special' versus integrated education.

Process   After reading through the article (and photo captions, or an adaptation of the article) in whatever way works for the group, facilitate a discussion about it. The following questions might help:

- What do participants think about the article/photos?
- What are the most important points that it raises for them? Why?
- How does it relate to the education available for disabled people in their country/region/community?
- Did participants find anything surprising in the article/photos?
- Could they use anything from the article/photos in their own advocacy work?
- What 'special measures' might they lobby their government to provide, in order 'to enable [disabled people] to enjoy equal access to all levels of education', as the author calls for in his final paragraph?

HANDOUT 32
Disability and literacy

One of the objectives of the United Nations Decade of Disabled People was to expand educational opportunities for all disabled people, regardless of the nature of their impairment. In this article (reprinted with permission from CBR News No. 16, 1994, published by Healthlink Worldwide, formerly AHRTAG), Khalfan H Khalfan, Chairperson of Disabled Peoples' International (DPI) Committee on Education, explains why education and literacy are so important for disabled people:

'Education for All' is a basic human right which is guaranteed in the Universal Declaration of Human Rights. Although education is a legal right in most developing countries, in practice it is generally still a privilege for a few people, particularly those who are richer or come from influential families, or who live in cities and big towns. In developing countries, women and girls are much less likely to receive education and therefore fail to learn how to read and write.

Literacy and rights

Literacy is a very important issue for people with disabilities, and it has become even more important in the United Nations Decade of International Literacy. About one billion people in the world today are unable to read to write. Among this group is a high proportion of disabled people. In developing countries more than 75 per cent of the disabled population cannot read or write.

Disabled people are caught in a vicious circle with regard to education and literacy. Many people, including those who are themselves disabled, think of disability as being an individual misfortune or as a punishment for past sins or as a curse. Society as a whole regards disabled people as 'useless'. The first step is to change our own attitudes and behaviour.

Disabled people who are uneducated and illiterate suffer a double disadvantage. In addition to being disabled, they are isolated by being unable to read and write. This makes them more dependent. Ironically, instead of working to give disabled people their basic human rights, such as education and training, society regards disabled people as 'burdens'. These negative attitudes further isolate disabled people from the educational, social, and cultural life in their community.

(continued)

Education and literacy is everyone's responsibility. It needs collective efforts by governments, non-governmental organisations, and international agencies to promote formal education in schools and non-formal education in the community. It is not a matter of financial resources but more a question of commitment and political will. To be long-lasting, literacy needs to go beyond the teaching of reading and writing skills. Education must work towards empowering disabled people and giving them equal opportunities with able-bodied people. Education liberates disabled people from the constraints of dependency. To be educated is to be politically conscious and aware. Education provides access to written knowledge, and knowledge is power.

Special or integrated education?

The political relationship between education and disability has been one of disorder rather than harmony and understanding. While the world claims to be working towards literacy for all people, disabled people are often ignored and neglected, as if they do not belong to the same society.

Some of the most exciting work currently undertaken is within the area of integrated education. This sector has a great deal of potential, both in terms of involvement in community programmes like CBR [community-based rehabilitation] and also in its own right.

The concept of integrated education is the subject of much debate, but it is a debate which should not be defined only by professionals. It is important to involve other people, especially the parents of disabled children. Parents can play an effective role in the development of their children's education, provided that they are empowered to do so, and if their contribution is valued by professionals. This can happen if professionals become flexible and willing to pass on their skills to non-professionals. In the long run this creates better skills and team building.

Why is the education of disabled children marked 'special', and what do we mean by 'special'? When we talk of 'special' education, we immediately think of education which is different or separate from the education of other children. How and why is this education 'special'?

The concept of 'Education for All', put forward at the World Conference on Education in Thailand in 1990, is a challenge to all nations to include disabled children in the education system. But the fact remains that, using the excuse of 'special' education, disabled children are kept out of school or given a poorer form of education than other children. They have little chance to fulfil their needs, even though their families may demand better standards for their disabled children.

Yet we are seeing only one side of the problem – that of disabled children and their parents. But have we ever thought that it is the schools who are failing to meet the learning needs and failing to create the right environment for the individual child?

Many countries develop education policies that include a disability perspective, but how much are disabled people involved in developing this concept? Sometimes professionals and policy makers decide on new concepts and programmes without involving those who are the target group. Disabled Peoples' International (DPI) believes in self-representation and determination; that is why we say *'nothing about us without us'*.

Let me give you an example. When DPI attended the International Task Force on Literacy (ITLF) conference, we insisted that learners must participate in the planning of literacy and post-literacy programmes, because it is the learners who are the target groups and they are the ones who know better than outsiders what their needs are and what their problems are. At the ITFL meeting at Mombasa, DPI insisted on the need for a learners' panel in which the learners and their teachers participated. From that panel, the professionals gained insights and learning which they could never have received by just consulting among themselves.

Therefore, it is essential for an effective programme to involve those who are supposed to benefit from it. But in many cases this is not done. How many countries have involved organisations of disabled people in the formulation of so-called 'special' education policies? What is the involvement of the community? Professionals working alone think only of their own theories and experiments, and the disabled children become experimental guinea pigs.

Even many partner agencies supporting special or integrated education don't have a clear policy when funding education programmes. For example, an agency might fund schools, but the same agency does not consider the policies followed in those schools. They may believe that they are supporting integrated education, but, in practice, they are supporting segregated education.

Today, more than ever before, we need to be aware of the importance of 'Education for All'. Until planners, administrators, and policy

(continued)

makers are aware that people with disabilities are part of the mainstream of humanity and are not 'abnormal' or a 'burden', successful programmes for integrated (mainstream) education and universal literacy will remain only a dream.

In addition, development agencies, both governmental and non-governmental, need to put special emphasis on 'Education for All' and on literacy as part of their programmes. United Nations agencies (such as UNESCO and UNICEF) and international donor agencies should clearly state that a certain portion of the funds they provide for education and literacy programmes should be earmarked to serve the needs and interests of disabled people.

Yet, when I consider the present situation, I am pessimistic. Looking at current literacy programmes, they clearly show that in most developing countries there is little hope of reaching even 75 per cent literacy rates. The size of the task means that it is difficult to achieve a rapid solution. We need to look at various ways to provide education and literacy to people with disabilities, so we can give them support to integrate into mainstream education.

The way forward

People who cannot read or write are not a random sample of the world's population. They are the oppressed, the exploited, and the disadvantaged. The lack of good-quality education for disabled people is both a cause and a consequence of injustice and isolation.

Therefore, we have to lobby our governments and international aid agencies to ensure that attention is given to the educational needs of disabled people and, where needed, special measures are taken to enable them to enjoy equal access to all levels of education. Only then will we truly achieve 'Education for All'.

9.3.14   Puppets exercise

Facilitator's note

The fundamental right to self-determination – to make decisions about one's own life – is frequently denied to disabled people. This exercise and the next one may be used to prompt consideration and discussion of this important issue. Using puppets is often helpful, because participants can make their puppet say something that they would normally be too shy or embarrassed to say themselves.

Preparation

Make two paper puppets, as in Handout 33. Cut them out and stick them on to stiff card.

Process

Ask two people to volunteer to take part in an improvised sketch. Take them away from the rest of the group. Explain that you want them to prepare a five-minute sketch to show to the rest of the group, about getting involved as an activist in the local disabled people's organisation (DPO). Outline the role that each should play (but encourage them to add their own ideas).

The male puppet wants to join his local DPO. He has a friend who is an active member, who has told him about the organisation and the community centre that it runs. He thinks that joining the DPO is a good way for him to meet (other) disabled people and to help to improve the circumstances of disabled people's lives.

The female puppet thinks that there is no point in trying to improve disabled people's lives, because of the political crisis in the country. She thinks that until the crisis is over, there is nothing to be done for disabled people. She thinks it's a waste of time to join the DPO.

Explain the scenario: the man puppet is visiting his cousin, the woman puppet, and tells her about joining the DPO. They talk about it, each saying what they think (according to the roles explained above). They argue about the purpose of the DPO, and what DPOs can and can't do. They can make the sketch funny. The puppets can get very angry.

Give the volunteers 10 minutes to prepare their sketch. Then ask them to come back and show it to the rest of the group.

Ask the audience which puppet do they agree with? Why? What are the rights involved? Why is it important for disabled people and their organisations to control their own lives? What happens if they don't?

Learning points

DPOs are an important means for disabled people to represent themselves, their wishes and needs, and work to make positive changes in their lives.

Political or economic crisis does not mean that disabled people's rights are not important: they and their supporters can start to make positive changes NOW.

HANDOUT 33
Puppets

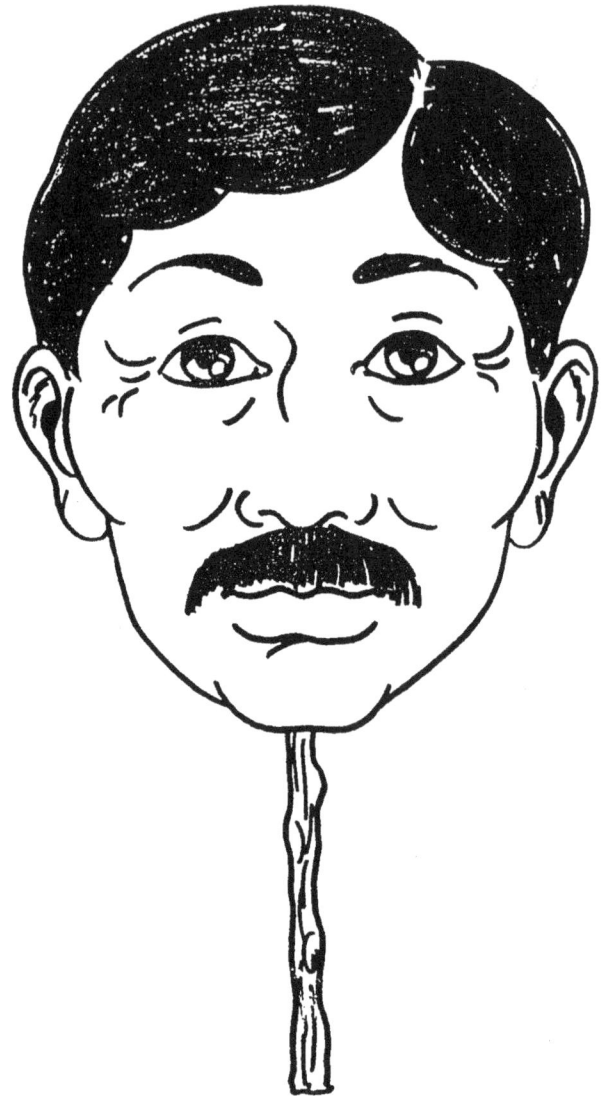

9.3.15   Two ways to cross a river

This activity can be used to promote discussion of issues related to education, development, and empowerment. Its main purpose is to look deeply at the question of dependency and self-reliance. It raises the question of doing things *for* people or doing things *with* people, and shows that people learn better when they are actively involved in the process. This is a key concept for people who are in training to facilitate group learning. But it is also vital for DPOs (especially for those with a tradition of autocratic leadership) to think critically about how they work to achieve full human rights for/with their members. It is a key concept for non-disabled people to grasp in their professional or personal relationships with disabled people. It stresses people's fundamental right and need to have a voice and role in determining and controlling their own lives.

Time   45 minutes

Preparation   Draw two lines, fairly wide apart, on the floor in chalk (or use string) to represent the banks of a river. Use pieces of paper to represent stepping stones in the river, and a piece of newsprint to represent an island in the middle of the river.

Process   Ask for three volunteers to take part in a mime, or a play without words. Take them away and explain what will happen:

- Two people come to the river and look for a place to cross. The current is very strong, and they are both afraid to cross.

- A third person comes along and notices their difficulty. S/he leads them up to the river and shows them the stepping stones. S/he encourages them to step on them, but both are afraid, so s/he agrees to carry them across, one at a time. By the time s/he gets to the middle of the river, the person being carried seems very heavy, and s/he has become very tired, so s/he puts him/her on the little island in the middle.

- The third person goes back to fetch the second, who also wants to be carried. But the third person refuses. Instead s/he takes the hand of the second person and encourages him/her to step on the stones him/herself. Half way across, the second person starts to manage alone. They both cross the river. When they get to the other side, they are extremely pleased with themselves and they walk off together, completely forgetting about the first person, sitting alone on the island. S/he tries to attract their attention, but they do not notice his/her frantic gestures for help.

After the mime, prompt a discussion by asking the following questions.

Questions   What did you see happening in the mime?

What types of approach were used to help the two people to cross the river?

Why was one approach more successful than the other?

Whom might each character represent in real life?

What does each side of the river represent?

In what ways can facilitators (or humanitarian aid workers, or DPOs, or non-disabled people working with disabled people, etc.) create a sense of dependence?

What must we do to ensure that those with whom we work maintain or develop a sense of independence? How can we *enable* others, instead of disabling them? What are some other benefits of doing this?

Option   If no one in your group can carry a person or be carried, they should work out a different way to represent this through the mime. One group's solution was for a wheelchair user to carry the first person on his lap, leaving him on the island when he became too heavy half way across.

(adapted with permission from *Training for Transformation*, Book 1, by Anne Hope and Sally Timmel)

9.4 Gender and disability

The activities in this section are presented in the format of a whole workshop, designed for people with little or no prior experience of the formal analysis of gender issues, and/or for people who are not familiar with the application of gender analysis to the situation of disabled people. For people with a well-developed understanding of gender equity, but no experience of applying it to disability, less time needs to be spent on general gender issues, and more time should be given to considering the disability-related aspects of the subject.

It may be appropriate to stress at the beginning of the session that you will be dealing with some sensitive issues, and to remind the group of any agreed guidelines that are relevant, such as a commitment to support and respect each other, and the right not to participate in activities which cause discomfort.

Overall objectives

By the end of the workshop, participants will be able to:

- explain the difference between sex and gender;

- list some of the key gender roles assigned to men and women by their community;

- describe the differences in the life experiences of disabled men and women, and explain the reasons behind them;

- start to think about some issues that are of particular importance to disabled women.

9.4.1 Who am I?

Time 45–60 minutes

Preparation No materials to prepare

Objectives To start the process of thinking about oppression and oppressed groups.

To make the group a safe place for people to be who they are.

For groups of people who do not know each other: to help participants to get to know each other.

Process Explain the objectives of the exercise, and what will happen.

Ask participants to find a partner with whom they would like to talk, whom they do not know very well. They will take turns to speak for five minutes about their identities, in terms of the groups that they belong to and where they come from; they may choose to describe themselves in terms of sex, race, class, religion, caste, disability, place of birth, being a son or daughter, or any other factors that seem important to them. The partner listens attentively and does not interrupt. After five minutes it is the turn of that person to talk.

With the whole group, ask each participant to share the key facts about who they are and where they come from.

Facilitate a discussion, drawing out the following learning points:

- Identity has many aspects (we each have many different identities).
- For people with impairments, disability is one aspect of their identity.
- The elements of our identity that are important to us at any given time may change, depending on the context/situation.
- In society, groups of people with a certain identity (often women and disabled people) are discriminated against and oppressed. This can make some people in these groups feel inferior, insecure, or resentful. People in the privileged or oppressor groups may feel guilty or ashamed. But we can all fight against oppression – no matter who we are. We are all equally welcome and accepted in the fight.

Facilitator's notes This activity may feel rather risky if the group is used to pretending that there are no differences between people, or that difference does not matter. Thus, with a group of people who do not know each other it should not be the very first activity that is done in the course or workshop.

See Handout 10 for guidelines on good listening. The important thing is that the listener should totally accept whatever the talker says, without interruption; but if the speaker dries up, the listener may ask a key question, to prompt a response.

This activity will give additional information to facilitators about the composition of the group, and a warning about difficult internal dynamics that are likely to develop. Be particularly aware of people who are in a minority of any kind, and consider what support they might need in order to feel safe in the group: ask them privately – outside the session.

Emotions will be aroused in this activity! Be prepared for them, and encourage the participants to be prepared for them. Allow extra time if necessary.

Link   We have seen that many things make us who we are, but for now this workshop will focus on two elements of identity: masculinity (being male) and femininity (being female).

(adapted from *The Oxfam Gender Training Manual*)

9.4.2   **The gender quiz**

(Reproduced from *The Oxfam Gender Training Manual*)

Time   30 minutes

Objective   To introduce the term 'gender' to participants who are unfamiliar with the concept.

Preparation   Copy Handout 34 (without the answers) on to a large sheet of paper or a blackboard.

Process   Ask the group if they understand the difference between 'gender' and 'sex'. If not, explain the difference quickly and simply.

Read out the list of statements from the board or flipchart.

Participants write down (quickly, based on their immediate response): **S** if they think the statement is about a sex-related (biological) factor, or **G** if they think it is about a gender-related (cultural) factor.

Then each participant exchanges papers with a neighbour and marks the responses as the facilitator gives the answers.

The participants receive their marked papers.

Conduct a whole-group discussion, drawing out the following learning points:

- Sex doesn't change.
- Gender roles change over place and time: they are different in different cultures.
- In some places men take on 'women's' roles, or women take on 'men's' roles.
- Often conflict, economic hardship, and modernisation alter gender roles.
- Age, race, class, and disability are also major factors which determine our gender roles.
- We can choose to change aspects of the gender roles of women and men if we think they are negative.

HANDOUT 34
Gender quiz

1. Women give birth to babies; men don't.

2. Little girls are gentle; boys are tough.

3. In one case, when a child brought up as a girl learned that he was actually a boy, his school marks improved dramatically.

4. In India, female agricultural workers are paid 40–60 per cent of the male wage.

5. Women can breast-feed babies; men can bottle-feed babies.

6. In Britain, most building-site workers are men.

7. In Ancient Egypt, men stayed at home and did weaving. Women handled family business. Women inherited property; men did not.

8. Men's voices break at puberty; women's do not.

9. One study of 224 cultures found five in which men did all the cooking, and 36 in which women did all the house building.

10. According to UN statistics, women do 67 per cent of the world's work, yet their earnings for it amount to only 10 per cent of the world's income.

Answers: Sex: 1, 5, 8. Gender: all others.

(Adapted from *The Oxfam Gender Training Manual*)

9.4.3   Sex and gender

Time   30 minutes

Objective   To summarise and reinforce learning about gender.

Process   Explain that, as seen in the previous exercise, our identity as men and women consists of two important factors: sex (a biological factor) and gender (a cultural factor). Sex is determined by our chromosomes and reproductive organs; these make us either male or female. Gender is a question of social rules and cultural roles; these dictate what is 'masculine' behaviour and what is 'feminine' behaviour.

Conduct a brainstorm with the whole group. Ask them to name the roles and qualities that their society expects of women and men respectively. Write up their answers in two columns on a flipchart or board. Unless the workshop is taking place in an exceptionally liberal country, you are likely to end up with a list like this:

Women	**Men**
mother	father as leader
carer	fighter/worker
follower	decision-maker
involved in domestic work	involved in work outside home
physically attractive	physically strong
sensitive	focused on action
nurturing	thinking
protective	brave
emotional	rational
(Reproductive roles)	(Productive roles)

Explain that our social rules about male and female identity – who women and men are, and what they do – are (usually) based on a rigid separation of prescribed tasks and assumed characteristics. For example, some women in rural Albania take on male roles in their community, dressing like men, working with them, and sharing privileges and space in the café with them. In return they have to give up their female identity completely, and cannot marry or have children. Social rules define the roles that men and women are expected to play. In some circumstances they are punished if they do not conform.

These rules may restrict the life choices of both men and women, and they form the basis of inequality between men and women. But, as we have already seen, we can change the rules if we want to. People who don't want to change the rules often talk about them as if they are determined by biology – but in fact they are cultural conventions.

9.4.4 Restrictive gender roles

Time   One hour

Objectives   To identify restrictions imposed on men and women.

To share personal experiences of gender roles.

To consider whether, in the group's experience, women encounter more restrictions than men.

To apply these insights to the life-experiences of disabled people.

Process   Introduce the exercise and give some examples of occasions (maybe one from childhood and one more recent) when you were prevented from doing something because social rules did not allow someone of your sex to do it.

Participants work in pairs, having chosen partners with whom they feel comfortable. Allow them ten minutes to think of a time when they were prevented from doing something because of being male or female. What happened, and why? How did they feel? The partners share their experiences with each other for ten minutes.

The whole group discuss in general terms what they have learned from the exercise. Bring out the point (if true for local circumstances, and if the group does not raise it) that women's lives are generally more restricted by social rules and gender roles than men's lives are – and that many women experience this as oppression.

Introduce the question of how gender roles might affect disabled men and women. They often experience discrimination if their impairment is perceived as preventing them from fulfilling their gender roles. For example, most societies assume (wrongly) that disabled women cannot or should not be mothers. Disabled women may even be prevented from marrying, and may be forcibly sterilised. It is more common for disabled men to be married than disabled women, because society expects men (disabled or not) to be looked after at home by women.

Another example: it is considered possible for a physically disabled man to fulfil his gender role of bread-winner or community leader, by using his rational or intellectual faculties, or by skilled manual work (even if, for example, his legs are paralysed). On the other hand, one of a woman's prime gender roles is to be physically attractive, according to her culture's definition of beauty. In many societies this definition does not include difference from the accepted norm, so many physically disabled women are not considered to fulfil their role.

Can the group think of similar examples from their own experience?

Sum up the discussion.

9.4.5   Gender roles: whole-group discussion

Time   30 minutes

Objective   To give a global overview of the oppression of women.

Preparation   Draw pie charts on flipchart paper or blackboard, based on the following statistics (all supported by UN research).

- 51 per cent of world's population are women
- 66 per cent of the world's work is done by women
- 10 per cent of the world's income is earned by women
- 66 per cent of the world's illiterate people are women
- 1 per cent of the world's property is owned by women

Process   Introduce the topic: this exercise will give a worldwide overview of the cultural restrictions on women's lives, which in general are greater than the cultural limitations on men's lives.

Show the pie charts, one by one.

How do participants feel about these facts? Allow time for comments, questions, and discussion.

Link   Explain that the next step is to consider how gender-related rules affect disabled men and disabled women (sometimes the same – sometimes differently).

Ask if the group thinks that these statistics take into account, or represent, the situation of disabled people. (No, it's even worse.) What about the situation of disabled women, as opposed to disabled men? (Worse still.)

What do the group think would be the corresponding statistics for disabled men and women? (Rough guesses are all that is required.) Take care when discussing how much of the world's work is done by disabled women: while it is often harder for them than for non-disabled women to gain paid employment, like their non-disabled sisters they also do a lot of the unpaid, unrecognised work in families and communities.

In the next activity we will consider the status of disabled women and men in the local community.

9.4.6 **The game of life**

Time   One hour

Preparation   Adapt the story used in this activity to make it appropriate to local circumstances.

Process   Ask the group for four volunteers to line up across the middle of the room. The rest of the group should sit around the edges, where they can see the volunteers. (You need a large room for this, or an outside space.)

Tell one volunteer to think of him/herself, for this exercise, as a non-disabled man; the second to play the part of a disabled man; the third that of a non-disabled woman; the fourth that of a disabled woman. (It is a good idea to have people assume different identities from their real identities.)

Explain that this exercise is to help us to examine how experiences of life may differ, depending on who we are and how our community sees us. You will go through the main stages of a typical life story, one by one, and each of the volunteers must respond to each stage, according to how they think it would affect their assigned character (or their family):

- Two steps forward for a very positive or very successful experience.
- One step forward for a positive or successful experience.
- One step back for a not-so positive or not-so successful experience.
- Two steps back for negative or unsuccessful experience.

Emphasise that they are each representing a group of people, so they should respond accordingly (rather than basing their response on their own experience, or the experience of one individual, which may not apply to the majority).

Emphasise that their response should be based on what they think is currently accurate for their culture and situation, not what they think it ought to be.

After each life stage, and the response by the volunteers, you will allow time for the rest of the group to react and comment on the moves made by the volunteers. If there is disagreement, the rest of the group should decide by consensus and instruct the volunteer (if appropriate) how to change the move that s/he made.

It is important for the facilitator to judge when to intervene and comment, to clarify reasons for decisions, and bring out and discuss any prejudicial points.

Start with the first life event, as if you are telling a story...

- *'One fine day, after a long wait of nine months, your character is born. How does your family feel when they see who you are? Make your moves.'* Comments/suggestions by the rest of the group?

  (Example to facilitator of what might happen:
  If the family is very happy (non-disabled son born): two steps forward
  Quite happy (disabled son/non-disabled daughter): one step forward
  Not happy (disabled son): one step back
  Very unhappy (disabled daughter): two steps back)

- *'Now you are a bit older, and it's time to start thinking about school. How likely is it that you will be able to attend school? Make your moves.'* Comments/suggestions by the rest of the group?

- *'Now you are 20 years old, Spring is in the air, and you would like to get married, or form a relationship. How much do you think this will possible for you? Make your moves.'*

- *'You like to keep busy and want to make some money for your family. You try to get a job. How easy will it be for you to find one?'* Comments/suggestions by the rest of the group?

- *'A few years go by, and everyone in your age group is having babies. How much will this be a possibility for you?'* Comments/suggestions by the rest of the group? (Check if the disabled woman takes two steps back, or is instructed to do so by the group. Why did this happen? They may say that it's because most disabled women are physically unable to have children – a common myth. Two steps back may well be an accurate response for a different reason: disabled women often don't have children because society thinks that they can't or shouldn't.)

- *'Now you are in your 40s, and you have a lot of experience of life. You want to help your community by becoming involved in local politics. How likely are you to achieve this goal?'* Comments/suggestions by the rest of the group?

Questions   When all the moves have been made, ask the group:

Who is in the best position? Who is in the worst position?

Ask the volunteers (especially those in the best and worst positions) how they feel about being where they are.

Are there any surprises?

At what point(s) were the experiences of disabled men and disabled women the same/different?

Do they think that this accurately reflects the general situation for men and women, disabled and non-disabled, in their community? Can they explain why things are like that? How do they feel about it?

What have they learned from this exercise about different people's experiences?

Summarise the discussion.

Facilitator's notes

This exercise needs particularly careful introduction and facilitation. To many participants it dramatically reveals things about which they had never consciously thought before. It can be fun, the humour taking the edge off the hard facts exposed by the game; but some participants have found it distressing, because it makes plain some very painful and personal truths. We include it here because we think that, at the right time and in an appropriate way, taboos and difficult issues need to be identified and spoken about, so that we can all recognise where the core of discrimination lies, and from there work out strategies for change.

In a way, this exercise shows how arbitrary the game of life really is, depending on the chance facts of one's birth. It can be an effective way of revealing to non-disabled people how much disabled people are discriminated against (directly and indirectly) in their community; and of helping non-disabled and disabled people alike to recognise that disabled women usually face worse discrimination than disabled men. (This is a fact that is often hotly denied by disabled men and DPOs, and used as a justification for not including women, or not working on disabled women's issues.)

In groups with a mixture of disabled and non-disabled participants, it is essential that participants have worked together enough, and know each other well enough, to feel comfortable with each other.

Options

With groups of disabled people, it is sometimes more effective to address these issues in another way, for example through small-group discussions, each group considering one of the major life-events and the personal issues involved, with feedback to the whole group. The reason for this is that the game's outcome is all too obvious from the outset for most disabled people, and the time may be better spent on deeper discussions of the issues. It is good nonetheless for disabled trainee facilitators to learn the Game of Life, in order to be able to facilitate it with other groups, whatever their composition.

Especially with groups consisting entirely of disabled people, or groups of any composition who already have a good understanding of the discrimination faced by disabled people, you may decide to omit the contrast between disabled and non-disabled lives and shift the focus of the game to emphasise male/female issues, changing the characters of the four volunteers to (for example) urban disabled man, rural disabled man, urban disabled woman, rural disabled woman.

Another alternative, for use with any type of group in a different context, is to use this exercise to raise differences in the likely life-experiences of people with various types of impairment, for example, learning-disabled people and people with physical or sensory impairments. Or to explore the question of whether disabled people (or disabled and non-disabled people) from different racial or religious groups receive different treatment within the broader community.

9.4.7 Disabled women's voices: diamond-ranking exercise

Time One hour

Objective To raise awareness of the following facts:

- Disabled women have issues in common with disabled men and non-disabled people. They may think the same or different things, but their voices are usually not heard.

- Disabled women also have their own issues, but again their voices are not heard.

Preparation Prepare one set of nine statement cards for each small group. Each statement should be numbered (for easy reference) on a separate card. Draw or print the numbers very large so that they can be seen from a distance for the whole-group feedback.

We used the following statements, taken from *Gender and Disability: Women's Experiences in the Middle East*, by Lina Abu-Habib, published by Oxfam, and *Disabled Women In Europe*, published by Disabled Peoples' International Europe and reproduced here with permission.

1 'We are all fighting for the same cause, so let us join together and not be divided. We are weak as it is. Now you want to divide the disabled people's movement into men and women.'

2 'To confront barriers, the most important thing is to have a fierce determination to be like other women and get rid of any feelings of inferiority or uselessness.'

3 'Health-care services were the biggest problem for me as a disabled woman. The nurses had a very negative attitude.'

4 'I have to fight against the belief that a disabled person is an object of pity who always needs assistance. The problem is made worse by the fact that I am a woman. Being a disabled woman is a double disadvantage.'

5 'My oldest brother makes all the decisions for us disabled girls in the family. The role of our mother is just to take care of us.'

6 'As a disabled woman I am allowed to go out, but my non-disabled sisters cannot. I guess my parents are not concerned for my honour and safety. They probably think, "She's disabled: who in the world would want anything to do with her?"'

7 'It is necessary to lift the veil on certain aspects considered taboo or unacceptable for disabled women: child-bearing has long been considered impossible for disabled women.'

8 'My father is disabled too. He is totally against the idea of marriage for disabled women like me. He says a disabled woman can never satisfy her husband's needs; the physical ones or the housekeeping, or raising children.'

9 'Education is the most important thing. A proper education will put a disabled girl on an equal level with other children.'

Process   Ask participants how often they hear disabled women speaking about their own lives, their wishes, their problems, the state of the country, the economy, etc. on TV, radio, in the community, at home.

Then explain that they will now spend some time hearing from women about some issues that are important to them.

Ask them to form small groups of four or five. Give each group a set of statements, a piece of flipchart paper, a marker pen, and some sticky tape.

Ask them to read and discuss each of the statements. Then they should agree, as a group, how to rank the statements, depending on how much or how little they agree with them. The ranking should be in a diamond pattern. Draw an example on a flipchart sheet:

X   completely agree
XX   agree
XXX   partly agree
XX   disagree
X   completely disagree

They should stick their cards on to their flipchart sheet to illustrate their ranking. As an alternative, the small groups can simply arrange their cards on the floor, and the feedback can be done with a walk around the room. One person from each small group should be prepared to present to the whole group, explaining briefly the ranking that their small group chose. (Five minutes each.)

Facilitate the feedback. This could lead into a whole-group discussion, and/or you could close the session with Handout 35 to take home, explaining that it contains some more disabled women's opinions. You could also recommend participants to read a complete chapter of *Gender and Disability: Women's Experiences in the Middle East*, not reprinted here for reasons of space. This could be done as homework, and then discussed in a future session.

Facilitator's notes   For this type of introductory workshop, the use of the statement cards, as opposed to asking women in the group to identify issues, is a safe way of addressing topics that women might think too personally revealing if they raised them themselves. This is especially true in mixed male/female groups.

HANDOUT 35
Disabled women's voices

'Pity can disappear from one day to the next. It makes you dependent on the whims of the person who is dispensing it. The issue of rights and equality is more lasting. It is this that disabled people are increasingly demanding. Charity has too often robbed us of our dignity and independence.' (Khadija)

'I must point out that the education I received was of paramount importance in my life. It is the foundation for what I am today. A proper education is necessary to put a disabled child on an equal level with non-disabled children.' (Apoka)

'It is almost impossible for a blind person to use public transport without a guide or companion, because the drivers are undisciplined and commuters compete viciously with each other for space and to grab the handles. Taxis could be easier. But they are risky, because few cabdrivers are absolutely trustworthy.' (Soledad)

'Designers, architects, builders, and engineers should keep in mind that disabled people also live in the city and that they have needs such as ramps, parking spaces, and access. We are all part of society.' (Paulina)

'The most difficult part of my life was my adolescence. Many parents did not want me as their daughter-in-law. They chased their sons away when they saw us together. Or a boyfriend would come simply out of curiosity, without any feeling, and deceive me in the most cruel way because he was ashamed to have me for a wife.' (Marie-Therese)

'Getting appropriate contraception for family planning was not easy for me as a disabled person. The nurses at the clinic had a very negative attitude.' (Gloria)

'Organise media campaigns to make the public aware of the needs and abilities of disabled people.' (Marie-Therese)

'My involvement with organisations that deal with disability also contributed to my achievements. It made me realise that I had to fight to survive. As I was one of the lucky few who had a better chance despite my disability, I had to help others in the same situation. The strong and progressive image that I portray encourages other disabled people who would otherwise sit back and suffer in self-pity.' (Gloria)

(continued)

'I had to learn to manage all alone, to confront numerous challenges. To all of these efforts must be added my fierce determination to be like other women, and my deep conviction that I could make a contribution to society. I got rid of any feelings of inferiority or uselessness.' (Diarietou)

'My main objective is to be an effectively contributing member of the community at large and thus contribute to the development of my country. The problem is the negative attitude in society towards the active participation of disabled people in community development. I have to counter the belief that a disabled person is an object of pity who always needs assistance from somebody else. This problem is compounded by the fact that I am a woman. Being a disabled woman is a double disadvantage in my country.' (Gloria)

(Reprinted with permission from *Disabled Women in Europe: A Resource Kit*, published by Disabled Peoples' International Europe)

9.5 Images and language of disability

This section considers how society's perceptions of disabled men, women, and children are reflected in the use of language and images in everyday life and in the media; and how the language and images that we use affect our perceptions, influencing us and our actions in potentially negative or positive ways.

9.5.1 Media search

Time   One hour

Objective   For participants to assess the public image of disabled people, presented in various media.

Preparation   Two weeks before the workshop, ask participants to conduct a media search to investigate how disabled people are portrayed, spoken, and written about in the media (radio, TV, newspapers, magazines, movies, documentaries, novels, traditional songs and stories, graphic images, etc.). They should not make a special effort to hunt out examples, but rather should collect what they come across in their usual contact with the media over the two-week period (in order to get an idea of what the general public are exposed to). But if the group includes the staff of humanitarian and development agencies, ask them in addition to include the publications on the shelves in their offices.

Ask them to gather articles or be prepared to make a brief (oral) summary of the content of radio/film/news etc., focusing on the role played by the disabled person(s) and the impression of disability given to the viewer.

Process   In the round, ask participants to share their research with the whole group.

Then ask for their comments or conclusions about the overall findings.

You could use the following questions to facilitate the discussion and draw out learning points.

Questions   How are disabled people generally being represented?

How do participants feel about that?

What impact do they think these kinds of image make on the general public?

What is the impact on disabled people themselves?

Were any particular sources especially positive or negative in their presentation of disability? Can participants suggest reasons for this?

Did they find any media sources where disabled people represented themselves? If no, why? If yes, was the disabled people's self-representation different from the impression given by non-disabled communicators? Why? Why not?

Were there any types of media where disabled people were not featured at all? What does this tell us?

If participants worked in the media (maybe some of them do already), how would (do) they represent disability and disabled people?

Facilitator's notes   The word 'media' is used here in the broadest sense to mean any shared, public form of communication, for example stories or news passed down through song, or on television.

The absence of disabled people in the media (both as producers and as subjects) is one reason why they are invisible 'non-people' in many societies. Where people with impairments are featured, it is usually in one of three stereotypical ways: tragic and suffering, therefore in need of pity; or bitter, twisted, and evil as a result of their condition; or heroic and brave superhumans or saints. None of these images is real, and all are (at best) patronising. They all start from a conscious or unconsciously assumed position of superiority on the part of the non-disabled person, who passes judgement on the person with an impairment.

The stereotypes do not enable non-disabled people to start to understand the varied reality of disabled people's lives; and they do not provide disabled people with images of disabled people to whom they can relate, or who can serve as positive role models. The media play a major role in informing and shaping public opinion, so modifying their representation of disabled people is one important method of raising awareness of disability.

Disabled people are more or less completely absent from publications about humanitarian relief and development (unless the publication specifically concerns disability or landmines). The three co-facilitators of the DETOT course in Kosovo could not remember ever having seen more than one picture of a disabled person used in a context other than disability. Between us we had read hundreds of books about micro-enterprise, gender, water and sanitation, sustainability, food security, rural development, etc., with never a disabled person in sight! This both reflects and perpetuates the exclusion of disabled people from mainstream life.

9.5.2 Using positive and non-stereotypical images of disability

Time   One hour

Objective   Participants will analyse a variety of ways in which visual images are used, and how they affect the perceptions of disability – by both disabled and non-disabled people.

Preparation   Find four different newsletters produced by DPOs from various places, using graphic imagery in different ways. The language used is not important. For example, in the DETOT course we used one newsletter from Serbia, one from Bosnia, one from the UK, and one from the USA. One contained a few photographs of disabled people – but mostly they were posed very passively; one contained a lot of text and a variety of photos, of which some gave the impression of activity and many were portraits of smiling disabled babies and children; one had (excellent) text only, no photographs or artwork; in another, a large amount of the space was given over to photographs and artwork, showing disabled people doing a broad range of activities.

Assemble two sets of four posters which focus on or include disabled people. A good source of positive images is the Greater Manchester Coalition of Disabled People – for details, see the Resources section at the end of this book. Major charities which raise funds for welfare projects often produce posters featuring less positive images.

Process   Divide participants into three groups. Group 1 will work on the newsletters, Group 2 on four of the posters, Group 3 on the other four posters.

Group 1 should look through the newsletters, focusing on the images used, not on the text. Ask them to discuss together the following questions:

- What are the main differences in the use of images in the four newsletters?
- Which newsletter do you think is most successful in presenting a positive image of disabled people? Why?
- Which picture would you choose to be on the front of your newsletter? Why?

Groups 2 and 3 should look at the images on their set of posters (not the text, if there is any) and make a list of all the issues or messages that they see in the posters. They should discuss which poster in their set is most successful in presenting a positive image of disabled people. What are the reasons for their choice?

Each group should report back to the whole group. This could lead into a discussion, based on the following questions.

Questions   Why is it helpful to use images in newsletters, on posters, and in other media (technology permitting)? (To catch people's attention and get them interested; to promote your message to a broader range of people – including those who cannot read, and those who might not take the time to read an article, no matter how well written; to make an impact; to reinforce the text, etc.)

What makes an image 'positive'? (It's not necessarily about smiling into the camera!)

What conclusions can participants draw about how to convey positive or non-stereotypical images of disability?

9.5.3 Posters exercise

Time One hour

Objectives To introduce participants to non-stereotypical images of disabled people with various types of impairment.

To encourage participants to identify with or empathise with people in the images.

To challenge participants' prejudices in a non-confrontational way.

Preparation Gather posters which present images of disability.

Process Ask participants to form pairs, and give one poster to each pair. If the poster has accompanying text, cover it up so that people focus initially on the picture.

For 10–15 minutes participants should study their poster and consider:
- Who is in the poster?
- What are they doing?
- Why?
- How are they feeling?
- What can you tell about their lives?
- How does the poster make the viewer feel?
- What message is the poster intended to communicate?

Bring the group back together and ask each pair to show their poster and report back.

If the posters contain text, you can read this aloud immediately after the relevant pair has reported back, and ask them if the text changes their ideas or understanding of the poster.

Give the rest of the group an opportunity to comment on and discuss each poster (with text).

9.5.4   The impact of language: Mr Biswas photo exercise

Time   40 minutes

Objective   For participants to experience how the choice of words can change perceptions.

Preparation   Prepare sufficient copies of Handout 36: the photograph of Mr Biswas (taken from *The Oxfam Gender Training Manual*, p.529).

Process   Participants should work in pairs. Give each pair one copy of the photograph.

Ask them to take ten minutes to think up two different captions to accompany the photo. One caption should be worded so as to make the image look negative. The other caption should be worded so as to give the viewer a positive impression from the photo. They can write their captions on flipchart paper if they want to.

Bring the whole group together and ask each pair to share their captions.

Tell them that the original caption was: 'Two English visitors to Calcutta photographing Mr Biswas, Director of the Fellowship of the Disabled'.

Facilitate discussion to bring out the learning points, which may be based on the following questions.

Questions   Was it easy or hard to think up the captions? Why?

What do they think most people would think about the photo if they saw it without the original caption?

How would most people react when they then read the original caption? What might they learn about themselves?

What can we conclude about using language, in this case with images?

HANDOUT 36
Photograph of Mr Biswas

9.5.5 **Word-list exercise**

Time 1 hour 15 minutes

Objectives To consider how language can reinforce positive or negative attitudes.

For participants to start thinking about and discussing what words are suitable to use in their own language.

To give participants information about some methods used by other groups of disabled people in determining appropriate terminology.

Preparation Prepare copies of Handout 37.

If the participants are multilingual, work out groups of four according to their first language.

Process Divide participants into groups of four; give out flipchart paper and pens.

Ask them to draw a line down the middle of the page and mark one side with a cross and the other with a tick.

They should think about all the words that are commonly used (in their language) to name, describe, or talk about disabled people.

Next they should write the words, on one side of the paper or the other, depending on whether they think the word is a good one (accurate, appropriate, etc.) or bad one (offensive, patronising, etc.) to use.

After 20 minutes, bring everyone back together, and ask each small group to present its list in turn. Give the rest of the participants an opportunity to seek clarification about any words on the lists, before moving on to the next small group's presentation.

If some words remain unclear or seem incongruous to you (as facilitator), ask for clarification from the presenting group, and then get the whole group to discuss them.

Display all the lists where they can be seen, and ask participants if they see any common features or can draw any conclusions about what makes words acceptable or unacceptable.

Distribute Handout 37 for participants to read at home for further ideas.

Facilitator's notes This exercise is not intended to produce final conclusions about appropriate terminology, but to start participants thinking about the significance of language and its impact in their own culture. It is intended only to start what is necessarily a long and dynamic process. Language responds to culture and is always in a state of change.

Finding appropriate language to represent disability is not a matter of being 'politically correct'. Appropriate language is an important aspect of Disability Equality, because language carries intent: the words that people usually employ reflect how they think and feel about what they are talking (or writing) about. Thoughts and feelings are translated into action. Also, to a large extent the choice of words determines what listeners actually hear, and it may influence their opinion of what is being talked about.

However, in most countries appropriate terminology is not used, or sometimes does not even exist. The fact that people use the words that are commonly employed does not always necessarily reflect how the speaker or writer feels about disability – it may simply be evidence of the lack of appropriate words. Where this is the case, people should be encouraged not to judge others who use the 'wrong' words, but to take action to create and promote an adequate vocabulary for disability. Where appropriate terminology does already exist, people should be encouraged to use it.

Part of the work of the disability-rights movement worldwide is for people with impairments to determine what is appropriate terminology in their own language, and to use terminology and the media to shape the personal and public image of disabled people. Disabled people need to give the rest of society a language that it can use and that will be acceptable to people with impairments.

Literal translations of acceptable terminology from one language to another language are usually not helpful. Even where different countries use the 'same' language, they probably use different words and definitions, depending on local nuances of understanding and perception.

Whatever words are chosen, three basic principles seem to be common factors in determining what disabled people and their groups classify as acceptable:

1. The language of disability should emphasise that someone who has an impairment is an individual, a person first and foremost. But the impairment should not be ignored: many disabled people feel that it is an important element of their identity, and they would endorse the statement: 'I am what I am because of my disability, not despite it.' Both parts of the equation are needed. Acceptable terminology includes *disabled people, a person who has cerebral palsy, people with paraplegia, a blind person, a hearing-impaired person, a person with learning difficulties*, etc.

2. The language of disability should emphasise the ability and activity of disabled people, e.g. *walks with crutches, a wheelchair user, employs a sign interpreter*, etc.

3. Words which reinforce commonly held prejudices or which make
    value judgements should be avoided. Many commonly used words
    imply that disabled people are either tragic, sick, or abnormal.

Examples of words about disabled people to avoid: *crippled, patient,
case, retarded, suffering from Downs Syndrome* (Downs Syndrome does
not cause suffering: prejudice does), *afflicted with, victim of, sick, deaf
and dumb, abnormal, people with limited/restricted abilities* (we all,
disabled and non-disabled alike, have limits!).

Examples of words about non-disabled people to avoid (when
distinguishing them from disabled people): *healthy, normal, able people.*

Understanding the disability movement's interpretation of the word
'disabled' may help people to think through what they can do to
determine or reclaim appropriate terminology: someone who is
'disabled' has been made disabled (made less able than they actually
are) by something or someone. Many people think that a person is
disabled if (and because) s/he has an impairment. But the disability
movement says that what disables a person is not the impairment
itself, but society's negative response to it. The word 'disabled' refers
therefore not to impairments, but to the effect on people with
impairments of society's disabling structures and attitudes.

Some people may question why there needs to be any special
terminology: why can't we just use our given names? Isn't all
terminology just a way of labelling people? Some people do not want to
identify themselves as disabled at all, and that is their legitimate
choice. But other disabled people choose to use disability-related
terminology with which they feel comfortable in order to describe that
part of their identity, and in order to have a collective identity to use in
lobbying and political or social organisation. The difference is between
labelling (of one person or group by another, usually from a position of
assumed superiority) and self-determination by disabled people.

Options   Spend time during the workshop reading Handout 37, and then divide
participants into two groups to devise a final list of appropriate and
inappropriate words, using their own lists and the handout for ideas.
Each of the two groups presents its list, which after the workshop you
could then combine into one final text and distribute to everyone.

In groups where you have observed that participants have a significant
level of negative attitudes towards disability, you may want to give
them food for thought by devising a short presentation, using the
facilitator's notes (above) and Handout 37, before introducing the
Word List Exercise.

HANDOUT 37
Guidelines for acceptable language about disability

(adapted with permission from 'Guidelines for Reporting and Writing about People with Disabilities', sixth edition, © Research and Training Center on Independent Living, University of Kansas; see Resources section for further details)

1. Do not sensationalise a disability by saying *afflicted with, victim of, suffering from*, and so on. Instead, say (for example) *a person who has multiple sclerosis.*

2. Avoid amassing individuals into faceless groups, as in *the disabled, the deaf, an arthritic.* Instead say *people who are deaf, people with disabilities,* etc.

3. Emphasise the individual, not the impairment. Say *person with paraplegia,* not *paraplegic* or *paraplegic person.*

4. Emphasise abilities and action, rather than what a person cannot do. Avoid words that sound passive: *uses a wheelchair* or *hears with an aid* rather than *confined to/in a wheelchair* or *can't hear without an aid ... walks with crutches* rather than *is crippled ... is partially sighted* rather than *partially blind.*

5. People with disabilities should not be referred to as *patients* or *cases* unless they are receiving medical treatment. If under medical care, they should be referred to as patients or cases only in the context of that care.

6. Disabled people are not 'sick', 'abnormal', or 'unable'. Therefore do not call non-disabled people 'normal', healthy', or 'able-bodied' when distinguishing them from disabled people.

7. Use the same language for disabled people as you do for non-disabled people, in order to keep the power relationships equal. For example, if you are giving a non-disabled person a lift (ride) somewhere, that is the expression used. If you are giving a disabled person a lift (ride), often the expression used is 'taking the person'(as you would take a child somewhere). These subtle changes are usually unconscious but significant: they indicate an underlying (unrecognised) unequal power relationship, and by their continued use they help to perpetuate that relationship.

(continued)

Words to avoid	**Words to use**
disfigured, deformed, abnormal, invalid	disabled
a victim of cerebral palsy	a person who has cerebral palsy
a cerebral palsy case/patient	(as above)
spastic	(as above)
suffering from cerebral palsy	(as above)
crippled, lame	physically disabled
confined to a wheelchair, wheelchair-bound	wheelchair user
deaf and dumb, deaf-mute	person who is deaf/hearing-impaired/hard of hearing
sightless	person who is blind/visually impaired/ partially sighted
has fits, throws fits, epileptic	has epilepsy, has seizures
retarded, subnormal	person with a learning difficulty/ who has a developmental disorder
healthy, normal, able-bodied person	non-disabled person

These are some suggestions which fit the English language. It is not easy to translate them into other languages, especially not literally. Each language has its own ways of expressing a concept with negative, positive, or neutral connotations. Disabled people have to decide what is right for their own language, according to their connotations.

As an example, in Serbia disabled people use the expression 'invalid', or *invalidna lica*, to translate 'disabled' or 'disabled person'. To an English-speaking person this sounds offensive, because 'invalid' is the opposite of 'valid', meaning 'having worth'. However, since the word 'valid' does not exist in the Serbian language (there is a completely different word to express that meaning), 'invalid' carries no suggestion of somebody who is not valid. In that language, 'invalid' is not offensive: it simply means a person who has an impairment.

9.6 Definitions of disability

As with images and languages, the definitions that we assign to a concept like disability determine the action or approach that we take. However, there is sometimes a danger that giving a definition to anything, let alone a concept as broad and complex as disability, will limit the reality to which it refers. Sometimes a particular definition is adopted and seems never to change, despite on-going processes of development and growth.

However, if these pitfalls are avoided, thinking about definitions can be very useful, for example when trying to change existing harmful definitions and gain broad acceptance of a new way of defining and acting; or to influence public or political opinion. For example, if you define disability as 'bodily or mental dysfunction', then politicians (the overwhelming majority of whom are not disabled) will not see disability as something relevant to themselves. If, however, you define disability as 'the exclusion of 10 per cent of the population from everyday life, including the political process', politicians may suddenly wake up to the fact that there is a potentially election-winning sector of the population who currently vote for no one and who might be persuaded to vote for them. Politicians might then be motivated to create the physical and legal conditions that enable disabled people to vote, and may even give them a reason for voting.

Additionally, for many of us definitions help to give cohesion or structure to an idea, which we can then articulate and/or act on.

With these points in mind, it was decided for the DETOT course in Kosovo to do the following exercise, which is recommended to be introduced after all (or a combination of) the components of the 'Disability Equality' section of this manual have been worked through.

Make clear to participants that in this case 'definition' means neither a literal, dictionary-style definition of the word nor a medical diagnosis. We mean a definition or description of the concept as a whole. The aim is for participants to bring together all the ideas and experiences shared in the workshop(s) so far, as well their personal, everyday experiences of disability, and to produce their own definitions of what disability is: what it means to them. By doing this, and by hearing other people's definitions, participants will, it is hoped, reach new levels of understanding. And how we understand an issue influences how we act.

9.6.1   'Our definitions' exercise

Time   One hour

Objective   For participants to define disability for themselves, taking into account their experience of disability and their society's response to impairments.

Process   Divide people into groups of four. Ask them to spend five minutes thinking individually about how they would sum up disability in a definition of their own. Explain that you do not mean a tight definition of the word as can be found in a dictionary, but a definition which conveys the whole reality of disability. They can draw on their own knowledge and experience, and on what they have learned about disability during the course of the workshop(s) to help them. They should bear in mind all the different aspects of disability that have been explored – human rights, the three models, barriers, etc.

After the five minutes of individual reflection, they should spend 20 minutes with the rest of their small group, working out their collective definition.

One person in the group should be prepared to tell and explain their definition to the whole group. This can be done orally, or in writing. Or, depending on the composition of the groups, you could suggest that they draw a picture to illustrate their verbal definition. Allow extra time for this.

After the report back, ask participants for comments and questions, and facilitate their discussion. The questions below might help you to focus the discussion.

Questions   Do they think it is a good idea to make definitions like this? Why? Why not?

Can participants think of examples of situations where a definition of disability would be helpful? Or unhelpful?

After seeing all the various groups' definitions, does anyone now think differently about their previous definition?

Does anyone disagree with any, or all, of the definitions? Why?

Which definition do participants like best?

Facilitator's notes   This last question may not be appropriate if you are trying to explain how the use of a single definition may exclude people, or to emphasise that on an individual level disabled people should define for themselves what disability is. It might set up the idea that there is one 'right' definition. On the other hand, in some sessions where we did this exercise, one of the groups produced a definition that put into words what the group as a whole was trying to express; so arriving at consensus in favour of that definition produced a high-energy and satisfying conclusion.

This exercise is not recommended for groups which do not include a significant number of disabled people. The appropriate people to define what disability is are disabled people themselves.

9.7 Self-determined living

The Independent Living Movement has made a significant impact in many countries, empowering disabled people to take control of their own lives. (Some people prefer to use the term 'self-determined living', rather than 'independent living', because it more clearly describes their aspirations.) Handout 38 offers a personal definition by Adolf Ratzka of the Institute on Independent Living in Sweden; it could be used to supplement the materials and exercises in this section. The first few activities are designed to stimulate thinking about interdependence, independence, and dependence.

HANDOUT 38
A personal definition of Independent Living

[Self-determined or Independent] Living is a philosophy and a movement of people with disabilities who work for self-determination, equal opportunities, and self-respect.

Independent Living does not mean that we want to do everything by ourselves and do not need anybody, or that we want to live in isolation. Independent Living means that we demand the same choices and control in our everyday lives that our non-disabled brothers and sisters, neighbours and friends take for granted. We want to grow up in our families, go to the neighbourhood school, use the same bus as our neighbours, work in jobs that are in line with our education and abilities, start families of our own. Just like everybody else, we need to be in charge of our lives, think and speak for ourselves.

To this end, we need to support and learn from each other, organize ourselves and work for political changes that lead to the legal protection of our human and civil rights.

(Adolf Ratzka, Institute on Independent Living, Sweden)

9.7.1   In/ter/dependence drawings

Time   60–90 minutes

Objectives   For participants to understand that no one is totally 'independent' or totally 'dependent', and that society functions by being 'interdependent'.

For participants to understand that everybody contributes to society in some way, but sometimes that contribution is not recognised or valued.

Preparation   Prepare three pieces of flipchart paper, headed **Alone, With someone,** and **By someone else.**

Provide three sheets of A4 paper per participant, plus coloured pens.

Process   Give each participant three pieces of A4 paper and coloured pens. Ask them to think about their typical day and to list on the appropriate sheet:

1. things that they do completely **alone** (either for themselves or for someone else);

2. things that they do **with other people's help** or participation;

3. things that **someone else** does for them.

You can give them examples from your own daily life to illustrate what you mean, and to share some information about yourself. (Examples: 1: Decide what to wear/lead the singing at family celebrations; 2: Communicate at work with help of interpreter; 3: Mother goes to market to buy food for me.)

For each of the three types of activity, participants should choose one example from their own lives and draw a picture of it, on the reverse of the sheet of A4 paper. They have 20 minutes for this.

Each person shares his or her pictures with the rest of the group. After each person's turn, stick their pictures up on the corresponding pieces of flipchart.

Make a (mental) note during this feedback of any activity that appears on two or three of the lists (if one participant does it alone, and another has someone else do it for them, etc.).

Facilitate a discussion, using the following questions.

Questions   What did this activity reveal?

Are there any overlaps across the lists? What were they?

What would life be like if we all had to do every single thing alone for ourselves?

If a non-disabled person needs someone to do something for him or her (for example, a man whose wife cooks dinner for him; a politician who is driven everywhere by a chauffeur), how is that perceived by other people? Is that person considered dependent and incapable?

Why are disabled people, who also need people to help them with certain things, often perceived as dependent and incapable? Is that fair?

Are there any activities in the drawings that participants do not currently do for themselves, but could do if they had training, or resources, or enabling aids?

What conclusions can participants draw? (*Control* is the important factor in determining whether someone is perceived as powerful or dependent when something is done for them. Whatever assistance you need, if you control the process, you are not likely to be labelled as dependent, nor feel dependent. This is one of the basic principles of Independent or Self-determined Living.)

9.7.2   My contribution

Time   40 minutes

Objectives   For participants to acknowledge and value their own contributions to their interdependent community, and thus to raise their self-esteem.

Process   Ask participants to spend five minutes in individual reflection, thinking about the various things they do that help other people; they might be practical, physical, intellectual, spiritual, or emotional types of help. What would happen if they did not offer this help? (Depending on the identity of the participants, you might decide to focus the discussion on family life, the community, or work situations.)

Ask them to join up with a partner and take ten minutes to share their thoughts; but there will not be individual feedback to the whole group.

Bring the whole group back together and ask for general feedback, based on the following questions:

- How did you feel while you did this exercise?
- Did you learn anything about yourself?
- Were you surprised by what you learned about yourself or your partner?

If individuals want to share with the whole group examples of how they help others, they should be encouraged to do so, but do not ask everyone to do this.

Options   In place of the above exercise, you can achieve similar objectives by playing the energiser game '*What I like about you*' (7.2.7), adapting it so that participants have to write on each other's backs what quality or skill they are grateful to the other person for bringing to the group.

Facilitator's notes   These are simple exercises, but very useful in societies where it is not customary to think well of oneself or give praise to others; and in societies where disabled people are not used to thinking about themselves in a positive way. Disabled people are often socialised into devaluing themselves, or taking themselves for granted, even though they contribute a lot to their families or community or the group. Having the time and space (and in some senses 'permission') to value oneself can be very empowering. We found that most disabled people actually have a lot of responsibility – for looking after and raising children while the rest of the adults in the family work the land, for supporting the family financially through a crisis, for being peace-makers, etc. – but they are never given (or give themselves) credit for it.

9.7.3 Independent (Self-Determined) Living: presentation and discussion

Time One hour

Objectives To introduce participants to the concepts of the Independent Living Movement and Personal Assistance services.

Optionally, to compare the principles that define rehabilitation and independent living (see Handout 39).

Presentation Explain that DPOs in various countries have founded a new movement (and philosophy) to try to end the enforced dependence (both perceived and actual) of disabled people on non-disabled people. The movement is often called 'Independent Living' (but more commonly now people are using the term 'Self-Determined Living' as a more accurate description of the concept). Not all the countries involved in this movement are rich, stable countries. It is also active in countries with economic and political problems, such as India, Brazil, and Hungary.

Self-Determined/Independent Living does not mean disabled people living alone, or doing everything for themselves. It is about finding ways in which disabled people can be in control of their own lives, fulfil their potential, be empowered, and be included in the rest of the community. It is based on four main principles (write up the key words as you speak):

- **Choices and decisions:** disabled people should make their own choices and decisions about what affects them, and they should participate in choices and decisions made by their families and communities.

- **Control:** disabled people must have control over their own lives (to the same extent that their non-disabled peers do).

- **Rights and responsibilities:** disabled people have the same rights as non-disabled people, but (like them) they must take responsibility for themselves, their decisions, their actions, etc.

- **Freedom to fail:** disabled people should have the freedom to fail. We all fail and make mistakes sometimes; this gives us the opportunity to learn and then to try again. Often, however, disabled people are over-protected and are not allowed to take risks or even to tackle the most ordinary tasks. Or if they try and fail, the failure is automatically seen as a result of their impairment, not as a normal part of learning.

Actions to achieve Self-Determined Living are often organised around, and co-ordinated by, an Independent Living Centre (ILC), formed by disabled people and their allies.

(Allow time for questions and comments about Self-Determined/Independent Living. Give participants a ten-minute coffee break before continuing with the presentation.)

One of the main services identified by ILCs as important is known as 'Personal Assistance'. The concept was created by and for disabled people who need a high level of assistance with mobility and/or communication in their daily living activities (for example, wheelchair transfers, dressing, personal hygiene, typing at work, speaking, etc).

In most societies, such people are prevented from leading active lives, and have no control over their own lives, because the person who helps them is either a relative who is very busy or ignorant of how to help, or a 'home help' who is financed and controlled by the State, or an over-worked care assistant in a nursing home or institution.

The types of help that a disabled person receives are often decided by someone else; and the assistance is usually limited in scope (for example, it does not include support at school or work, with the result that the disabled person is denied education or employment). When, and how often, the help is available is usually decided according to someone else's priorities (for example, a disabled adult may have to go to bed at 7 o'clock every night, because the home help can't come later).

In addition, some institutions, nursing homes, and home-help services are notorious for the physical and sexual abuse to which disabled people are subjected, and the disabled person is not in a position to challenge his or her treatment.

In some countries where the State usually provides home helps or institutions, Personal Assistance services have been introduced as an alternative. Other countries are trying out small-scale pilot schemes.

How Personal Assistance schemes work (write up key words on a flipchart or board as you speak):

- Instead of paying for a home help, or an institution, the State pays the money directly to the disabled person (or sometimes to a collective of disabled people).
- The disabled person employs his or her own personal assistant (PA), deciding and controlling what assistance will be given, when, and how often.

- ILCs train disabled people how to employ PAs.
- Disabled people (with the help of the ILC to begin with) train PAs in what to do. The role of the assistant is to help the disabled person with physical activities or communication, not to make decisions for them or tell them what to do.

The benefits of PA schemes (write up key words on a flipchart or board as you speak):

- Disabled people manage their own assistance and therefore have much more control over their lives.
- PA schemes are often cheaper and more cost-effective than centrally managed home-help schemes or nursing homes.
- Disabled people are in a position to sanction or dismiss employees who are incompetent or abusive.
- Assistance is given in the right way and at the right time.
- Studies show that providing accessible housing costs less than half what it costs to keep people in institutions. When given accessible housing, PAs, and appropriate enabling aids, people with impairments often require much less assistance than they would if they lived in institutions. A couple who when institutionalised needed 33.5 hours of help a week moved to their own accessible home. Initially they needed eight hours of help, which was reduced over a few months to 1.5 hours per week (according to Gini Laurie: 'European Concepts of Independent Living').
- Many disabled people do not need a PA. Those who do are usually the people whose lives are most restricted, who are usually most severely excluded by the rest of society. So PA schemes enable some of the most isolated, marginalised disabled people to participate in society (education, employment, social life, etc.) and to exercise choice and control in their lives. They also enable society to benefit from the contributions of people who previously have been prevented from participation.

(Note that even though a PA scheme may not suit every country's socio-economic circumstances, the principle of putting assistance under the control of disabled people can be applied anywhere. There will be an opportunity to discuss this in the next activity.)

Give time for questions and comments. You can stimulate further discussion by posing this situation: a disabled student who employs a PA has an examination tomorrow morning. The night before the exam, the student goes to a party, accompanied by her PA, intending to stay for only a short while. But she has a good time and ends up staying late. Should the PA say or do anything about this?

Facilitator's notes

This is a good opportunity to bring in a guest speaker, for example a member of a Centre for Independent Living who can present its philosophy, or a disabled person from a local DPO who has visited such a centre or has links with one. They might also have photographs or a video to show. If no suitable guest speaker is available, you could do a presentation (see outline above), supplemented by a video or photographs if possible, followed by the small-group discussion exercise below (9.7.4).

Non-disabled people commonly react to the idea of Self-Determined Living by saying, 'There are lots of things in my life that I can't control or decide about, so why should disabled people have that freedom?' The point is that none of us can control or decide about everything, but disabled people are usually denied choice and control over things that non-disabled people automatically can choose or control. Self-Determined Living seeks only to give disabled people the same degree of choice and control that non-disabled people already have.

HANDOUT 39
The principles of rehabilitation
('the medical model'), compared with the principles of independent living ('the social model')

	Rehabilitation concept	Independent living concept
What is the problem?	The disabled person is a deficient being whose ability to play roles in society is restricted.	The disabled person is made dependent on other people, including experts, rehabilitation centres, and environmental and political conditions.
Where is the problem situated?	In the disabled person.	In the environment, the rehabilitation process, and social and political circumstances.
How is the problem solved?	By the expert procedures of doctors and other specialists. The disabled person is 'cared for' by certain people and organisations.	By self-help, peer counselling, self-organisation of assistance, the reduction of pyschological, social and other barriers, consumer control.
What is the role in society of the disabled person?	Patient, client, dependent family member	Consumer, decision maker, participant.
Who is competent?	Other people (experts, rehabilitation workers, family).	The disabled person
What is the desired result?	Psycho-physical independence, reduction of the 'disability', or institutionalisation.	A self-determined life, possibly a profession, the ability to organise and accept assistance. Assistance structures close to the consumer.

(This chart was originally created by Gerben de Dejong in 1982. It appears on the Internet at www.dpa.org.sg/DPA/publication/dpadec99/p12.htm)

9.7.4   Putting Independent (Self-determined) Living into practice

Time   50 minutes

Objectives   For participants to discuss how the principles of Independent Living, and services like Personal Assistance, relate to their own circumstances.

To identify ways in which the principles might be put into effect at the local level.

Process   Introduce the exercise by saying that Personal Assistance services are just one way in which Independent Living can be put into practice.

In countries where there is no kind of State-provided support that could be used to establish PA services, the principles of Independent Living on which PA services are based are still relevant, and have been successfully applied (for example in India). How might they be put into practice locally?

Divide people into small groups and ask them to spend 20 minutes discussing this. They should be prepared to share their ideas in a whole-group feedback session.

Facilitate the feedback and allow time for questions, comments, and discussion.

10 Action planning

This section includes a range of activities from which facilitators may select, using them as appropriate to encourage workshop participants to put their learning into action. Ideally, all workshops will include at least one exercise, towards the end, which gets participants to think about 'what next?'. For the DETOT course in Kosovo, which ran for 19 days over five months, we gave a whole day to action planning (and that was still not enough time!). If time is short, remember that action planning need not end with the workshop: participants can use the exercises as tools outside the workshop, to carry on with the planning and implementation.

10.1　Short and half-day activities

10.1.1　Individual reflection

This is the simplest and quickest method (but not necessarily the best).

Time　30 minutes

Objective　For participants to reflect upon and share ideas for implementing their learning.

Process　Ask participants to spend five minutes quietly reflecting, on their own, about what they have gained from the workshop.

They should then take 5–10 minutes to note down two new things (actions, ways of behaving) that they will start to do, and two things that they will do differently from now on, as a result of the workshop (at work, at home, in the community, etc.).

Encourage people to identify practical, do-able things. It is better to make a personal commitment to something small which will have an impact, than to propose something grand which you will never be able to achieve.

Bring the whole group back together and ask each person to share with the rest of the group one of his or her proposed actions. Remind people of their right to pass if they do not want to share their thoughts.

10.1.2   Objective setting

Time   One hour

Objectives   To introduce participants to the SMART objectives tool.

For participants to reflect upon, set, and share objectives for action.

Preparation   Work out an example to use with the group (see sample below).

Process   Introduce the topic: in order to plan and carry out actions successfully, it helps to have a clear idea of what you are trying to achieve – in other words, to define your objectives. The clearer your objectives, the easier it is for everyone to work in a focused way towards them, and to know when they have been met.

Explain that there is a method of setting (describing) realistic objectives, known as SMART objectives. On a flipchart or board, write the letters:

S
M
A
R
T

Then go through them in turn, explaining what each stands for:

Specific: not general and vague, but practical and concrete

Measurable: how many? how much? to what degree?

Achievable: do you have enough people? the resources you need?

Realistic: is it possible to do what is being proposed?

Timebound: within a fixed time limit

Work through an example with the whole group (see the sample in the facilitator's notes below).

Divide participants into groups of four or five. Or, if participants are from various organisations, ask them to work with people from the same organisation as their own.

Ask them to work together to set four objectives for themselves, for putting into practice the things that they have found valuable in the workshop: in their work, their community, their home life, etc. (choose one, depending on the type of workshop).

Set a maximum time limit of three or six months from the date of the workshop, but make it clear that they can set different timescales within that limit for different objectives, depending on how long they think, being realistic, it will take to achieve.

Remind participants to be very specific about their objectives, to think about achievable practical actions, rather than big ideas; go around during the group-work time to find out if they need help with this.

Give out flipchart paper and pens. They have 30 minutes to discuss and write up their objectives.

Bring the whole group back together. Each small group presents its objectives to the rest. Allow time for questions and comments.

Explain that by using a SMART objective as a starting point, you can then plan all the actions needed to reach the objective.

Facilitator's notes

Here is an example to work through. Participants are activists from several rural women's groups, who attended an introductory disability-awareness workshop. An objective such as 'to make disabled women's lives better' is too vague, as is 'to raise awareness of disabled women's issues'. They are not focused on action, and are not SMART. Ask the group to suggest why not, letter by letter if necessary.

A truly SMART objective would be: *Within the next two months, to work with two other group members to identify all the disabled women living in my village, and visit each one to tell her about our group and invite her to meetings.*

Options

Depending on the focus of the workshop, you may wish to omit some of the SMART elements, especially if you are concerned to set objectives that are concerned with putting attitudes into action. For example, not patronising disabled people; not pushing a wheelchair user's chair without asking if that is what s/he wants and where s/he wants to go. These are specific and relevant objectives, but they are not fully SMART.

10.1.3 Eight sunrays of planning

You may want to move on next to the 'Eight sunrays of planning' (described in detail in 8.3.1). Ask participants to return to their small groups, as in the SMART objectives exercise, choose one of the objectives and work out plans to achieve it, using the sunrays as a guide.

10.1.4   'Nothing about us without us'

This is a good exercise for action planning with NGOs, intergovernment agencies, and other organisations.

Time   One hour

Objective   For participants to identify actions that they can take to include disabled people at all stages of programme planning and implementation.

Process   Write up on flipchart paper or a board: 'Nothing about us without us'. Explain that this is the motto of Disabled Peoples' International. It refers to disabled people's participation in all aspects of life, and the need for consultation with disabled people on all matters that affect them.

Divide people into groups of three or four (according to the organisation that they represent, if appropriate). Ask them to decide how they will put this motto into effect in their work, and to agree on four actions that they will take (possibly using SMART objectives, if helpful).

After 20–30 minutes, bring everyone back together. Each small group presents its ideas in turn.

Allow time for questions and discussion of any issues of particular interest or concern.

10.1.5   More planning exercises

There are other exercises elsewhere in this manual that might also be used as part of action planning – for example, in order to plan a public event to mark the annual International Day of Disabled People (3 December); or to plan a meeting to lobby international NGOs and agencies to ensure that disabled people are included in their programmes; or to plan a project to identify disabled people among the refugee population and assess their needs. The approach used in exercise 8.3.2 and the 'Identifying allies' exercise (9.3.12) could also be used in action planning.

10.2 Half-day or whole-day session on action planning

Facilitator's notes For the DETOT course in Kosovo, which was training disabled and non-disabled rights activists, we divided action planning into two sections. The first explored what participants could do now, in their current situation, using resources that they already had. The second explored what they wanted to start to do, in the short- to medium-term future, which would be totally new: activities which might require more planning, or training, different or more resources, or whatever. Part of the reason for this division was to stress the idea that many things could be done right away without additional resources, despite the grave political and economic problems prevailing in Kosovo at the time.

The activities for these two sections are presented below. They could be combined with one or more of the exercises suggested in the previous section.

10.2.1 Immediate action

Time 45 minutes

Objective For participants to recognise and specify how they can use experiences and learning from the training course in their current situation and activities.

Process Ask participants to spend five minutes thinking individually about all the things they can do to implement their learning now, in their local DPO, community centre, family, etc.; in their rehabilitation work, during outreach visits, etc.

Then ask people to form pairs and discuss their ideas. (20 minutes)

Bring the whole group back together for feedback in the round, one pair at a time.

Write up their ideas on a flipchart or board as they speak.

Allow time for questions and comments, and conclude by noting the wealth of positive changes and ideas that they can put into practice.

10.2.2 Future actions: a competition

Time 30 minutes

Objective To give free expression to participants' aspirations for their disability-rights activism.

Preparation Buy or make small prizes.

Process Divide participants into two groups; give each group flipchart paper and pens.

Explain that they should think about new things that they would like to start doing as disability-rights activists, using what they have gained from the workshop. These activities might need preparation, resources, planning, etc.

They should write down every suggestion made, no matter how impossible it currently seems. They may use symbols instead of words if they prefer.

Tell them that this is a competition, to see which group can produce the greatest number of good ideas.

Bring the whole group back together and review the two lists.

Give prizes to participants in the winning group (and consolation prizes to the other group if you want to).

10.2.3 Future actions exercise: diamond ranking

Time 1 hour 15 minutes

Objectives To set priorities for future actions.

To do this as a consensual group process.

To discuss the relevance of consensus in prioritising (or planning) situations.

Preparation Make four sets of nine blank index cards (or similar).

Process Ask each of the two groups from the previous exercise to divide in two, making four small groups.

Give out the sets of cards. Explain that as a group they should decide on the nine most important suggestions, taken from either of the two lists compiled in the previous exercise. Stress that decision making should be by consensus, i.e. accepted by all members, not by majority vote. (15 minutes)

Then they should write one suggestion (in words or symbol) on each of the index cards.

Next, they should decide as a group how to rank their nine chosen suggestions in order of importance. They should illustrate their priorities by putting the cards in a diamond shape, where the one at the top is most important, and the one at the bottom is the least important.

```
    []
   [] []
  [] [] []
   [] []
    []
```

Bring everyone back together. Each group has five minutes to show its diamond and explain the priorities.

Discuss the decision-making process that took place: was it hard? easy? Why is it important to reach consensus? Are there times when decision making by consensus is not appropriate? Can they give examples?

11 Evaluation

Evaluation of each workshop, or other group activity, is an invaluable part of the learning process for both facilitators and participants. Depending on what type of activity you choose, evaluation can do the following:

- Help facilitators to gauge what/how much participants have learned, and what areas still need to be covered.

- Provide feedback from participants in order to improve future work.

- Give participants a safe space in which to offer criticism, to tell the facilitator what didn't work, or wasn't appropriate, and why. (In many cultures it is considered inappropriate or disrespectful to criticise someone in person – even if it is done constructively.)

- Create an opportunity for problems to be brought into the open and dealt with.

- Provide an opportunity to recognise and value everyone's contributions.

- Help participants to reflect on what they have learned.

- Close the session in a meaningful way, drawing together the key points, rather than ending in an abrupt or inconclusive manner.

11.1 Quick evaluations in the round

At the end of the day, each person in turn, including facilitator(s) and interpreter(s)

- gives one word to express how he or she feels about the day's events;

- gives three adjectives/words to describe the atmosphere in the group today;

- names the one thing that he/she liked most, and the one thing that he/she liked least about today;

- states one thing from the workshop that he/she wants to share with someone outside the group;

- says what he/she would do differently, in the facilitator's role;

- says what he/she would do more of, and what less of, in the facilitator's role;

- gives appreciation to the whole group, on a personal level, for the workshop and/or for people's contributions.

Use only one of the above options per workshop. Remind people before starting that they may 'pass' if they do not wish to comment.

11.2   Small-group and whole-group evaluation activities

11.2.1   Sketch/mime

In groups of three, participants take ten minutes to devise a sketch or mime showing the most important thing that they learned from the workshop. They then perform the sketches. Alternatively, you may decide to use the sketches as the start of the next session, as a refresher. This is particularly helpful if some considerable time has elapsed between two workshops.

11.2.2   Throw out or keep

Before the workshop, take a cardboard box, cut a hole into it, and cover it with scraps and bits of rubbish. For the evaluation, place the box in the middle of the floor, give each participant four pieces of paper and a pen, and ask them to write or draw anything they have experienced in the workshop that they would like to leave behind when they go home, and anything that they would like to keep and take home with them. The thing(s) they would like to throw out can be put in the rubbish box. Then ask them to share with the rest of the group one (of the) thing(s) that they would like to keep.

11.2.3   Song

Ask participants to work together in groups of four to produce a song that either expresses what they have learned today about whatever the main topic was; or sums up how they feel about today. Give them 20 minutes to prepare, then five minutes each to perform. Make it clear that this is just for fun, not a music competition. (If some people do not feel comfortable singing, they can do a spoken song, or poem instead.)

A variation on this activity, depending on what types of music are common in the country where you are working, is to write different styles of music, one per group, on separate pieces of paper before the workshop, fold them up and have each group draw a paper from a hat. They have to compose their song in the style named on their paper.

11.3 Mid-way evaluations

During a long course of workshops it is a good idea to devise some type of midway evaluation, which allows the facilitator to gauge how far participants have come and check whether plans for the next stage in the course are appropriate, or if they need to be adjusted – and how.

For the DETOT course in Kosovo, two exercises, incorporated at the end of the first section of training, which were concerned with facilitation skills, helped us to identify remaining gaps in participants' knowledge or experience about facilitation (which we then tried to address during the second part of the course); and helped us to find out how much participants had absorbed about the disability-awareness issues that were presented indirectly during the section on how to train/facilitate. This helped us to avoid unnecessary repetition and to focus our time and energy during the second section of the course, which dealt directly with disability awareness.

11.3.1 Reflecting on facilitation

Time   40 minutes

Objective   To conclude the focused work on facilitation skills, we included this exercise to give participants an opportunity to reflect on, share, and sum up their experiences from the practice sessions, as well as information taken from the facilitators' input and group discussions. It also gave the facilitators an opportunity to do an informal evaluation of participants' learning about facilitation to date.

Process   Working in pairs, participants take a few minutes to think back over their own facilitation of the practice sessions: what they thought was good, and what they found difficult. They should think also about everything they have heard from the facilitator and other participants about facilitation skills.

With their partners, they should make memory checklists for themselves – a reminder of points that they think are important to keep in mind for their next experience of facilitating.

Give each pair a sheet of flipchart paper, on which one partner should write for both people in the pair.

After 15 minutes, bring the whole group back together and display all the lists around the room.

Give people time to move around the room and read each other's lists. Ask them to make a (mental) note of anything that is not clear to them.

When everyone has read all the lists, bring them back together and give time for questions, clarification, and comments.

If the group includes people who are non-literate or who have impaired sight or restricted mobility, adapt the method of making the lists and the method of whole-group feedback to suit the circumstances.

11.3.2 **Writing and drawing**

Objective   As for the previous exercise.

Process   Divide people into groups of four. Ask them to take a few minutes to think back over all of the issues about disability that have arisen in the course of the workshops so far.

In their groups they should take ten minutes to write, or draw symbols to represent, each of those issues on flipchart paper.

Each small group presents its work to the whole group.

For each issue, make a note of how many of the groups mentioned it.

Allow time for questions and comments.

You can sum up by highlighting the issues raised most commonly, and explaining briefly what you hope to cover in the second part of the course.

11.3.3 Collage

This is quite a long exercise, but it is very satisfying to do at the end of a series of workshops or a course. It gives people a personal, creative, and collaborative way of evaluating their experience and learning. The finished collages serve as attractive and lasting reminders of what participants have shared. It is good to use as a balance to a detailed evaluation questionnaire.

Preparation Decide on the general theme for the collages (for example, 'Your group's message to the general public about disability').

Collect together a variety of materials: cloth, coloured paper, string, wool, shells, words or phrases cut from relevant articles or workshop materials, photographs, leaves, pebbles, shiny things, and other objects; plus pens, crayons, staplers, glue, scissors, and one large piece of thick white paper per group. If you explain the exercise to participants at the previous workshop, they will have time to reflect on it, and to bring in their own objects to include in their collage.

Process Ask people to form groups of four, and explain that as a way of evaluating the overall course you would like them to work together to make a collage to show their interpretation of whatever general theme you have chosen.

Put materials in the centre of the room for participants to take what they want. They have one hour to make the collage, and then five minutes for each group to share its work with the whole group. Use the feedback time as an opportunity to thank all the participants for their contributions.

11.4   Questionnaires

11.4.1   Questionnaire for general use at the end a day's workshop

Q1.   What do you think was the purpose of today's workshop?

Q2.   Give a mark from 1 to 5 (where 1 is low and 5 is high) to show your assessment of the effectiveness or value of the following:
  • subject matter/content
  • timing
  • facilitation
  • organisation
  • training methods used
  • balance between theory and practice. (If the balance was not good, was there too much theory or too much practice?)

Q3.   What was the most useful topic, item, or activity?

Q4.   What was the least useful topic, item, or activity?

Q5.   Please give any other comments or suggestions

11.4.2   To end a facilitation-practice session

Q1.   Which activity did you like best today, as a participant?

Q2.   Which activity did you like best today, as a facilitator?

Q3.   Which activity did you learn most from? Why?

Q4.   Were there any activities that you did not like? Yes / No
If Yes, which?
Why?

Q5.   Were there any activities that you did not understand? Yes / No.
If Yes, which?

Note: today's practice activities were:
A [name it]
B
C
D etc.

11.4.3 Detailed questionnaire for a final evaluation

For use at the end of a series of workshops. Handout 40 is a copy of the one that we used at the end of the DETOT course in Kosovo. You should adapt it to your own circumstances. Invite participants to complete it at home and bring it back to a final session or celebration.

HANDOUT 40
Final evaluation questionnaire

Please note that you should not put your name on the questionnaire, and that all the information that you give will be completely confidential. This is so that you can write freely what you really think.

1 **Our hopes for this course**

As a group, our hopes at the start of this course were as follows:

- to become more aware of the situation of disabled people
- to increase the independence of disabled people
- to share our experiences and opinions with each other
- to enable us to support (other) disabled people effectively
- to contribute to creating a better future for disabled people, and the realisation of our/their rights
- to discover together ways of designing workshops suitable for our society

Q.1. How far do you feel that we have met these hopes through the course? (Please mark 1–5, next to each of the above hopes: 1 means that we did not meet the hope, 5 means that we met it completely.)

2 **Your participation**

Q.2.1 How involved did you feel in the following (please tick the answer that applies in each case):

	very involved	involved	partly involved	not at all involved
In whole-group discussions?				
In exercises?				
In the practice facilitations?				
Overall?				

Q.2.2 What did you like most about being in the group?

Q.2.3 What did you like least about being in the group?

(continued)

3   Course content

Here is a summary of the topics that we covered in the two parts of the course:

Part 1: Training in facilitation skills

- Forming the group (introductions, hopes and fears, getting to know each other, agreeing group guidelines)
- Respect and listening skills; self-esteem; participation
- What is facilitation? The role of facilitators, and the skills required
- Learning process and rates; how adults learn; learning styles
- Practice in facilitation
- Designing training sessions: deciding on topic, content (skills, knowledge, attitudes, methods)
- Planning skills: planning an event
- Prejudice/diversity/valuing different people's contributions
- Role of Local Action Groups and role of disabled people in LAGs
- Methods of evaluation

Part 2: Disability equality

- Human rights/disabled people's rights
- Models of disability
- Barriers to equal participation/overcoming barriers
- Gender and disability
- Independent (self-determined) living; assertiveness
- Images of disability
- Language of disability
- Causes and prevention of disability (from a human-rights perspective)
- Feelings about being or becoming disabled

Q.3.1   Was it helpful to you to have the course divided into two parts like this?

Yes   No   Partially   (please circle)

If No or Partially, please say how you think we could have it done it better.

Q.3.2   Do you feel that we respected the priorities for topics that you set at the beginning of the course? (Please mark 1–5; 1 means that we did not meet them at all, 5 means that we did meet them completely.)

Q.3.3   Which two topics did you most enjoy in each part?

Part 1

Part 2

Q.3.4   Which two topics did you least enjoy in each part?

Part 1

Part 2

Q.3.5   Which two topics in each part were most useful to you as a LAG member?

Part 1

Part 2

Q.3.6   Which two topics in each part were least useful to you as a LAG member?

Part 1

Part 2

Q.3.7   Which two topics in each part did you find easiest to understand?

Part 1

Part 2

(continued)

Q.3.8   Which two topics in each part did you find hardest to understand?

Part 1

Part 2

Q.3.9   Please name any topics that did we not cover which you think should have been covered.

Q.3.10   Please assess the visual information (e.g. flipcharts, diagrams) used during the workshops. Was it

    a. understandable? (please mark 1–5; 1 means not understandable, 5 means very understandable) _____

    b. relevant? (please mark 1–5) _____

    c. too much? too little? the right amount? (please circle which one applies)

Q.3.11   Please assess the handouts that were given to you to take home. Were they

    a. understandable? (please mark 1–5; 1 means not understandable, 5 means very understandable) _____

    b. relevant? (please mark 1–5) _____

    c. too many? too few? the right number? (please circle which one applies)

Q.3.12   Could you understand the language used by the facilitators/interpreter during workshops

always / nearly always / sometimes / almost never / never?

(please circle which one applies)

Q.3.13   Do you think that there were enough opportunities for you to practise facilitating during the course?

YES   NO   (please circle which one applies)

Q.3.14   Which difficult or sensitive issues did we deal with appropriately?

Q.3.15   Which difficult or sensitive issues did we not deal with appropriately – and why?

Q.3.16   Did you learn anything about yourself during the training?

NO / YES   (please circle which one applies)

If YES, please explain.

4   **Facilitation methods**

The working methods that we used generally were the following:

- brainstorms
- whole-group discussion
- whole-group exercises
- small-group discussion
- small-group exercises
- pairs discussion
- pairs exercises
- individual exercises
- presentations by participants
- presentations by facilitators
- each person talking in turn around the group
- light-hearted games

Q.4.1   Which of the above methods did you like best?

Q.4.2   Which of the above methods did you like least?

Q.4.3   Which method(s) do you think you will use most in the future?

5   **The future**

Q.5.1   How in the future do you want to use the information, skills, etc. that you gained from this course: (a) with your work in the LAG/centre? (b) in your everyday life?

Q.5.2   How confident do you feel to use the information, skills, etc. from this course in the following situations? (please mark 1–5; 1 means not at all confident, 5 means very confident):

- doing workshops
- working informally with groups of people
- in your work in the LAG/centre
- in your everyday life

Q.5.3   What further training or support do you need to be able to use the information, skills, etc. that you gained from this course?

(continued)

Q.5.4   Which topics do you need more input on?

Q.5.5   If you were going to facilitate a workshop in the future, which two participants from our group would you choose as your co-facilitators ? (Remember, this information is confidential.)

Feedback about the facilitators and interpreter

Q.6.1   Please give marks from 1 to 5 for the following criteria (for example, 1 means not clear, not open, 5 means very clear, very open, etc):

	clear/ understandable	supportive	knows what s/he is talking about	open to other people's ideas/suggestions
name				
name				
name				
name				
name				

Q.6.2.   Do you wish to make any other comments about the facilitators or interpreter? And/or can you offer suggestions to help them to improve their work.

7   The venue

Q. 7.1   Please give marks 1–5 (1 means very bad, 5 means very good) for the following criteria:
- accessibility
- comfort
- room temperature
- refreshments (coffee, juice, biscuits)
- lunch arrangements
- room layout (could you always see, hear, and communicate well?)
- other facilities (such as kitchen, toilets, use of telephone)

Q.7.2   Can you suggest how to improve the venue?

8   **Timing**

Q.8.1   Was the length of the course (five months)

too long / too short / about right? (please circle the one that applies)

Q.8.2   Was the length of each weekly session (10.30–16.00)

too long / too short / about right? (please circle the one that applies)

Q.8.3   Did we try to put too much content into one day

always / usually / sometimes / never? (please circle the one that applies)

9   **Logistics and general arrangements**

Q.9.1   Please describe any other problems that you had and/or please make suggestions for improvements.

Thank you again for you time and assistance!

12 Case studies

12.1 Individual case studies

This set of six studies may be used with a variety of participant groups, to learn about the lives of disabled people in different countries and examine what barriers they encountered and how they overcame them, as well as their on-going problems. Participants may be able to identify parallels with (and differences from) their own experience, or that of disabled people in their country, and maybe will find ideas for action. The case studies may be used to stimulate discussion about the role of disabled people and their organisations in working on issues which affect the lives of disabled people. They may be edited or shortened as required.

Oxfam acknowledges the valuable contribution of Action on Disability and Development, whose staff supplied the first four case studies in this section, and all the case studies in section 12.3.

12.1.1 Shapla, Bangladesh

Mahfuja Akhter Shapla, now 18 years old, was born in a village in Bangladesh. Her family's income was less than $2 a day. Clean water and nutritious food were in short supply, and the children were not immunised against common childhood diseases. Shapla contracted polio at the age of 3; it affected both her legs. Unable to walk, and not provided with crutches or callipers, she had to be carried to school by her mother. Other children teased her, and she gradually lost confidence in herself because the teachers discouraged every initiative that she tried to take. Eventually she stopped going to school, and her mother was left worrying about her future. Since Shapla's family were not aware of the cause of her disability, her mother was blamed, and the girl was regarded as a burden to her family. Her parents separated as a result.

When Shapla was a little older, she joined a self-help group in her village, supported by ADD (Action on Disability and Development). The group made her aware of the rights of disabled people, and gave her confidence to take part in meetings and decision-making. She was encouraged to return to mainstream education and learn computer skills. She has now completed her secondary education, and with the help of ADD she has established a computer training centre for young people. She supports her mother and young brother, who have no paid work, although her mother runs an informal school in their community, with Shapla's help.

Shapla says: 'I feel proud, because I am a disabled woman running a computer centre. There is no competition in this area. I train many non-disabled people, as well as disabled students. It has involved me in the community. I now attend more disability groups and I have been elected as the secretary of our federation. I would like to support many more disabled people in income-generating activities, and I want to participate in the regional and national disability movement, to establish the rights of disabled people in Bangladesh.'

(Case study adapted from *The ADDvocate*, Issue 13, Spring 2002), published by Action on Disability and Development (ADD))

12.1.2   **Mamadou, Mali**

Mamadou Mahi Coulibaly lives in the town of Ségou. His father, a jeweller, took him out of school to train as an apprentice with one of his own former apprentices. Mamadou quickly learned the trade, and after three years he went to work with his father.

'In 1995 I was approached by a friend to join an association of disabled people that was being formed. At first I couldn't see any point in it. I had not experienced any problems because of my disability. My father gave me responsibility when I was very young; this obliged the rest of the family to respect me, and I learned to value my own abilities. But my friend kept on insisting. That night I gave it some thought and I decided to join. I joined the association to exchange ideas with others. It has been a space for me to think about what it is to be disabled; for example, different people have different levels of impairment. Now when I meet other disabled people, I tell them that joining a group can open up your mind and change your ideas.'

Mamadou began working for himself as a jeweller, but could not make enough profit to enable him to buy raw materials and therefore take on orders. 'When I joined the association I didn't expect money, but in 1999 I got a loan to help me to expand my business. I had not considered taking a loan from anywhere before joining the group. I was too poor to take a loan from a credit and savings organisation whose interest rates were too high, and I was scared of handling money. But now I have had one experience, a good one, it has given me the confidence to consider expanding a bit further.

'Before I got the loan, I had to do a 45-day literacy course in Bambara, the language that everybody here uses for trading; and a five-day course in business management and accounting. When I got the loan, I bought raw materials and extra tools. I had to repay it within one year, which I have done. Now I can take orders, and I also send things to my sister, who lives in Nieno. She sells them for me and sends me the money.'

Mamadou has now taken on an apprentice of his own, who is also disabled. 'Disabled people are often stuck sitting around, with no purpose. My door is open to anyone who would like to be trained in the jewellery trade.'

(Case study adapted from an interview conducted by an ADD staff member in 2000)

12.1.3 Lao Sonn, Cambodia

Dr Lao Sonn, 52 years old, was blinded by a bomb explosion while hoeing in a field in 1976.

'This happened during the early months of the Pol Pot regime. I was formerly a doctor in the provincial hospital and a surgeon in the army. The explosion caused injuries to my upper body and total blindness to both of my eyes. In the past, I just stayed in the house, not going anywhere, and feeling sad about my situation. I didn't want anybody to see my condition, as I was afraid that they would ridicule me.

'One day, the staff of ADD came to our village and gathered all the disabled people to meet together. For twenty years I had been hoping for someone, or some organisation like ADD, to assist me. We formed an association in 1998, and my life became more hopeful. I am more confident in myself and happier to participate in life. We help each other to solve problems, such as acquiring crutches and other prosthetics. The group also gives me inspiration and counselling support.

'I was divorced from my wife after being disabled, because her family looked down on me. She still comes once in a while to check on me, but she cannot and will not live with me. That occasionally angers me, and it drives me to teach my two sons well, so that they can have a good future.

'I used to live in a small house with my parents. Later I was able to build my own house, and now my son and daughter-in-law live with me. This son works for an NGO. My other son is a teacher. I take pride in the fact that despite my visual impairment I was able to tutor my children through primary school and high school.

'I now walk around the village by myself and communicate with others. I know how to lead a group and how to conduct meetings. There are nine other members in my group, but one [the sole woman member] died last month; she was 76 years old and in poor health. There are other people in the community with minor disabilities, such as those who lost a finger, and a few others who have not been willing to join. We have a credit programme, which is also open to non-disabled people.

'I have accepted my disability and become used to it. My daughter-in-law helps to take care of the house, and I continue to do the cooking myself. I am raising five chickens, which I hope to profit from. I plant apple trees around my house and harvest the fruit to be sold in the market. Even though I am blind, I can do things like everyone else, and I take pride in that fact. My family treats me well, and I think the community respects me because of my capacity.'

(Case study taken from an interview with an ADD staff member)

12.1.4 **Françoise, Burkina Faso**

Françoise Diarra lives in Banfora, Burkina Faso. She struggled to get through school, because her parents did not think that it was worth sending her. So she wrote to an aunt who had moved to France, and the aunt agreed to support her until she had completed her education. Françoise trained as a secretary, but has not been able to get regular employment.

'They think that if you can't walk, you can't work in an office – that you can't do anything. And then they pity you. I don't want pity, I want to show what I am capable of. In my last work placement I think I at least changed people's thinking. The boss wasn't sure whether to take me on, but I was able to show him that being disabled didn't prevent me from doing my job. I encouraged people there not to fear for me, thinking that I couldn't manage, or worrying that I would fall down the stairs.'

Unable to make her living from office work, she had the idea of setting up a project to make and sell *soumbala* – black spice balls. She invited other women in her DPO to collaborate with her. Four decided to join her venture. They all invested the same small amount each month, until they could buy a special bowl for preparing the seeds.

'We needed to keep the rest of the money back, to buy seed stock throughout the year. So we could not afford to buy the fuelwood that we needed. I went to a wood merchant in the town and explained our situation. He gave us a stock of wood and told me to come back when we ran out. I think he took pity on us, but also he wanted to help because we showed our capacity and our determination to do something with the little money that we had.

'Our business is successful. I use the money that I make to repair my tricycle, to send my younger son to school, and to support the other one in his mechanic apprenticeship. You know, there are things that we can do that people who aren't disabled can't do: we have courage that they don't have.'

(From an interview with an ADD staff member in 2000)

12.1.5 Annya, Abkhazia

Annya became disabled after the war between Georgia and Abkhazia. She and her family were threatened and forced to leave their town of Sukhumi after being caught hiding in a neighbour's house.

She writes: 'After the initial shock of becoming disabled and losing my old life and home and surroundings, I started to re-assess things. I have always been positive, and even though everything had been taken, I saw that I still had life. It was difficult at first – particularly when my mother died, a year after being forced to leave Sukhumi. I was treated as a second-class citizen. I taught German to other children and adults, but no one paid me money, because I was disabled and I wasn't considered to be of enough worth to be paid.

'I wanted to help my family and the people whom I saw around me. I didn't know how, until I heard about the Disabled Women's Group in Zugdidi. I went along. They needed an English-speaking interpreter. After a while, a job opportunity presented itself. It was my first job interview. I never thought I would get paid work, because I was a disabled person. I gave everything I had. I got the job on my own merit. I was very proud. And now I see that my life has even more meaning and purpose than before. I am a disabled person. I have a cause. I "belong" to an oppressed group. I can work hard and long.'

(From an interview with an Oxfam staff member)

12.1.6 Caroline, Kenya

I was born with cerebral palsy in the Machakos district of Kenya.
I am able to walk but not to speak. As a child it was difficult for me to
attend physiotherapy sessions regularly, because of the nature of my
father's job: he got transferred from town to town very often.

Eventually my mother and I went back to our rural home in Mt Elgon
district. I stayed there, but life was difficult for me, because my sisters
had begun school and I was home most of the time on my own, only
with a cousin. In 1985 my father moved to Nairobi. He met a doctor
who told him that he could treat me. So father came home to take me
to that doctor, who gave me some medicines. After I took them, I went
into a coma for five days; then I had convulsions and I did not sleep for
four days. My parents took me to another doctor. He gave me some
other medicine and I stopped having convulsions; but I was weak, so I
stayed in Nairobi for six months. Afterwards I went back home. Many
people were not interested in becoming my friends, for fear that they
might become like me. But my family was friendly to me.

Then in 1989 my father moved to Nakuru, and he and my mother decided
to take me to school. The first days in school were difficult for me, because
I was not able to use a pencil to write. So that time I hated myself, because
I was wishing to write like any child in that class. But my teacher tried his
best. He cut wood into small pieces and wrote the letters of the alphabet
on them. He taught me how to write my name, and I learned a lot of
things. I was able to read and write. But I wished to have a computer, so
that it would be easy to write without the help of someone else; because
when I used the small pieces of wood to write things, I needed someone
to help me by writing everything down on the paper or in the book.
Sometimes it was difficult to get someone to help me, and it was hard for
me to get a computer, until in 1999 I met someone from Germany in
school. She made a communication board for me. It helped me a lot: it
meant that I could communicate with anyone, although I am speechless.
My friend has also assisted me in another way: she sent a computer for
me. It was brought by other friends from Germany. They trained me how
to use a computer. I have even had a chance to represent my school in
certain seminars, and I am glad to say that I can now operate a computer.

My life is just to show you an example of how far a little help given to a
disabled person can do wonders in their life and in the life of others,
and in developing the whole world.

*(Reproduced with permission from 'Disabled in Kenya' by Caroline
Sakura; with acknowledgements to Susanne Klug and Astrid Keller.)*

12.2 Disabled refugees and internally displaced people: case studies with questions

This set of case studies was used in an Oxfam workshop where participants were a mix of expatriate staff and local NGO employees in Eastern Europe, working with refugees and displaced people. All the participants were non-disabled. The workshop aimed to make NGO staff aware of the following:

- the existence of disabled people among the refugee/displaced population;
- the responsibilities of NGOs in respect of disabled people's rights;
- reasons why those responsibilities are often not met;
- the types of problem that disabled people may face as part of the refugee experience (in particular, becoming subject to the control and charity of others, and being excluded from decision-making and resource allocation).

Each of these situation studies is based on the real experiences of a disabled refugee or displaced person; only the names and personal details have been changed. It is important to encourage workshop participants to see the disabled people themselves as the first source of information and possible solutions. What resources and strategies did they use before the current crisis to organise their lives?

12.2.1 Hassan

Hassan is affected by polio and uses a wheelchair. He and his family
fled from his home town, where he had his own small business
repairing clocks and watches. His family are Emina, his 73-year-old
mother; Sanja, his wife, who walks with crutches, also as a result of
polio; and their seven-year-old son, Amir. After an exhausting six-day
journey, the family arrive at a refugee reception centre (a school sports-
hall) and are accommodated there for a week. During this time Hassan
forces himself to eat and drink only the bare minimum, because the
toilets are inaccessible (his wheelchair cannot pass through the narrow
door), none of his family is strong enough to carry him in, and mostly
the other refugees in the centre are too caught up in their own
problems and trauma to help him regularly. He can't drag himself
across the floor, because it is wet and filthy: the plumbing system
backs up because it is not designed to deal with so many people using
it. On the occasions when Hassan has managed to get someone to help
him, he found it humiliating and painful, as they did not know how to
lift him properly. He is also worried that he might develop a urinary-
tract infection, which could lead to serious health complications.

Questions   1. What immediate problems are Hassan and his family facing?

2. What rights-related issues are raised by their predicament?

3. How might their problems be resolved? What could your NGO/
   agency do? Who else might be mandated and able to assist?

4 What further problems do you think they may have to deal with?

Suggested   1   Lack of appropriate hygiene and medical resources to meet basic needs.
answers   2   The rights to life, health care, adequate living standards,dignity,
               and control.

3   Ask Hassan what he needs and wants. Possibilities include:
    widening the toilet door (he will be able to tell you the correct
    dimensions); solving the toilet back-up problem and keeping stalls
    clean; providing a portable toilet chair (or having a simple one made);
    arranging for Hassan to see a doctor; putting him in contact with
    the local disabled people's organisation; providing hygiene supplies.

4   What type of accommodation will they be allocated when they move
    from the reception centre? Will it be accessible? Will the authorities
    try to move them to an institution? Will the family be split up?
    If Hassan becomes ill, he may be left too weak to work, or may even
    die. He is the family breadwinner; without him the family will
    become impoverished and dependent on the State or aid agencies.

12.2.2 **Suada**

Suada is a deaf person. She is a single mother of a seven-month-old baby. She lost her husband when their home was attacked two months ago, and she escaped to the other side of the country, leaving everything behind. She is now living alone with the baby. Most nights she makes herself stay awake all night long, because otherwise she will not hear when the baby is crying to be fed. In addition to that, she has a problem when she takes the baby to the local clinic for a check-up. She cannot hear when her name is called by the receptionist, so she misses her turn and has to wait hours and hours in the unheated waiting room. She gave the receptionist a note, asking her to put her name up on a piece of paper when it was her turn, or to come and get her, but the receptionist says she is too busy to do this.

Questions
1. What do you think are the causes of Suada's problems?

2. What rights-related issues are raised by Suada's situation?

3. What possible solutions can you identify? What could your NGO/agency do? Who else might be mandated and able to assist?

4. What other problems do you think that Suada might encounter as a female head of household who is displaced and deaf?

Suggested answers
1 Having to leave behind her possessions when she fled; lack of simple basic resources; the receptionist's attitude; the clinic system, which ignores the needs of the deaf community; social isolation.

2 The child's right to health and health care; Suada's right to accessible information.

3 Ask Suada what she needs and what she wants. Possibilities include: vibrating alarm (or other enabling aid available locally) to wake her when the baby cries; moving to shared accommodation with a woman or family willing to help; sign-language interpreter; contact with other deaf people in the community and/or organisation of deaf people; contact with local women's group; meeting with clinic director to discuss accessible information systems.

4 Grief over the loss of her husband and home; isolation, no one to communicate with; access to aid may be limited if she has no way to find out about it; how will she be able to communicate her needs? As a lone woman with a child to support, she is particularly vulnerable to abuse and exploitation; as a deaf woman she is likely to face discrimination when she tries to find employment.

12.2.3 Milica

Milica is a refugee from Osijek who fled to Serbia with her 10-year-old daughter, Vesna. Milica has muscular dystrophy. She and her daughter were accommodated in a refugee hostel when they arrived, and the State-run home-help service provided her with two hours of assistance a day. When all the refugees from the hostel were moved to other places, a social worker decided to transfer Milica to an institution for people with learning difficulties in another town, and to move her daughter to an orphanage in the town where they had first arrived, so that she could continue attending the regular school.

Questions

1. What problems are Milica and Vesna facing? Do you think the child is being properly looked after? Why? Why not? Do you think Milica is getting the type of assistance that she needs? Why? Why not?

2. Did the social worker resolve the basic problems in the most appropriate way?

3. What rights-related issues are involved?

4. What possible solutions to the current situation can you identify? What could your NGO/agency do? Who else might be mandated and able to assist?

Suggested answers

1. Separation from each other, which will increase the trauma they have already gone through as refugees; the possibility of abuse in institutions; the abuse of rights and freedoms. Vesna needs to be with her mother, who has raised her for 10 years already; Milica's daily life will be severely restricted in the institution, and she may become confined there indefinitely if her problem is seen as resolved. Her special physical needs are unlikely to be cared for in an institution for people with learning difficulties.

2. No, the social worker's response did not take into account Vesna's and Milica's rights and needs.

3. The rights to life, family life, protection, dignity, control.

4. Ask Milica (and Vesna) what they need and want. How did they manage before? What resources do they need in order to return them to that situation? Find accommodation to keep the family together. Arrange for assistance as needed (Milica will tell you what, how often, etc.). Arrange contact with a local women's group and disabled people's group or community group who can assist with these things. Ensure that the mother receives the humanitarian aid to which she is entitled and that she is enabled to participate in other programmes (for example, trauma-support group, seed-distribution programmes).

12.2.4 Flora

'I am from a village in the Drenica region of Kosovo, but I've been in Pristina for six months now. I've been in several places since arriving in the city. The first two months I was with a family, but had to leave as agreed. Then another family hosted me in a caravan for two weeks, but there was no water, so a doctor found me this apartment. When I first came here, they were still building the flat, so it was totally messy with the labourers continuing their work. We had to leave our homes. I came alone with the children. When I found this place, I was so happy that I started clearing it myself, although the owner had told me he would get people to do that for me. I was just so happy to have my own place.

'I am 35 years old and had worked as a nurse since the age of 17. My disability started six years ago. My daughter is 9 years old, and my son 6 years old. My husband is dead.'

Q: Do you know what happened to your home?
A: I visited my village four days ago. My home has not been destroyed, but it has been locked and is totally empty.

Q: Are your children going to school here?
A: Both the children are good pupils and have began their schooling here again, but because of the recent shocks they have suffered they are under observation and don't attend the school full time.

Q: Did you have relatives here in Pristina?
A: No, not originally. My sister is here now with her family; they live on the other side of town, but she spends a lot of time here with us to help me out. Her home (in another village in the same region) was totally destroyed.

'My physical condition is deteriorating. Up to a month ago I was able to move around using crutches, but I no longer have the strength. The association donated my wheelchair, and it was one of the happiest days of my life. It was my sister who brought it round, so I didn't meet them at first. But because I'd been so happy I wanted to meet them, know them. Then I met Amir in the street, and he brought me to the centre. It was a big and happy day for me to see the centre and to meet people with disabilities there. Then Blerim asked me if I'd want to join the association, and I've been going back as often as possible. Blerim told me about the centre's work. It's great. In fact I wanted to know if they had a similar centre in the Drenica area at home, and so now I know that there is indeed a branch of the association there, it's just that I didn't know about it. So when I go back home, I want to be more involved with that branch because now I know what disabled people need and how important it is to help people as I was helped. I know what my situation was and I know the happiness I felt when they brought me a wheelchair, and I would like to help this organisation to help others. I can't wait to go back home and start. I will do so as soon as the basic conditions are ready.

'I had planned to go there three weeks ago. I got as far as the bus could take me, but I couldn't get a car to the village. But finally I managed to get there four days ago. That's when I found that the house had been looted. It's better to live in your own house, but my home is far, and it's difficult for the children.'

Q: What about your living conditions here?
A: The most difficult things are the stairs; then it's hard to provide food for ourselves. People who are working find it difficult to provide for their families – and I have no income. The children are very young. They want to continue their education and they've been ill, and I need money to buy medication because they are good pupils, and they've been studying and I want them to continue their studies. As you can see, the space we're living in isn't very big, and the doors aren't accessible for my wheelchair. We don't have hot water: I must boil the hot water that we use for cleaning dishes and things.

'I would like to be active when I get home, because I personally know 14 people there who have disabilities. You know, although it's important to have help from your family when you are disabled, it's even better to help yourselves and help each other. That's the most difficult thing for me right now: knowing that I need my family's help. My sister helps me a lot, but I would like to be more independent, because I have my life and she has hers: she has her own family, her own children.'

12.3   Case studies of social and political action by disabled people

12.3.1   Grassroots representation in Cambodia

Cambodia has the second highest per capita rate of disability in the world, caused by malnutrition, land mines, and the breakdown of immunisation campaigns and medical services – a legacy of the regime of the extremist communist group, the Khmer Rouge, in the 1970s. Since 1991 international aid has focused on rehabilitation. Despite real progress since then, Cambodia still faces a huge task of rebuilding its social, legal, and economic structures. Cambodia has one of the world's highest proportions of amputees, due to the indiscriminate laying of land mines, which are still a threat today. As a result, disability was first understood as a health-related issue, despite disabled people being among the most marginalised citizens and disproportionately among the poorest in the country.

Action on Disability and Development (ADD) established a programme in the capital city, Phnom Penh, in 1995. ADD development workers began by visiting individual disabled people in their homes, working closely on a one-to-one basis with them to assess their needs. Often ADD staff met with disabled people who were isolated, grossly neglected by their families, and forced to live in appalling conditions; because of the deeply religious culture, disability is often perceived as punishment for a person's sins in another life, or as his or her personal destiny. ADD staff had to work with patience and sensitivity in order to convince disabled people of their own worth and their rights. After working with individuals, ADD went on to address wider social issues, focusing on the discrimination and prejudice that disabled people face within their communities. Disabled people were encouraged to form self-help groups – the first such groups in Cambodia. These are important forums for disabled people to meet with other disabled individuals for social and economic purposes.

> 'I didn't know anybody else with a disability in my village; we never met. Only after ADD came to the village was I aware of the other disabled people.'(Kor Morn, Lompaing Ream village)

ADD organises training for self-help groups in skills such as leadership, so that each group becomes self-sufficient and ADD can move into a new area and start new groups. More recently these groups have been joining forces to form federations of self-help groups, which are more powerfully equipped to effect social and political change.

At the national level, another international organisation had established the Cambodian Disabled People's Organisation (CDPO) in 1995, but it lacked a democratic structure, and local groups felt that the CDPO did not represent them. They did not feel involved, because there was no system at village level for individual groups to influence the actions of CDPO. When CDPO hit a funding crisis in 2001, a Reforming Committee was founded to debate how best to move forwards. It included many disabled people's organisations in Cambodia which were not previously involved with CDPO. The Committee decided to restructure, reorganise, and re-launch CDPO, with the following new principles:

- To be democratic, with leaders and representatives elected by disabled people.
- To be accountable to members.
- Not to deliver services, but to campaign for these services to be provided by the government.
- To build a representative and inclusive movement.
- To provide a unified voice for disabled people

ADD has always taken a rights-based approach to disability and has worked hard with groups of disabled people in order for disability to be understood as a social issue, not a health issue. 'Progress towards anti-discriminatory legislation continues, but at a slow pace,' reports Srey Vanthon, ADD's Programme Manager in Cambodia.

The struggle of the disability movement in Cambodia shows that, while it is always difficult for disabled people to fight for their rights, these difficulties are amplified in a political and social climate such as Cambodia. It takes time to develop a movement that is democratic and effective, and sometimes there are fundamental flaws in the development process. What is evident from the disability movement in Cambodia is that external intervention is not always successful; the voices of disabled people need to be heard from the grassroots level.

12.3.2 The Soroti Agricultural and Craft Association of the Blind, Uganda

In Uganda, a country where two-thirds of the population live in poverty, people with visual impairments are severely disadvantaged: they are isolated within their communities, or they have families to support, and they lack skills because education and training courses for blind people simply do not exist. They have a great need to learn the skills that will enable them to lead independent and respected lives.

After the National Resistance Movement came to power in 1986, civil war in Eastern Uganda forced hundreds of people to flee from the town of Soroti and the surrounding regions to Sudan, leaving behind terrified and displaced blind people. People such as Angela Sifrosa, who had worked hard for years to become proud owners of farmland, had their houses, food, and crops burnt.

However, the blind people of Soroti managed to find enough food to survive until the civil war ended and the refugees returned. A group of people with impaired vision were able to get places on an agricultural training course, something that had been denied them when they were younger. After they had graduated from the course, in 1992, they decided to unite in order to take action: the Soroti Agricultural and Craft Association of the Blind (SACAB) was born.

The group, which included Angela Sifrosa and John Stephen Okello, now had the knowledge and skills necessary to farm successfully and independently. Angela and her friends were determined to show others that 'blind people can be independent'. But they had no land of their own. 'If we continue asking for help, will you be able to go on assisting us for all those years? We think it is better for you to give us land whereby we can try to do something for ourselves. We have the skills,' argued John Stephen, presenting their case to the local district authority. After a long fight, SACAB were eventually given the land that they needed in order to establish themselves.

The members of the group were malnourished and exhausted and had to clear the land of a high, dense scrub with their bare hands. They desperately needed extra resources. In 1995 Action on Disability and Development was approached by SACAB, who asked for help to make their vision for the Association a reality. SACAB wanted to do more than simply produce enough food to live on; their vision was to give training to other blind people in independent living and agriculture; and to raise the profile and status of blind people within their community and to give others new opportunities. They themselves had overcome the odds and wanted to provide the very things that were lacking in the Soroti region: essential training and education for the blind.

A grant from ADD enabled them to buy four oxen, a plough and some tools. SACAB now farms a variety of crops, including millet, maize, beans, and tomatoes, together with 40 goats, in addition to the original oxen. SACAB trains blind people of all ages in agricultural skills, which include the handling of crops and livestock, cooking, collecting firewood, and reading and writing Braille. Basic accommodation is provided for the trainees by the Association, which is paid for by the local authority of the sub-county of each trainee. The aim is for graduates of the SACAB courses to run their own independent courses for other blind people on their return to their villages, which creates a new unity between blind people and dispels isolation and poverty.

'We are free now,' says Angela, who now teaches Braille at SACAB and attends council meetings regularly, where she lobbies hard for the districts to contribute to the trainees' fees. This is a continuing problem,because some districts refuse to pay the full fees. Angela is active and respected within the wider community of Soroti. John Stephen Okello is now the Training Manager of SACAB, and also teaches Braille.

SACAB is an example of how disabled people are able to break free from the confines of social exclusion and escape the disenfranchisement caused by poverty and conflict. Their achievement demonstrates how disabled people do not need or want charity, but support to enable them to develop sustainable, independent lives. Disabled people have the right to freedom and independence, and they will fight for these rights with dignity to become newly empowered members of their communities.

12.3.3 Election monitoring and the right to vote in Ghana, Bangladesh, and Zambia

In 2000, Action on Disability and Development (ADD) launched a project in Ghana to enable disabled people to vote in the national elections freely and fairly, and to train as accredited election observers. This ground-breaking project provided disabled people with the information and resources that they needed to bring about a new political equality for the first time in their history.

'People with disabilities comprise at least ten per cent of the population of developing nations. Yet they remain largely invisible to the decision- and policy-makers who design and implement government programs.'(International Foundation for Electoral Systems (IFES))

In many countries, disabled people can't and don't vote, for two main reasons:

- Inaccessible polling booths, long queues, and the lack of tactile ballot papers (for blind and partially sighted people) mean that disabled people are excluded from the voting process by physical circumstances.

- As the vast majority of disabled people have never been able to vote, it is assumed (by both disabled and non-disabled citizens) that people with impairments don't have the right to take part in the democratic process. They are excluded by negative attitudes and lack of awareness.

ADD worked with disabled people's organisations in Ghana to gain the vote for disabled people in the 2000 Presidential and Parliamentary elections. Success in this venture encouraged similar projects in Bangladesh and Zambia in 2001. Further to this, ADD worked in partnership with the US-based International Foundation for Electoral Systems (IFES) to train disabled people as election monitors. It was the first time that disabled people had observed elections in all three of these countries.

Workshops were held to raise awareness and educate disabled people about the electoral process and their right to vote. Dramatisations and music were performed by groups of disabled people, and the message was carried further by advertisements, posters, television features, and printed t-shirts. Press conferences were held, and there was an overall positive reaction from the national press in each of the countries. The BBC World Service carried a feature on the work that was taking place in Bangladesh, which included an interview with a disabled man who said, 'The significant volume of media coverage has raised the level of awareness of the issues relating to disabled people to a new height.'

Extensive discussions were held with electoral officials to ensure that disabled people had fair access to the electoral process. This included securing permission for blind people to be accompanied in the polling booth by a person of their choice, making the booths accessible, and allowing people who could not stand for long periods to 'jump the queue' in order to cast their vote.

Disabled people were trained to serve as accredited election monitors, responsible for ensuring not only that the elections took place freely and fairly, but that the needs of disabled people were met, and that they were able to vote independently and privately. ADD and IFES trained and co-ordinated the teams of election monitors to develop skills and strategies to deal with the possible negative reactions of non-disabled people. The aim was to build the confidence of the new election monitors.

Throughout Ghana, Bangladesh, and Zambia more than 400 disabled people trained as election monitors for the first time. 'Our presence at polling stations was at first met with surprise, then acceptance. The observation effort led to a greater awareness about disability,' reported Mercy Apoe, of the Ghana Association of the Blind. David Adeenzekangah, of the Electoral Commission of Ghana, commented: 'We gave accreditation for their participation with pleasure and joy. That, for the Commission, and Ghana, was a great historic event. I am told it was also a first-time event in the world!'

'People said they never knew that a blind person could observe.'
(Gladys Waadi, Ghana Association of the Blind)

Appointing disabled people as election monitors, and campaigning for disabled people's right to vote, has had a significant impact on the attitudes of mainstream society towards people with disabilities. The leadership of disabled people's organisations has been developed, and the disability movement as a whole has been strengthened. When disabled people have the right to vote, and are able to exercise this right, it promotes citizen participation from all sectors of society and strengthens democracy where it is fragile.

ADD sees these ventures as just the beginning of major social and political change, brought about by and for disabled people.

13 Some useful quotations

Quotations can be used as the basis for discussions and small-group activities. Make a collection for your own use, or adapt the following to fit your context.

1. 'Impairments can be endured, but the lack of human rights, the marginalisation and exclusion, the deprivation of equal opportunities and the institutional discrimination that disabled people face cannot be endured and can no longer be tolerated.'– Maria Rantho, Disabled Peoples' International (DPI)

2. 'The destiny of human rights is in the hands of *all* our citizens in all our communities.'– Eleanor Roosevelt (emphasis added)

3. 'Nothing about us, without us.'– The motto of Disabled Peoples' International

4. 'If people feel good about themselves, they can start to create change.'– B. Venkatesh (India)

5. 'Design it right the first time.'– Principle of engineering

6. 'Do what you can, with what you have, where you are.'– Theodore Roosevelt

7. 'We live by encouragement and die without it. Slowly, sadly, and angrily.'– Celeste Holm

8. 'Self-deprecation is a characteristic of the oppressed, which derives from their internalisation of the opinion the oppressors hold of them. So often do they hear that they are good for nothing and incapable of learning anything – that they are sick, lazy and unproductive – that in the end they become convinced of their own unfitness.'– Paulo Freire

9. 'No one is going to put your rights on the table for you. You have to ask for them. It's also important to remember that if you think you can't fight the system by yourself ... find someone to help you fight.'– T. J. Monroe, People First, Hartford, Connecticut (USA)

10.   'Speak up for what you know is right and speak as one united voice. Remember: we have power in our hearts and in each other. We must break the silence.'– Bob Williamson, People First, Washington DC (USA)

11.   'Your attitude is my only handicap.'– Slogan from ADAPT demonstration

12.   'Universal rights begin in small places close to home. They are the world of the individual person; the neighbourhood he lives in; the school or college he attends; the factory, farm or office where he works. Such are the places where every man, woman and child seeks equal justice, equal opportunity, equal dignity without discrimination. Unless these rights have meaning there, they have little meaning anywhere.'– Eleanor Roosevelt, 1958

13.   'Piss on pity'– Slogan from ADAPT demonstration

14.   'Rights not charity.'

Other good quotations about disability-related subjects are to be found in Handout 23: How can I help? and Handout 35: Disabled women's voices.

14 Sample workshop agendas

These sample workshop agendas are intended as guidelines only. We strongly recommend adapting each workshop to suit the needs of the group and situation. Making activities accessible and relevant to participants' experience and interests is vitally important for achieving success in changing attitudes and translating attitudes into action. Some further suggestions for adapting the content to fit the participant group are given in Chapter 7.

14.1 One-day general introductory workshop for local and international NGOs and agencies

9.30–10.00 Introductions and expectations: say your name, who you work for, and three things that you hope to gain from the day, in the round. Review agenda. (If participants' expectations are very different from what is likely to be met through the planned agenda, consider changes.)

10.00–11.00 What is disability?

Brainstorm based on the question 'What do you think of when you hear the word "disability"?'. Use different-coloured pens to circle any words that relate to the three models of disability. This leads into the next stage:

Presentation and discussion of models of disability: medical, charity, and social. (See exercises 9.1.2 and 9.1.3.)

11.00–11.15 Break

11.15–12.15 Rights-based approach to disability

Introduce the topic by asking the whole group if they are aware of the Universal Declaration of Human Rights. Where in the UDHR does it say 'These rights do not apply to disabled people'? – Nowhere, but the rights of disabled people around the world are violated every day. Display and talk through some key statistics about rights abuses (see Handout 20).

Introduce the UN Standard Rules. Give out copies (Handout 31) and ask participants to read them. In groups of four, they discuss how the rules apply to their work, and prioritise five rules that are most relevant to what they do on a daily basis. Feedback to whole group.

12.15–1.15   Lunch

1.15–2.00   Barriers exercise, using activity 9.2.1, to draw out a description of three types of barrier to the full inclusion of disabled people in society: environmental, institutional, and attitudinal.

2.00–2.45   Situation studies about refugees and displaced people with disabilities (see Chapter 12). Three small groups each work on a case study for 20 minutes, then the whole group shares conclusions. What do participants know about the people with disabilities in their beneficiary population(s): how many are there, where are they, who are they, what are their needs, are their rights being respected? If they don't know, how can they find out?

2.45–3.00   Break

3.00–3.40   Action planning
'Nothing about us without us' exercise (10.1.4)

3.40–4.00   Evaluation and closure

14.2   One-day workshop on disability and gender for local staff of NGOs and agencies

9.30–10.00   Introductions and agreement on group guidelines. Review of agenda.

10.00–10.40   The situation of disabled people
Small-group exercise: 9.1.1, Option 2. *Drawings of disabled people's situation in the community*

10.40–11.00   Why is it like that?
Presentation of the three models (Exercise 9.1.2)

11.00–11.15   Break

11.15–12.15   Disabled women's experiences
Game of life (Exercise 9.4.6)

12.15–1.15   Lunch

1.15–1.30   Energising activity: *'Darling' game* (7.2.6)

1.30–2.15   Why is it like that? – gender roles
Quiz (Exercise 9.4.2)

2.15–2.30   Break

2.30–3.00   Why is it like that? – continued
Presentation and discussion on Sex and Gender, and the impact of gender-based discrimination on disabled men and women (Exercise 9.4.3). Handout 35: Disabled women's voices

3.00–3.45   Action planning: SMART objectives and exercise (10.1.2)

3.45–4.00   Evaluation: *Throw out or keep* (Exercise 11.2.2)

Handouts

14.3 Two-day workshop for members of local Disabled People's Organisations

Day 1

10.00–10.30   Introductions: interviews in pairs (Exercise 7.2.3)

10.30–11.30   Models of disability: Exercise 9.1.2

11.30–11.45   Break

11.45–12.45   Barriers that exclude disabled people from society (Exercise 9.2.1)

12.45–1.45   Lunch

1.45–2.45   Problem-trees (9.2.2)

2.45–3.00   Break

3.00–3.45   Overcoming barriers: a case study (9.2.5)

3.45–4.00   Evaluation in the round (11.1)

Day 2

10.00–10.30   Fairness and rights: Camouflage game (9.3.1)

10.30–11.30   What rights do we have? Calendar game (9.3.2)

11.30–11.45   Break

11.45–12.00   Global and local discrimination (9.3.7)

12.00–12.30   Documentation of disabled people's rights (9.3.8)

12.30–1.30   Lunch

1.30–2.30   Improvised drama about disabled people's rights (9.3.11)

2.30–2.45   Break

2.45–3.45   Action planning (9.2.3)

3.45–4.00   Evaluation: Throw out or keep (11.2.2)

14.4 Five-month training course for disability-awareness trainers

Five months, one day a week, 10.30 am – 4 pm

Week 1 Introductions; expectations, agreeing group guidelines; overview of proposed course content

Week 2 Completion of group guidelines; exercises in showing respect and listening; setting priorities for course content; use of personal learning diaries

Module 1

Week 3 Facilitation – what is it? Role and skills of facilitator

Week 4 Learning processes

Week 5 Designing training sessions (topic/objective; content, methods)

Week 6 Practising facilitation; discussion of learning points about facilitation methods and disability issues

Week 7 Practising facilitation; discussion of issues raised

Week 8 Skills for effective planning; planning workshops

Week 9 Practising facilitation; summary and review of progress and learning about facilitation and learning; preparation to move to Module 2.

Module 2

Week 10 Human rights and disability rights

Week 11 Models of disability

Week 12 Barriers to equal rights and participation; overcoming barriers

Week 13 Gender and disability

Week 14 Independent/self-determined living; Personal Assistance services; assertiveness (as a tool for independent living and facilitators)

Week 15 Images of disabled people

Week 16 Language and definitions of disability

Week 17 Dealing with difficult issues as facilitator: prevention of disability; personal issues

Week 18 Action planning

Week 19 Evaluation and celebration.

15 Conclusion

Humanitarian and development organisations such as Oxfam expend a lot of hard work and money on supporting vulnerable, marginalised people to survive and make positive changes in their lives. What could this mean in practice for disabled people, if organisations learned consistently to apply a disability-rights perspective to their work? What positive changes would be achieved by ensuring that all our work was informed by an awareness of the needs and potential contributions of disabled people?

When put into practice in the contexts of humanitarian relief and development work, the impact of Disability Equality is illustrated by examples like the following:

- The young woman who used to say 'better dead than disabled', but who developed enough confidence in herself and her considerable abilities to help other disabled people (and their non-disabled relatives) to survive the war and winter in Kosovo, distributing supplies of aid and tracing the displaced.

- The smart and eloquent man with a speech impairment, made to feel embarrassed and used to keeping quiet, who now shares his ideas and knowledge with others, gives public speeches, chairs meetings, challenges misconceptions, and is a role model for disabled children.

- An emergency-relief programme which acknowledges the existence of disabled people and actively seeks to protect their rights and provide for their needs, on a par with its support for non-disabled people.

- Thousands of disabled people in Uganda elected to every type of decision-making body, from village council to national parliament.

- A workshop on NGO management which brings together disabled women from a disability organisation and non-disabled women from a women's organisation to work together on matters of shared interest. They have never interacted before, and the disabled women have never before been invited to be involved in anything that is not specifically about disability. The women learn about and from each other, and go beyond any initial barriers. They make plans for future work together, and create networks and friendships.

- The development of programmes which aim for this type of impact, even though that impact may be hard to quantify and present in neat, statistical form.

- A report from Afrim, a member of a DPO in Pristina: 'Our group had a party, and one guy came who for eight years hadn't even wanted to go out on the balcony of his house. Now he comes to the community centre twice a week, asking what else he can do.'

Experience shows that people will not make lasting change in their lives unless they believe in themselves and their ability. Disabled people, like other oppressed groups, have an extra obstacle to overcome to reach the starting point of self-belief. Many have endured a lifetime of being made to feel useless, inadequate, and inferior.

That is why for many disabled people discovering the disability-rights movement is a life-changing experience. The idea of Disability Equality offers a completely different way of thinking about being disabled and about one's place in the world. Disabled people are no longer the problem, but the solution. One of the major impacts of Disability Equality is to make people feel good about themselves, and 'if people feel good about themselves, they can start to create change'(B. Venkatesh).

Disability Equality is a powerful tool, one which helps people to move from shame to pride, from passivity and dependence to activism and action. Myrvete from Kosovo sums it up: 'Learning about the human rights of disabled people ... we began to recognise the existence of barriers, but above all we began to realise that it is possible to break down those barriers ... we are the ones who have to create that environment [of equality]; we can't wait for others to do things for us.'

For non-disabled people, Disability Equality is no less rewarding. Most do not consciously seek to discriminate against others, and they find that learning how not to discriminate is liberating. It can change how disabled and non-disabled people relate to each other, opening up a space where genuine emotions of all kinds can flourish. You like or dislike someone for who they really are. You are liked or disliked for who you really are. Pity, fear, and other misplaced emotions, which can distort the reactions of non-disabled people to disabled people, are replaced by a willingness to learn, share, and co-operate on an equal basis.

As we have seen, attitudes and actions are closely linked. In the Disability Equality movement, the focus is not on lofty ideals, but on practical action. Whether we are disabled or not, dealing with our attitudes and emotions needs to be recognised as the starting point for action. Disability Equality helps the transition from attitude to action, because it shows what has to be done to overcome the 'problem' of disability: modify our physical environment; introduce transport and communication systems that work for everyone, not just part of the population; provide opportunities and resources for the equal participation of disabled and non-disabled members of our families and communities, at work, at school, and in legal, social, and political spheres.

Awareness of Disability Equality and the implementation of its principles can bring significant results in the disaster-relief context, where the overwhelming majority of workers and decision makers are (still) non-disabled. Disability Equality leads to decisions that are based on respect for all individuals, recognising their worth and dignity, and to actions which meet different people's basic needs in a variety of appropriate ways. This approach is more likely to save lives at risk than a 'survival-of-the-fittest' or 'one-size-fits-all' approach. Everybody gains if staff involved in water and sanitation provision, construction, medical care, public health, logistics, and distribution are given the opportunity to make their programmes inclusive.

Often the changes that need to be made in order to make Disability Equality a reality are simple and inexpensive. Sometimes they are not, but that is no justification for not making them. On a daily basis society spends millions of dollars on meeting the rights, needs, and wishes of its non-disabled citizens, without the slightest hesitation. The cost of being non-disabled is very high, but it is rare to hear anyone complain about it, or refuse to spend money because of it.

To conclude, Disability Equality helps disabled professionals and activists to reach out to their isolated brothers and sisters, those who feel themselves to be beyond hope. It helps emergency and development staff to reach in appropriate, effective ways the most marginalised and vulnerable within any marginalised group, be they disabled 'Untouchables', disabled street children, disabled flood survivors, or disabled refugees.

Putting Disability Equality into action saves lives that would otherwise have been lost, and changes lives that would otherwise have had little chance of change.

Resources

Sources and further reading

Abu-Habib, Lina (1997) *Gender and Disability, Women's Experiences in the Middle East,* Oxford: Oxfam (UK and Ireland)

BOND (British Overseas NGOs for Development) (1999) *Strengthening Disability and Development Work,* BOND Disability and Development Working Group, Discussion Paper

Coleridge, Peter (1993) *Disability, Liberation, and Development,* Oxford: Oxfam (UK and Ireland)

DAA (1997) *Disabled Women,* Resource Kit No. 6, Disability Awareness in Action, ISBN 1 898037 35 3

DFID (2000) 'Disability, Poverty and Development', DFID Issues Paper, London: Department for International Development

DPSA (2000) *An Empowerment Tool. Pocket Guide to Disability Equity for Leaders of Persons with Disabilities,* Africa Decade of Disabled Persons, Disabled People South Africa

Economic & Social Commission for Asia and the Pacific (1995) *Promotion of Non-Handicapping Physical Environment for Disabled Persons* – Guidelines, www.independentliving.org (Library page)

Hope, Anne and Sally Timmell (1984, revised 1995) *Training for Transformation: A Handbook for Community Workers,* London: Intermediate Technology Publications

ISO (1994) *Building Construction – Needs of Disabled People in Buildings – Design Guidelines* (ISO/TR 9527:1994), International Organisation for Standardization, www.iso.ch

Oliver, M. and C. Barnes (1998) *Disabled People and Social Policy: From Exclusion to Inclusion,* London: Longman

SCF (1998) 'Global Disability Strategy', London: Save the Children (UK)

SCF (2000) 'Community Based Rehabilitation: Global Review and Seminar Report', Knowledge Report, London: Save the Children (UK)

Sphere Project (2000) *The Sphere Handbook: Humanitarian Charter and Minimum Standards in Disaster Response,* published by The Sphere Project (www.sphereproject.org), distributed by Oxfam (GB) (www.oxfam.org.uk/publications)

United Nations (1991) *Self-Help Organisations of Disabled Persons,* New York: UN Economic and Social Commission for Asia and the Pacific

United Nations *UN Standard Rules on the Equalization of Opportunities for Persons with Disabilities*, full text available from local UN offices, or on line at www.un.org/ecosocdev/geninfo/dpi1647e.htm

VSO (2001) 'Including Disabled People', VSO Position Paper, www.vso.org.uk/publications

Werner, David (1990) *Challenging a Disabling World*, Milton Keynes: World Development Education Centre, now Global Education Milton Keynes

Werner, David (1998) *Nothing About Us Without Us: Developing Innovative Techniques For, By, and With Disabled Persons*, Palo Alto, CA: Healthwright

World Disability Report 1999, available from International Disability Forum, brooks@int-disability.org; fax 41-22-788-5954; tel 41-22-788-5988

Newsletters and websites

This is a selection of organisations with newsletters and websites provide good-quality, thought-provoking information and opinions. Their materials are available at low cost or free of charge, and some are on the Internet.

Action on Disability and Development (ADD) Vallis House, 57 Vallis Road, Frome, Somerset, BA11 3EG, UK. *add@add.org.uk; www.add.org.uk*

Disability Awareness in Action 11 Belgrave Rd, London, SW1V 1RB, UK. *www.daa.org.uk*

Disabled Peoples' International 101–7 Evergreen Place, Winnipeg, Manitoba, Canada, R3L 2T3. *www.dpi.org*

Downs Syndrome Association 155 Mitcham Rd, London SW17 9BG, UK. *www.dsa-uk.org*

Institute of Independent Living *www.independentliving.org*

Research and Training Center on Independent Living, Robert Dole Human Development Center, The University of Kansas, 1000 Sunnyside Avenue, Room 4089, Lawrence, KS 66045-7555, USA. *www.rtcil.org*

Spinal Injuries Association 76 St James Lane, Muswell Hill, London N10 3DF, UK. *www.spinal.co.uk*

UN Disability Rights Resources Site *http://esa.un/socdev/enable*

Posters

Greater Manchester Coalition of Disabled People *gmcdp@globalnet.co.uk*

Spinal Injuries Association (address as above)

Radio

Disability Radio Worldwide broadcasts to more than 100 countries from Costa Rica via Radio for Peace International on shortwave frequencies 6975, 15050, and 21460, Mondays at 19:00 UTC, Fridays at 17:00 UTC, and Saturdays at 22:00 UTC, each with a second broadcast eight hours later. A programme list and individual shows are available on-line at *www.independentliving.org/radio*. Cassette tapes of shows may also be ordered; for details phone 1-303-355-9935 or email *global3@concentric.net*

Appendix
Oxfam's policy on disability

As part of its overall mandate to overcome poverty and suffering, Oxfam GB is committed to working for equal rights for disabled people and non-disabled people, both internally within the organisation and externally in its programmes of development, advocacy, and humanitarian work.

Oxfam is striving to increase the social and cultural diversity of its workforce. Its Diversity Strategy, adopted in May 2000, states:

> In carrying out our work we will seek to positively include and equally value, for example, black people as well as white people, women as well as men, disabled as well as able-bodied, and older people as well as younger people.

Oxfam's corporate Disability Policy recognises the prejudice and negative discrimination that disabled people commonly experience, and aspires to address them in the following particular ways:

- improving the recruitment of disabled people;
- making every effort to ensure that employees who become disabled remain in employment;
- developing greater awareness of disability among all staff and volunteers;
- providing (where reasonable) accessible services, environments, and buildings;
- reviewing progress on an annual basis.

To try to turn these commitments into reality, Oxfam has adopted a range of initiatives.

- Targets have been set for the increased representation of disabled people, with milestones to measure annual progress.
- The UK government's scheme, *Two Ticks – Positive about Disability*, has been implemented, with the aim of improving the employment opportunities of disabled people.
- Oxfam is working with local disability organisations to improve the recruitment of disabled people into Oxfam as paid staff and as volunteers. Advice is available to help managers to identify appropriate publicity channels in order to reach different identity groups, including disabled applicants.
- Staff training schemes in recruitment and selection skills incorporate an awareness of the rights, needs, and potential contributions of people with impairments.

- Disability-awareness workshops for staff aim to challenge prejudiced attitudes and increase people's understanding of disability-related issues.
- Guidelines have been produced to encourage the production of communications materials which are accessible to people with various impairments.
- Other guidelines help staff and volunteers to organise inclusive events which will be accessible to people of all identities, including disabled people.
- All new Oxfam office and shops, and existing premises where possible, must be accessible by disabled people. This is in accordance with anti-discrimination legislation in the UK.
- A workbook for volunteers on providing good customer service in Oxfam shops includes meeting the needs of disabled customers, also in compliance with UK legal requirements.
- Stories gathered from disabled colleagues about their experiences of working in Oxfam are used to help others to learn about the issues.

Despite this recent progress, Oxfam still has a long way to go. So far, most of the initiatives described above have been limited to the UK context; but all staff and volunteers must be enabled to implement these schemes and use these tools, consistently and across the entire organisation.

Bimla Ojelay-Surtees
Oxfam Diversity Adviser
Oxford, UK
January 2003

General index

Since the whole of this manual is about disability, the term itself has been used very sparingly in the index. Please consider what aspect of disability you are looking for, and search under that.

The codes used in the index are as follows:
E   Exercise
H   Handout
P   Presentation

Abkhazia, case studies 305H
acceptance 116–17H
accessibility 24–5, 30, 31, 77–8, 185E, 189E, 215H, 307E
    of workshops 79–81
    see also environmental discrimination
accidents
    and disability 160H
    prevention 162–3E, 164H
Action on Disability and Development (ADD) 301H, 302H, 303H, 313–14H, 315–16H, 317–18H
action plans 188–90E
    developing 116–17H, 277E, 280E
    future 282E, 283E
    immediate 281E
    see also goal setting; objectives; priority setting
Action-planning to overcome barriers 188–90E
activism *see* social and political action
activities
    accessibility of 80–1
    evaluation of 123E
    see also workshops
ADD *see* Action on Disability and Development
adult learning 112–13E, 114H
Africa *see* Burkina Faso; Ghana; Mali; Sierra Leone; Uganda; Zambia
Agreeing guidelines 101–2E
aid *see* emergency aid; relief; technical co-operation
aid agencies
    action planning for 188–90E
    sign-language interpreters in 185–6E
    workshops for 321–2H

see also Oxfam
aims *see* objectives
Annya, Abkhazia (case study) 305H
Applying the UN Standard Rules to real life 213E
Asia *see* Bangladesh; Cambodia
assumptions 89E
    see also stereotyping
attitudinal discrimination 11, 16–17, 177–9E, 180H, 181–2H, 188E

Bangladesh
    case studies 20, 301H, 317–18H
'Banking education' and 'problem-posing' education 128H
Barriers: a case study 191E
barriers to participation *see* participation, barriers to
blindness *see* visual impairments
Bosnia, refugees in 3, 22, 23
Bosnian conflict 21, 25
built environment, design for disabled people 24–5
Burkina Faso, case study 304H

The calendar game 196–7E
Cambodia, case studies 303H, 313–14H
Cambodian Disabled People's Organisation 314H
Caroline (case study) 306H
charity model of disability 16–17, 32, 170P, 172H
children
    rights 197E
    see also disabled children
'Choosing' rights 203–4E
civil society, development of 25

co-ordination, of disability rights 218H
Collage 289E
Come to Work programme, Bangladesh 20
communication *see* instruction; interpreters;
    language; listening; non-verbal
    communication
community centres (KAPP) 43, 44–5
community development, and disability 18–20,
    25, 329
community-based rehabilitation 19
Components of training 121P, 122H
conflict situations *see* Bosnian conflict; crisis
    situations; Croatian conflict; Kosovar
    conflict; Sierra Leone conflict
consultation *see* participation
costs
    of accessible environments 24, 30
    of disability-related development work 53
Creating a learning environment: four needs of the
    group 116–17H
Creating a positive learning environment 115P
credit schemes 19, 20, 302H
crisis situations 20–2, 160H
    needs of disabled people 53, 54–5
    and rights 22–3, 204E
Croatian conflict, effect on disabled people 22
cultural activities 216H
cures, for impairments 15

'*Darling' game* 90E
deafness *see* hearing impairments
decision making *see* participation; planning;
    problem solving
dependence *see* independent living;
    interdependence
The development of codified rights for disabled
    people 212H
development work
    and disability 18–20, 24–5, 26, 31, 48, 329
    Disability Equality perspective 49–50
    and Disability Equality training 51
    disability-related costs 53
    participation of disabled people 52–3,
        189–90E
    and policy development 50–1
    and the social model 50
    see also reconstruction work
Different rates of learning 120H
disability
    definitions 5–6, 11, 263, 264–5E
    and gender 12, 235, 241E, 323H
    language of 256E, 258–60E, 261–2H
    misconceptions 29–32
    prevention 155–6

    psychological impact 153–4
    see also impairment; models of disability
disability awareness 31
    developing 214H
    workshops for trainers 325H
disability discrimination *see* discrimination
Disability Equality
    benefits 326–8
    development in Oxfam 48
    in development work 49–50
    in disabled people's organisations 56–7
    policies 46–7, 332–3
    and policy development 46–7, 48, 50–1
    principles 27–8
    role of donors 56
    statistics 209–10H
    in Uganda 25
    see also disability rights; discrimination
Disability Equality training 28–9, 51, 218H
    components 121P, 122H
    course structure 69–73
    methodology 74–5
    process of 150H
    role of facilitators 62, 128H
    of trainers 39, 325H
    see also manual; workshops
Disability Equality training (Kosovo) 39
    activities 64
    aims and objectives 62–3
    course structure 63
    evaluation 65–7
    facilitators 62, 66–7
    funding 64–5
    language use 63–4
    methodology 62
    participants 62
    transport for 64
Disability and literacy 227–30H
disability professionals, role 175E, 176H
disability programmes, evaluation of 218H
disability rights 18, 27–8, 165–6E, 192–3,
    222–3E
    co-ordination 218H
    in crisis situations 22–3, 204E
    development of 211P, 212H
    and economic policies 217H, 219H
    and fairness 194–5E
    and international co-operation 219H
    organisations 14
    personal values 203–4E
    quotations 319–20H
    and relief and development programmes 26
    and technical co-operation 219H
    see also Disability Equality; discrimination;

human rights; social and political action;
Standard Rules
disabled children, work with (KAPP) 40, 44–5
disabled people
allies of 224–5E
effects of disasters/conflict 20–2
images of 251–2E, 253–4E, 255E, 256E
invisibility of 30, 251–2E
needs of 53, 54–5, 168E, 176H
organisations for 13–14, 16
organisations of *see* disabled people's
organisations
participation *see* participation and
reconstruction 24-5, 44, 48
specialist interventions for 31, 32
statistics 316
stereotyping 16, 205–6E, 251–2E
support when isolated 155
see also disabled children; disabled refugees;
disabled women
Disabled Peoples' International 14, 227–30H
disabled people's organisations 14, 25, 218H
action planning for 188E
Cambodia 312–13H
case studies 301H, 303H, 311–12E
Disability Equality in 56–7
newsletters 253–4E
staff as workshop participants 78
value 231E
workshops for 323H
see also Action on Disability and Development;
Kosovo Association of People with
Paraplegia; social and political action
disabled refugees 21, 22, 23, 43, 306, 308–12E
case studies 305H
disabled women
discrimination against 12, 242E, 243–6E,
247–8E, 249–50H
work with (KAPP) 40
disabled women's groups (KAPP) 45–6
Disabled women's voices 247–8E, 249–50H
disaster situations *see* crisis situations
discrimination 208E, 236–7E, 243–6E
against disabled women 12, 242E, 243–6E,
247–8E, 249–50H
allies against 224–5E
gender 240E, 241E, 242E
shared experiences 220–1E
see also attitudinal discrimination;
environmental discrimination;
institutional discrimination; stereotyping
Discussion of good and bad listening 129E
Discussion of the three models of disability 173E
donors, role in disability equality 56

doorways, accessibility of 79
DPI *see* Disabled Peoples' International

Eastern Europe *see* Abkhazia; Bosnia; Croatia;
Kosovo; Macedonia
economic policies, and disability rights 217H,
219H
education
styles 128H
see also integrated education; learning;
literacy; public education
Education for All 227–30H
The eight sunrays of planning 144–5P
*Election monitoring and the right to vote in Ghana,
Bangladesh, and Zambia* (case study)
316–17H
elevators *see* lifts
emergency aid 22–4, 26, 31, 53–6
employment of disabled people 47, 183–6E,
192–3, 216H
case studies 305H
in development work 52–3, 189–90E
see also income generation
empowerment
developing 233–4E
see also self-esteem
enfranchisement, case study 317–18H
engineers, as workshop participants 77–8
environmental discrimination 11, 17, 24–5,
177–9E, 180H, 181H, 185E
evaluation
of activities 123E
of Disability Equality training (Kosovo) 65–7
of disability programmes 218H
of facilitation 142–3E, 286, 287E, 291H
see also impact measurement; workshops,
evaluation
*The evolution of documented rights for disabled
people* 211P
Explanation of barriers 181–2H

Facilitation: brainstorm and discussion 125–6E
facilitation
characteristics 125–6E
evaluation of 142–3E, 286, 287E, 291H
practice activities 141, 142–3
techniques 127H, 137H
see also instruction; learning
Facilitation checklists 142E
Facilitation of groups and workshops 127H
facilitators
management of groups 66–7
role in training 62, 128H
Fairness and rights 194–5E

family life 216H
fathers, as carers 34
feelings 86E, 110–11E, 133H
Find someone who ... 84E
Fishbowl exercise 165–6E
Flora (case study) 310–11E
Françoise, Burkina Faso (case study) 304H
freedom of movement 192
Future actions: a competition 282E
Future actions exercise: diamond ranking 283E

The game of life 243–6E
gender
    and disability 12, 235, 241E, 322H
    and discrimination 240E, 241E, 242E
    and life events 243-6E
    roles 241E, 242E
    and sex 238E, 239H, 240E
    see also fathers; women
The gender quiz 238E, 239H
Gender roles 242E
Gesture energiser 97E
Ghana, case studies 317–18H
Global and local discrimination 208E
goal setting 116–17H
Good and bad listening 130H
Grassroots representation in Cambodia
    (case study) 313–14H
Group guidelines for a workshop in Kosovo 103H
groups
    management of 66-7
    observation of 131–2E, 133H
    selecting 106
Guessing game 89E
guidelines, for workshops 101–2E, 103H,
    104–11E
Guidelines for acceptable language about disability
    261–2H
Guidelines for giving instructions or information
    140H

Handikos *see* Kosovo Association of People with
    Paraplegia
Hassan (case study) 308E
health professionals, as workshop participants
    76–7
hearing impairments
    and accessibility of activities 80–1
    case studies 309E
    see also sign-language interpreters
Hopes, concerns, contributions, and needs 98E
How can I help? 175E, 176H
human rights 196–7E, 200–1E, 207H
    in emergencies 22–3, 204E

personal values 203–4E
    and responsibilities 202E
    see also children, rights; disability rights;
        United Nations, Universal Declaration of
        Human Rights; voting rights
Human rights: a summary of learning points 207H

I respect you/You respect me 110–11E
Identifying allies 224–5E
Identifying barriers: the wall exercise 177–9E
identity, aspects of 236–7E
IFES 316–17H
images
    of disabled people 251–2E, 253–4E, 255E, 256E
    see also stereotyping
The imaginary country 200–1E
Immediate action (action plans) 281E
The impact of language: Mr Biswas photo exercise
    256E
impact measurement, in emergency aid 54
impairment
    causes 20–1, 157–8P, 159–60H
    cures for 15
    definition 5, 11
    prevalence 12
    prevention 155–6, 157–8P, 161E, 162–3E,
        164H
    psychological impact 153–4
    statistics 12, 159–60H
    see also disability; hearing impairments;
        muscular dystrophy; polio; restricted
        mobility; speech impairments; visual
        impairments; wheelchair users
Improvised drama about disabled people's rights
    222–3E
income generation 46
    case studies 302H, 304H, 315–16H
    see also employment of disabled people
income maintenance 216H
independent living 266, 268–9E, 271–4P
    definition 267H, 271P, 275H
    developing 233–4E, 276E
    see also personal assistance schemes;
        rehabilitation
Independent (Self-Determined) Living 271–4P
Individual reflection (on action plans) 277E
information sharing, in groups 116–17H
institutional discrimination 11, 17, 177–9E,
    180H, 182H
instruction, good practice 138E, 140H
integrated education 215H
    Local Active Groups lobby for 41
    right to 226E, 228–30H
    work of KAPP 47–8

integrity 216H

inter-agency co-operation, and emergency aid 55

interdependence 268–9E, 270E

    see also personal assistance schemes

In/ter/dependence drawings 268–9E

international co-operation, and disability rights
    219H

International Day of Disabled People 41, 52

International Foundation for Electoral Systems
    317–18H

international NGOs

    effects on KAPP 48

    workshops for 321–2H

    see also Action on Disability and
        Development; Oxfam

interpreters

    in workshops 63–4, 137H

    see also sign-language interpreters

Interviews in pairs (on discrimination) 220–1E

invisibility, of disabled people 30, 251–2E

isolation, support during 155

KAPP *see* Kosovo Association of People with
    Paraplegia

Kenya, case study 306H

Know your apple 205–6E

Kosovar conflict

    effect on disabled people 21, 22

    relief work during 42–3

Kosovo

    attitudes to disability 13, 16, 154

    carers in 34

    disability equality policies 46–7

    disabled people in 13–14, 23, 25, 33–4, 64

    socio-economic situation 33

Kosovo Association of People with Paraplegia 1

    community centres 43, 44–5

    development of 34–5, 37, 41–2, 44, 48, 68

    effects of international NGOs 48

    and employment 47

    influencing government 41, 46–7

    media work 40–1, 45, 46

    public education work 46

    reconstruction work 44

    relief work during war 42–3

    support for returnees 43

    women's groups 45–6

    work with disabled children 40, 44–5

    work with disabled women 40

    work in integrated education 47–8

    see also Disability Equality training;
        Local Active Groups; Oxfam's work with
        KAPP

Krajina *see* Croatia

language

    of disability 256E, 258–60E, 261–2H

    impact of 256E, 258–60E, 261–2H

    see also disability, definitions

Lao Sonn, Cambodia (case study) 303H

learning difficulties *see* people with learning
    difficulties

learning environments 115P, 116–17H

learning processes 112–13E, 114H, 118P, 119P,
    120H

    see also facilitation

legislation, on disability rights 217H

leisure 216H

life events, and disability/gender 243–6E

Life stories 174E

lifts, accessibility of 79

Line drawing 139H

Line-drawing exercise 138E

listening 130H

Listening exercise 107–9E, 129E

literacy, right to 227–30H

lobbying (KAPP) 41, 45, 46–7

    see also social and political action

Local Active Groups (KAPP) 35, 36–8, 39, 41–2,
    43, 44

    disabled women's groups 45–6

local NGOs

    workshops for 321–3H

    see also disabled people's organisations

Macedonia, disabled refugees in 23, 43

magazines *see* media

Mali, case study 302H

Mamadou, Mali (case study) 302H

manual

    rationale 1–2

    usage 4–5, 6

    see also Disability Equality training

Mapping for Mars 104–6E

materials, accessibility of 80–1

media images

    of disabled people 251–2E, 253–4E, 255E, 256E

    see also language

Media search 251–2E

media work (KAPP) 40–1, 45, 46

medical care 214H

medical model of disability 15, 18–19, 32,
    169–70P, 172H, 275H

medical staff, as workshop participants 76–7

micro-finance programmes 19

    see also credit schemes

Milica (case study) 310E

models of disability 167–8E, 169–71P, 172H,
    173E, 174E, 175E

see also charity model; medical model;
    social model
movement
    freedom of 192
    see also restricted mobility
Mr Biswas photo exercise 256E
muscular dystrophy, case studies 310E
My contribution 270E
My life pie-chart 95E

Name game 88E
Name-badge exercise 94E
natural disasters *see* crisis situations
NGOs *see* aid agencies; international NGOs;
    local NGOs
non-verbal communication 89E, 97E, 133H
Nothing about us without us 280E

Objective setting 278–9E
objectives, of Disability Equality training 62–3
Observation exercise 131–2E
Open the day 86E
organisations
    for disabled people 13–14, 16
    see also aid agencies; disabled people's
        organisations; international NGOs;
        local NGOs
Organising the workshop 147E, 149E
'*Our definitions*' exercise 264–5E
over-protectiveness, effects 13
Oxfam
    development of Disability Equality 48
    policy on disability 331–2
Oxfam's work with KAPP 35
    overseas links 38–9
    peer-support initiatives 38–9
    programme objectives 36
    regional workshops 38
    relief work during war 42–3
    training of trainers 39
    work with Local Active Groups 36–8

Paired interviews and introductions 87E
participation 19, 25, 31, 50, 52–3, 55, 280E
    barriers to 177–9E, 180H, 181–2H, 183–6E,
        187H, 188–90E, 191E, 301H
    see also discrimination
    case studies 301H, 302H, 303H, 304H
    see also Standard Rules
peer pressure 97E
peer support 38–9, 52
people with disabilities *see* disabled people
people with learning difficulties, effects of
        disasters/ conflicts 21–2

personal assistance schemes 272–3P, 276E
A personal definition of independent living 267H
Photograph of Mr Biswas 257H
planning
    for emergency aid 53–4
    see also action plans; goal setting;
        objective setting; priority setting;
        workshop planning
Planning the agenda and contents of a workshop 151E
Planning a workshop: task list 148H
policy development 46–7, 48, 50–1, 217H
    Oxfam's policy 48, 332–3
polio, case studies 301H, 308E
political and social action *see* lobbying; social
        and political action
Positive feedback 93E
    see also self-esteem
Posters exercise 255E
poverty
    and disability 12–13, 160H
    see also income maintenance
Presentation of the three models 169–71P
Preventing accidents in the home 164H
Prevention in the home 162–3E
Prevention of impairment 157–8P, 161E
The principles of rehabilitation 275H
priority setting 99–100E
problem solving 183–6E, 187H, 188–90E
Problem triangle 186E, 187H
Problem-tree exercise 183–6E
The 'process of learning' exercise 112–13E
professionals *see* disability professionals;
        health professionals
project development, disability perspective 19
Psychological impact of impairment and disability
    153–4
The psychology of adult learning 114H
public education work (KAPP) 46
Puppets 232H
Puppets exercise 231E
Putting independent (self-determined) living into
        practice 276E

Quick evaluations in the round 284E
quotations 319–20H

radio *see* media
Rates of learning 119P
reconstruction work 24–5, 44, 48
    see also development work
recreation 216H
Reflecting on facilitation 287E
refugees 3, 78
    see also disabled refugees; women refugees

rehabilitation
  principles of 275H
  services 18–19, 176H, 214H
  see also independent living
relief staff, as workshop participants 78
relief work
  and disability 22–4, 25–6, 31
  Kosovo war 42–3
religion 217H
religious model *see* charity model
research, on the status of disabled people 217H
respect 54–5, 110–11E
responsibilities, and rights 202E
restricted mobility
  in crisis situations 21, 22, 23
  and workshop accessibility 80
  see also wheelchair users
Restrictive gender roles 241E
rights *see* children, rights; disability rights;
    human rights
Rights and responsibilities 202E
Room layout 135–6H

Sample activity cards 152H
schools *see* integrated education
self-determined living *see* independent living
self-esteem 91E, 92E, 93E, 96E, 270E
  see also empowerment; respect
self-reliance *see* independent living
Setting priorities 99–100E
sex *see* gender
Sex and gender 240E
Shapla, Bangladesh (case study) 301H
Sierra Leone conflict, effect on disabled people 21
sign-language interpreters 185–6E
Sketch/mime 285E
SMART objectives 278–9E
social exclusion *see* discrimination; poverty
social model of disability 17–18, 27, 170–1P, 172H
  case studies 20
  in development work 50
  and rehabilitation 275H
social and political action 231E
  case studies 313–18H
  see also disabled people's organisations
social security 216H
Song 285E
*The Soroti Agricultural and Craft Association of
    the Blind, Uganda* (case study) 315–16H
speech impairments, and accessibility of
    activities 81
sport 216H
Stages of learning 118P
Standard Rules (UN) 25, 56, 211P, 213E, 214–19H

steps, accessibility of 79
stereotyping 16, 205–6E, 251–2E
  see also assumptions; images
Stereotyping and discrimination: know your apple
    205–6E
Suada (case study) 309E
Sufia (case study) 20
support services 215H

teaching *see* education; facilitation; instruction;
    learning
technical co-operation, and disability rights 219H
terminology *see* language
The right to education: whole-group discussion 226E
theatre *see* media
Throw out or keep 285E
Timing and pacing 137H
toilets, accessibility of 79, 308E
training *see* Disability Equality training;
    facilitation; instruction; learning processes;
    workshops
Two ways to cross a river 233–4E

Uganda
  case studies 315–16H
  Disability Equality in 25
  micro-finance programmes 19
United Nations
  International Day of Disabled People 41, 52
  Standard Rules on the Equalisation of
    Opportunities for Persons with
    Disabilities 25, 56, 211P, 213E, 214–19H
  Universal Declaration of Human Rights 27,
    198–9H
*Using positive and non-stereotypical images of
    disability* 253–4E

visual impairments
  and accessibility of activities 81
  case studies 303H, 315–16H
  in crisis situations 21
voting rights (case study) 317–18H

Wall of barriers 180H
The wall exercise 177–9E
Wallpaper exercise 96E
war *see* crisis situations
What I am proud of myself for 92E
What I like about you 91E
What rights do we have? The calendar game 196–7E
What to observe in a group 133H
wheelchair users
  case studies 307E, 311–12E
  see also restricted mobility

Who am I? 236-7E
The whole training process 150H
Whole-group activity 123E
women
    statistics 242
    see also carers; disabled women; gender
women refugees, as workshop participants 78
Word-list exercise 258–60E
workshop planning 76–9, 144–5P, 146H, 148H,
    150H
    accessibility of workshops 79–81
    agendas 98E, 99–100E, 147E, 149E, 151E,
        152H, 321–5H
    questionnaires 81, 82–3H
    room layout 135–6H

workshops
    establishing guidelines 101–2E, 103H,
        104–11E
    evaluation 284, 284–5E, 288E, 289E, 290H,
        292–9H
    interpreters in 63–4, 137H
    management of groups 66–7
    selecting small groups 106
    see also facilitation
Writing and drawing 288E

Zambia, case studies 317–18H

Index of training methods

art work
>   *In/ter/dependence drawings* 268–9E
>   *models of disability* 168E
>   *My life pie-chart* 95E
>   *Wallpaper exercise* 96E
>   *Writing and drawing* 288E

brainstorms
>   *Discussion of good and bad listening* 129E
>   *Facilitation: brainstorm and discussion*
>   125–6E
>   *Future actions: a competition* 282E
>   *Models of disability* 168E
>   *Sex and gender* 240E

case studies 300, 307
>   *Annya, Abkhazia* 305H
>   *Barriers: a case study* 191E
>   *Come to Work* programme, Bangladesh 20
>   cures for impairments 15
>   *Election monitoring and the right to vote in*
>   *Ghana, Bangladesh, and Zambia* 317–18H
>   *Flora* 311–12E
>   *Françoise, Burkina Faso* 304H
>   *Grassroots representation in Cambodia* 313–14H
>   *Lao Sonn, Cambodia* 303H
>   *Mamadou, Mali* 302H
>   *Shapla, Bangladesh* 301H
>   *The Soroti Agricultural and Craft Association*
>   *of the Blind, Uganda* 315–16H

case studies with questions
>   *Hassan* 308E
>   *Milica* 310E
>   *Suada* 309E

craft work
>   *Collage* 289E
>   *Name-badge exercise* 94E

drama
>   *Improvised drama about disabled people's*
>   *rights* 222–3E
>   *Life stories* 174E
>   *Puppet exercise* 231E
>   *Sketch/mime* 285E
>   *Two ways to cross a river* 233–4E
>   see also role play

energisers
>   *'Darling' game* 90E
>   *Fairness and rights* 194–5E
>   *Find someone who …* 84E
>   *Gesture energiser* 97E
>   *Name game* 88E

introductory/ icebreaker exercises
>   *Agreeing guidelines* 101–2E
>   *'Darling' game* 90E
>   *Find someone who …* 84E
>   *Gesture energiser* 97E
>   *Guessing game* 89E
>   *Hopes, concerns, contributions, and needs* 98E
>   *My life pie-chart* 95E
>   *Name game* 88E
>   *Name-badge exercise* 94E
>   *Open the day* 86E
>   *Paired interviews and introductions* 87E
>   *Positive feedback* 93E
>   *Setting priorities* 99–100E
>   *Wallpaper exercise* 96E
>   *What I am proud of myself for* 92E
>   *What I like about you* 91E

pair work
>   *Action-planning to overcome barriers* 189–90E
>   *Facilitation checklists* 142E
>   *Global and local discrimination* 208E
>   *Guessing game* 89E
>   *I respect you/You respect me* 110–11E
>   *Immediate action* (action plans) 281E
>   *Interviews in pairs* (on discrimination) 220–1E
>   *Line-drawing exercise* 138E
>   *Listening exercise* 107–9E, 129E
>   *Mr Biswas photo exercise* 256E
>   *My contribution* 270E
>   *My life pie-chart* 95E
>   *Open the day* 86E
>   *Organising the workshop* 147E, 149E
>   *Paired interviews and introductions* 87E
>   *Positive feedback* 93E
>   *Posters exercise* 255E
>   *Prevention in the home* 162–3E
>   *Problem triangle* 186E, 187H

Reflecting on facilitation 287E
Restrictive gender roles 241E
Rights and responsibilities 202E
What I am proud of myself for 92E
What rights do we have? The calendar game
    196–7E
Who am I? 236–7E
presentations
    Components of training 121P
    Creating a positive learning environment 115P
    The eight sunrays of planning 144–5P
    The evolution of documented rights for disabled
        people 211P
    Prevention of impairment 157–8P
    Psychological impact of impairment and
        disability 154
    Rates of learning 119P
    Stages of learning 118P
questionnaires
    for facilitation evaluation 291H
    for workshop evaluation 290H, 292–9H
    for workshop planning 81, 82–3H
quizzes, *The gender quiz* 238E, 239H
role play
    Fishbowl exercise 165–6E
    The game of life 243–6E
    Observation exercise 131–2E
    see also drama
small-group work
    Action-planning to overcome barriers 188E
    Agreeing guidelines 101–2E
    Applying the UN Standard Rules to real life 213E
    Barriers: a case study 191E
    'Choosing' rights 203–4E
    Collage 289E
    Disabled women's voices 247–8E
    Fairness and rights 194–5E
    Future actions: a competition 282E
    Future actions exercise: diamond ranking 283E
    The game of life 245–6E
    Hopes, concerns, contributions, and needs 98E
    How adults learn 112–13E
    How can I help? 175E
    Identifying allies 224–5E
    Identifying barriers 177–9E
    The imaginary country 200–1E
    Improvised drama about disabled people's rights
        222–3E
    Life stories 174E
    Mapping for Mars 104–6E
    models of disability 168E
    Nothing about us without us 280E
    objective setting 278–9E
    Observation exercise 131–2E

'Our definitions' exercise 264–5E
Planning the agenda and contents of a workshop
    151E
Prevention of impairment 161E
Problem-tree exercise 183–6E
Putting independent (self-determined) living
    into practice 276E
Setting priorities 99–100E
Sketch/mime 285E
Song 285E
Using positive and non-stereotypical images of
    disability 253–4E
Word-list exercise 258–60E
Writing and drawing 288E
visual aids
    Components of training 122H
    Creating a positive learning environment 115P
    Different rates of learning 120H
    The eight sunrays of planning 146H
    Know your apple 205–6E
    Line drawing 139H
    Mapping for Mars 104–6E
    Mr Biswas photo exercise 256E, 257H
    My life pie-chart 95E
    Posters exercise 255E
    Preventing accidents in the home 164H
    Problem-tree exercise 183–6E
    Problem-triangle 187H
    Puppets 232H
    Room layout 135–6H
    Using positive and non-stereotypical images of
        disability 253–4E
    Wall of barriers 180H
    Wallpaper exercise 96E
    What rights do we have? The calendar game
        196–7E
whole-group work
    'Darling' game 90E
    Discussion of the three models of disability 173E
    Facilitation: brainstorm and discussion 125–6E
    The gender quiz 238E, 239H
    Gender roles 242E
    Gesture energiser 97E
    Global and local discrimination 208E
    In/ter/dependence drawings 268–9E
    Know your apple 205–6E
    Media search 251–2E
    Name game 88E
    Quick evaluations in the round 284E
    The right to education: whole-group discussion
        226E
    Throw out or keep 285E
    What I like about you 91E
    Whole-group activity 123E